IMAGES
of America

CRESTED BUTTE

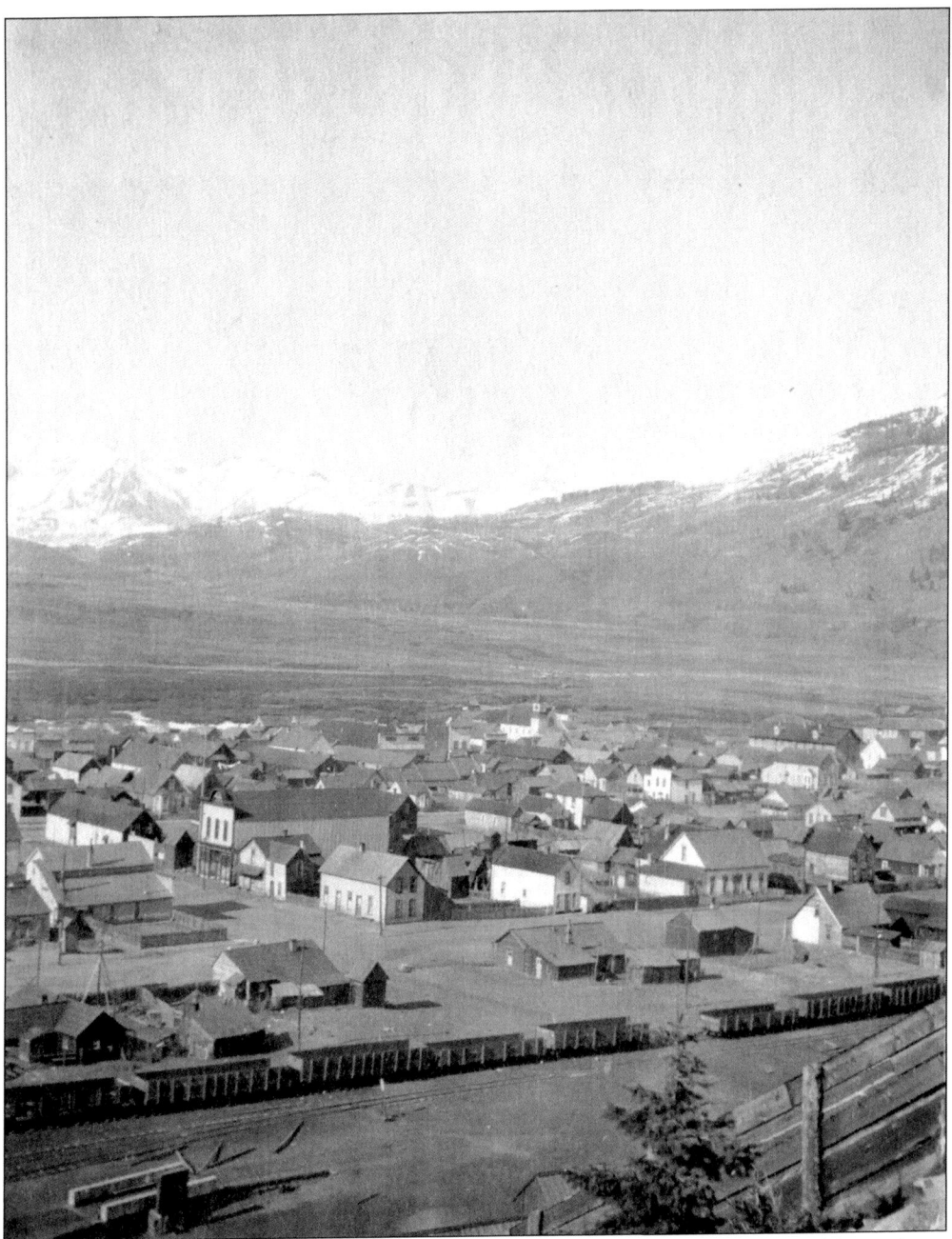

THE JEWEL OF THE ELK MOUNTAINS. Taken from the Big Mine located on "the Bench" just above Crested Butte, this picture shows the great coal town in 1915. The flank of Crested Butte Mountain and part of the Elk Mountains can be seen in the background. Empty Denver and Rio Grande Railroad cars wait to be loaded below the Big Mine.

ON THE COVER: A primitive dirt road runs by a ranch building and cattle loading pen between Crested Butte and Gothic in the 1940s. Below Crested Butte Mountain is the Malensek Ranch, which would become the Crested Butte Ski Area 20 years later.

IMAGES of America
CRESTED BUTTE

Duane Vandenbusche

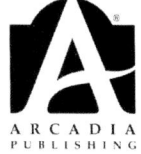

Copyright © 2011 by Duane Vandenbusche
ISBN 978-0-7385-7443-1

Published by Arcadia Publishing
Charleston, South Carolina

Printed in the United States of America

Library of Congress Control Number: 2010939112

For all general information, please contact Arcadia Publishing:
Telephone 843-853-2070
Fax 843-853-0044
E-mail sales@arcadiapublishing.com
For customer service and orders:
Toll-Free 1-888-313-2665

Visit us on the Internet at www.arcadiapublishing.com

This book is dedicated to the immigrant people of Crested Butte's past, whose work ethic made it a great town.

Contents

Acknowledgments		6
Introduction		7
1.	Elk Mountain Wonder	9
2.	Satellite Camps	17
3.	Crested Butte: Early Years	27
4.	Crested Butte: Later Years	43
5.	When Coal was King	57
6.	Pioneer, Rozman, and Early Skiing	69
7.	Denver and Rio Grande Railroad	89
8.	Age of Snow: The Crested Butte Ski Area	99
9.	Potpourri	111

Acknowledgments

Many individuals, libraries, and museums are to be thanked for the use of their photographs in this book. The Crested Butte Mountain Historical Museum, Bessemer Historical Society containing the Colorado Fuel and Iron Company (CF&I) Archives, Denver Public Library, Colorado State Historical Library, and Western State College Library were of great help in providing photographs and information.

Individuals who played major roles in this book's production include local photographers Sandy Cortner, J.C. Leacock, and Tom Stillo. Special thanks go to Staci Comden (Bessemer Historical Society), Glo Cunningham and Brooke Murphy (Crested Butte Mountain Heritage Museum), Nancy Gauss (Western State College Library), Coi Gehrig (Denver Public Library), and Jennifer Vega (Colorado Historical Society) for their great help.

Throughout the years, my interviews with Crested Butte old-timers like Frank Hodgson, Lyle McNeill, John Panion, Paul Panion, Joe Saya, Cloe Spann, and Philip Yaklich have added immeasurably to the information in this book. History papers written by Bob Lee, Lynda MacLennan, and Gary Sherman were also of great value to me.

Unless otherwise noted, the images in this book are from the author's collection. Additional images appear courtesy of the Colorado Historical Society (CHS), Denver Public Library (DPL), Bessemer Historical Society (BHS), Sandy Cortner (SC), Tom Stillo (TS), J.C. Leacock (JCL), and the Crested Butte Mountain Heritage Museum (CBMHM).

I am very grateful for the support, guidance, wisdom, and expertise of my editor, Jerry Roberts, and Arcadia Publishing. Very influential in my work on this book was Pam Williams of historical Island Acres Resort in Gunnison, Colorado, who scanned all the photographs contained herein. Her knowledge and guidance were of great importance to me. Lastly, I thank the people from the Gunnison Country, where I have spent almost half a century, for their friendship and inspiration.

Introduction

High in the Elk Mountains of Colorado's Western Slope is one of the most beautiful and historic towns in the American West. Crested Butte towers 8,885 feet in elevation, and its panorama is unmatched in Colorado. The Slate River from the north and Coal Creek from the west join near the historic mining camp. Crested Butte was named for the 12,171-foot mountain that towers over the town to the east. Early surveyor Ferdinand Hayden thought it resembled the crest of a Spanish helmet, hence the name.

Crested Butte is only 25 miles or so as the crow flies from Aspen to the north. Between the two great mining camps are six mountains in the Elk Range (Capital, Castle, North and South Maroon Bells, Pyramid, and Snowmass) that rise over 14,000 feet. Placer miners prospecting for gold entered the Elk Mountains in the 1860s, but the area proved to be very dangerous. Tremendous snow, numbing cold, isolation, and the Ute Indians kept all but the bravest away. Despite the dangers, the lure of gold brought hundreds of miners into the Elk Mountains during the 1860s and early 1870s. Famed Methodist missionary John F. Dyer preached to 250 placer miners at a camp called Minersville near the head of Washington Gulch, just north of today's Crested Butte, in 1861.

A decade and a half of placer mining ended in the Elk Mountains in the mid-1870s with the streams panned out. In 1878, Howard Smith laid out Crested Butte near the junction of Coal Creek and the Slate River because of the discovery of large bituminous coal deposits found there the year before. However, silver created the most excitement in the late 1870s. Across East and West Maroon Passes, Aspen became one of the great silver camps in the nation. Crested Butte soon became known as the "Gateway to the Elks," the jumping off point to all the speculative silver camps springing up nearby. By the early 1880s, Crested Butte was the major supply town for Gothic, Aspen, Schofield, and Irwin. When the silver boom ended by 1882 because of low-grade ore, transportation problems, and falling prices, Crested Butte never lost a beat—it turned to coal.

The age of coal began in Crested Butte in 1880 and continued unabated until the closing of the Colorado Fuel and Iron Company's Big Mine in 1952. Crested Butte was surrounded by rich coal deposits in nine different coal mines—Jokerville, Pershing, Peanut, Anthracite, Floresta, Robinson, Bulkley, Pueblo, and the Big Mine. The Denver and Rio Grande (D&RG) narrow gauge railroad arrived in Crested Butte on November 21, 1881, insuring the success of the new coal mines. By 1884, 154 coke ovens were built in Crested Butte; these ovens turned out 175 tons of coke a day. The coke was taken by rail to the CF&I mills in Pueblo, where it was used in the production of steel. Coal mining was hard and dangerous work. The Jokerville mine blew up in January 1884 because of seeping methane gas, killing 60 miners in one of Colorado's worst mining disasters.

By 1900, Crested Butte had grown to 1,500 residents. The early people of the mining camp were from Wales, Scotland, England, and Ireland. The 1890s brought a new group of immigrants from southern and central Europe—Italy, Austria, Croatia, and Slovenia. Tensions remained high between the two immigrant groups well past World War I.

Crested Butte hit on hard times when the last coal mine—CF&I's Big Mine—closed in 1952. Three years later, the railroad tracks were pulled between Gunnison and Crested Butte. During the 1950s, the population plummeted to 300, and many predicted Crested Butte would soon become a ghost town. In 1960, however, two Kansans, Dick Eflin and Fred Rice, purchased the Malensek ranch three miles northeast of town at the base of Crested Butte Mountain and announced they would start a winter recreation area. Crested Butte's "Age of Snow" had arrived. The Crested Butte Ski Area opened during the winter of 1961–1962, and the following year Colorado's first gondola lift was put in.

The Crested Butte Ski Area marked the revival of the town. By 2010, Crested Butte's population was 1,500. A new town, Mount Crested Butte, began in 1974 at the base of the ski area. Condominiums and lodges were built, property values soared, and during the winter of 2009–2010, Crested Butte Mountain Resort experienced 342,000 skier days.

Today, Crested Butte is a great year-round recreation area. The town is the center of world-class skiing at Crested Butte Mountain Resort and is surrounded by a vast complex of Nordic ski trails. Crested Butte is also one of the great mountain bike areas in the nation, with high-altitude single-track trails that take one's breath away. The National Mountain Bike Hall of Fame is located in Crested Butte. Along with the great skiing and mountain biking, Crested Butte is also famous for its four-wheel drive roads, hunting, fishing, and wildflower and music festivals, which attract people from all over the world. All of the outdoor activities fashioned Crested Butte into a summer and winter wonderland. Gold miners, missionaries, surveyors, coal miners, immigrants, railroaders, and skiers—all with dreams—have made Crested Butte what it is today.

One
ELK MOUNTAIN WONDER

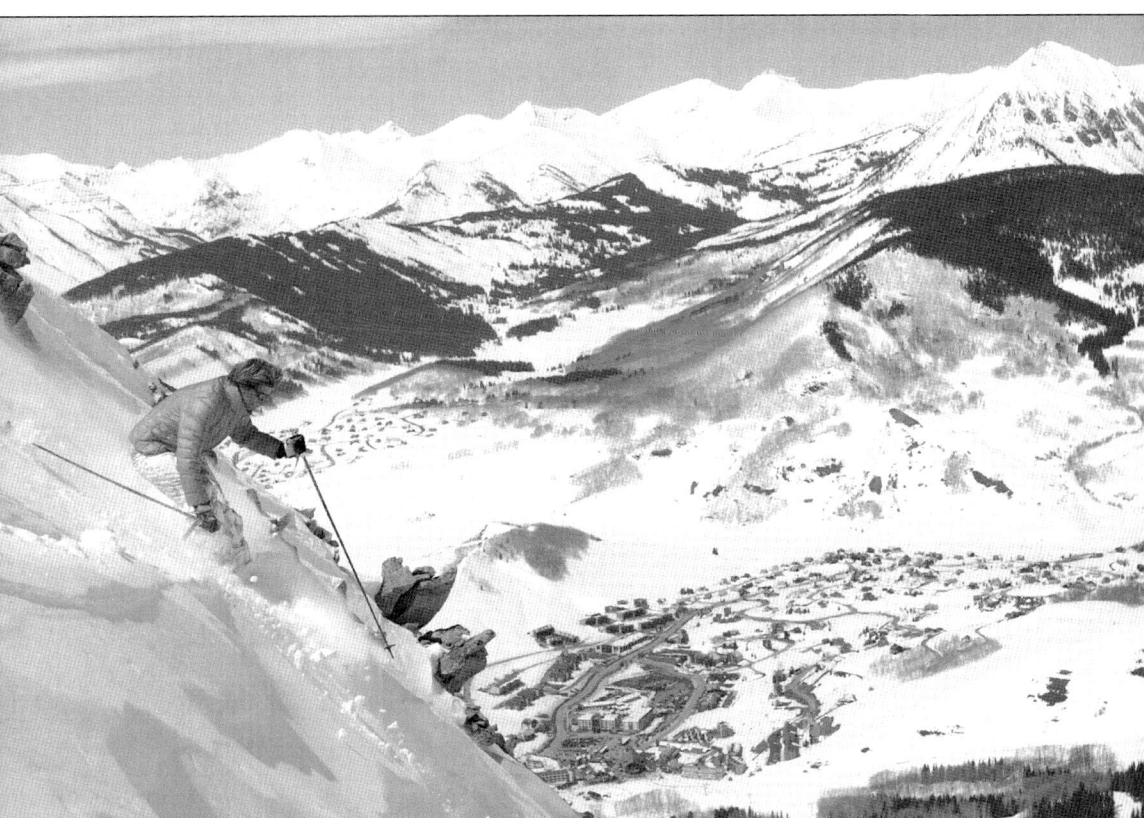

SKIING THE PEAK. One of the world's top extreme skiers, Kim Reichhelm skis precipitous Crested Butte Peak in great powder conditions. Almost 3,000 feet below are the town of Mount Crested Butte and the base of the ski area. (TS.)

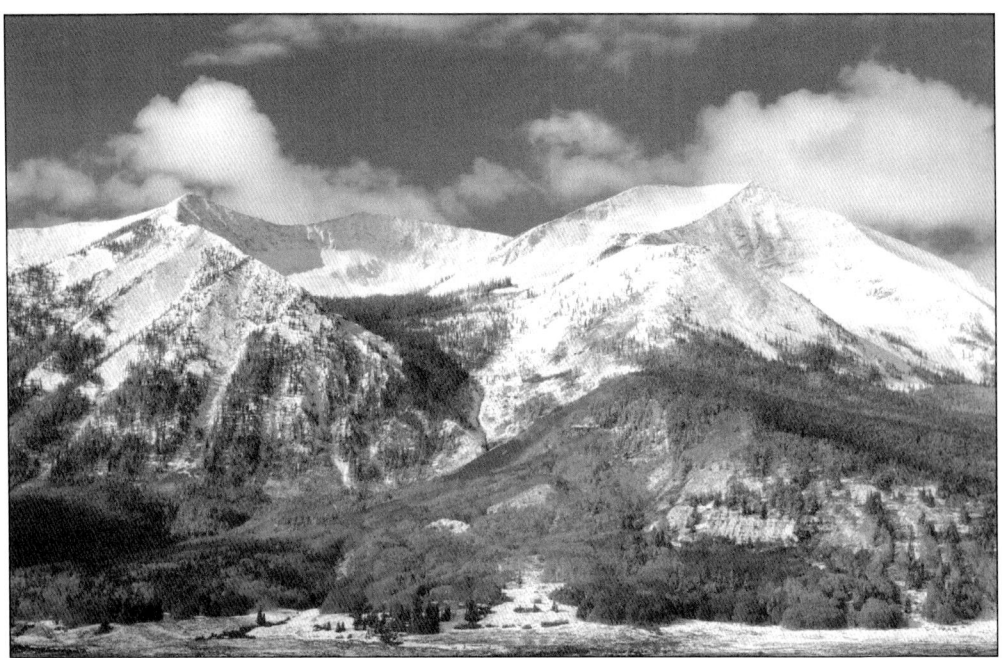

MOUNT WHETSTONE. Towering 12,500 feet into the clouds, Mount Whetstone forms the entrance into Crested Butte just to the west of the main road into town. The mountain provides locals with some sensational backcountry skiing, especially in the spring when the threat of avalanches lessens. (TS.)

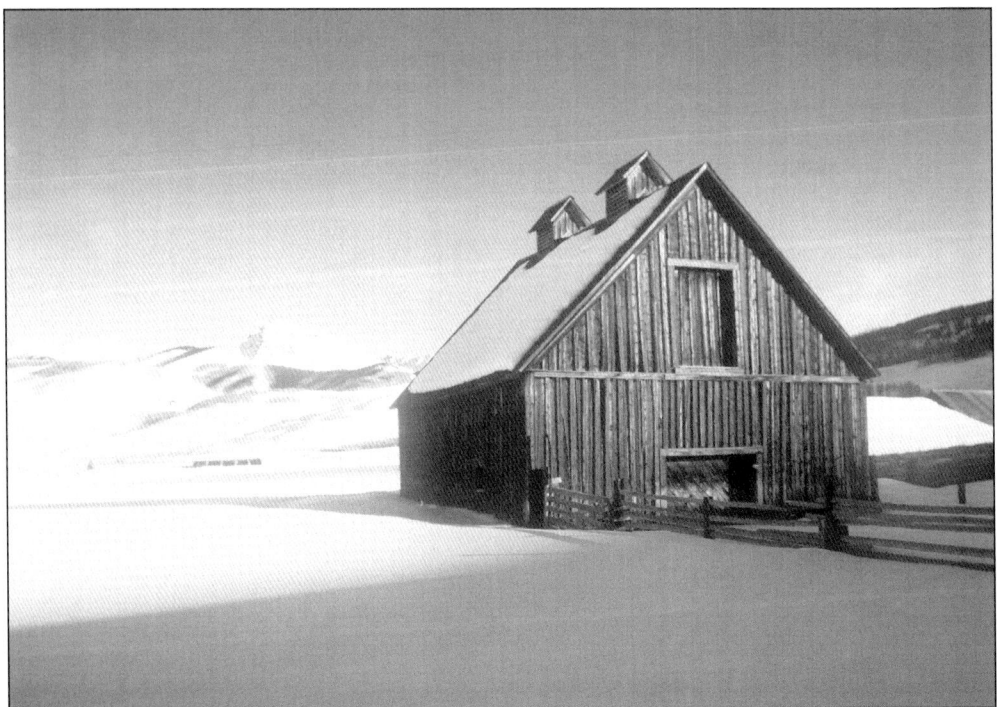

BRUSH CREEK BARN. An old barn sits in the magnificent beauty of the Brush Creek Valley southeast of Crested Butte. Mount Teocali, over 13,000 feet high, provides the background. (JCL.)

SNODGRASS SPLENDOR. Two mountain bikers pedal uphill on a beautiful trail on Mount Snodgrass north of Crested Butte, the mountain biking mecca of the West. The National Mountain Bike Hall of Fame is in the Crested Butte Mountain Heritage Museum. (TS.)

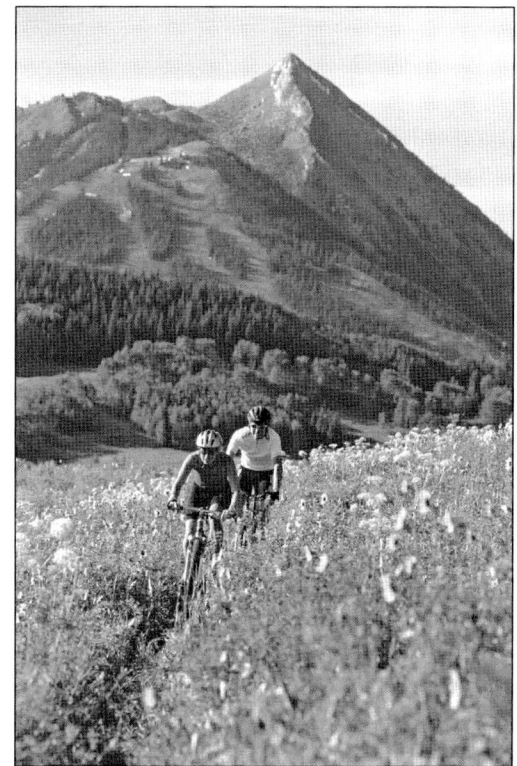

RAINBOW'S END. After a heavy rain, a rainbow appears over Crested Butte, with Crested Butte Mountain in the background. At almost 9,000 feet and on the edge of the Elk Mountains, some of which rise to over 14,000 feet, Crested Butte is one of the most beautiful towns in the West. (TS.)

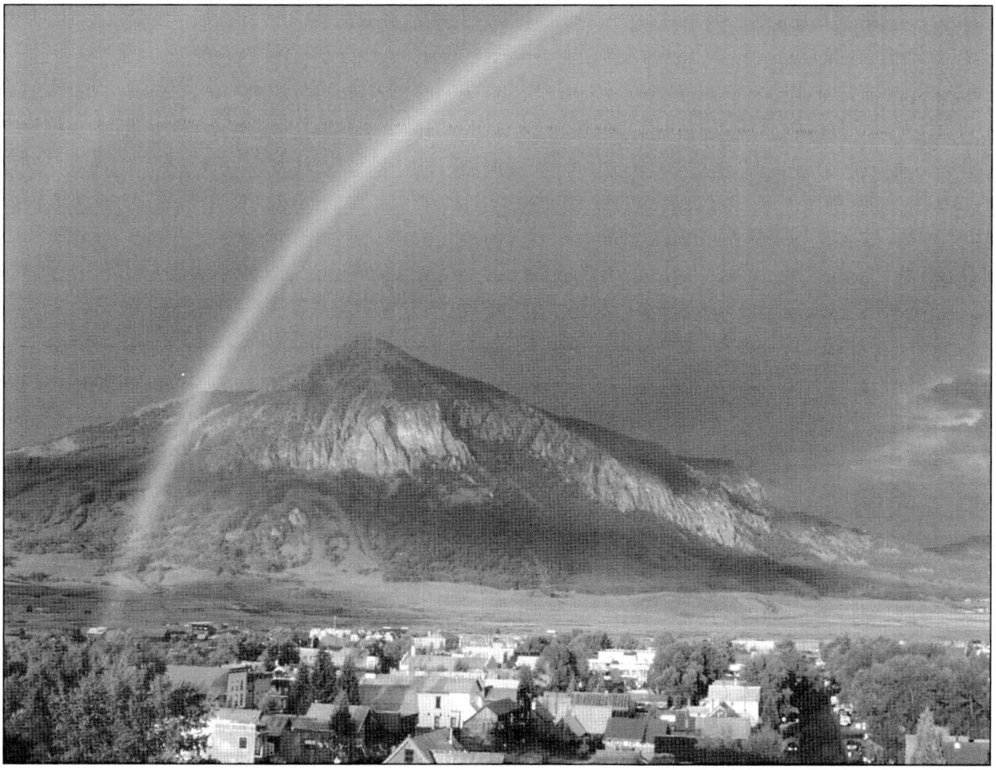

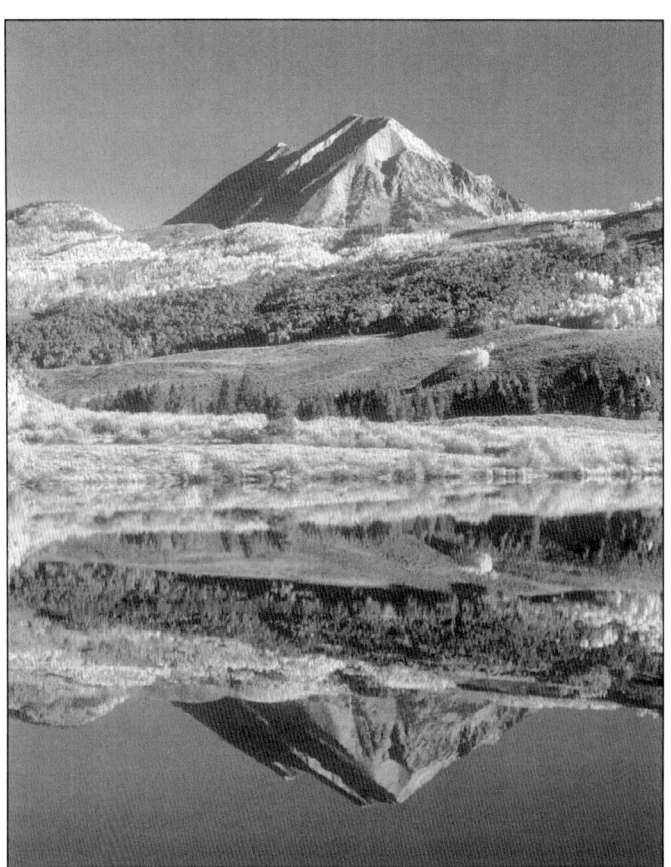

PEANUT LAKE. Towering Gothic Mountain is in the distance in this beautiful fall scene taken from Peanut Lake. One of Crested Butte's most stunning and well-used mountain bike trails, heading north at over 9,000 feet, passes right by the lake. (JCL.)

UNION CONGREGATIONAL CHURCH. One of the most beautiful churches in Colorado, the Union Congregational was built in Crested Butte in 1881. Behind the church is Gothic Mountain, rising 12,500 feet into the clouds. The Union Congregational has been the scene of many weddings because of its beauty and the stunning scenery that surrounds it.

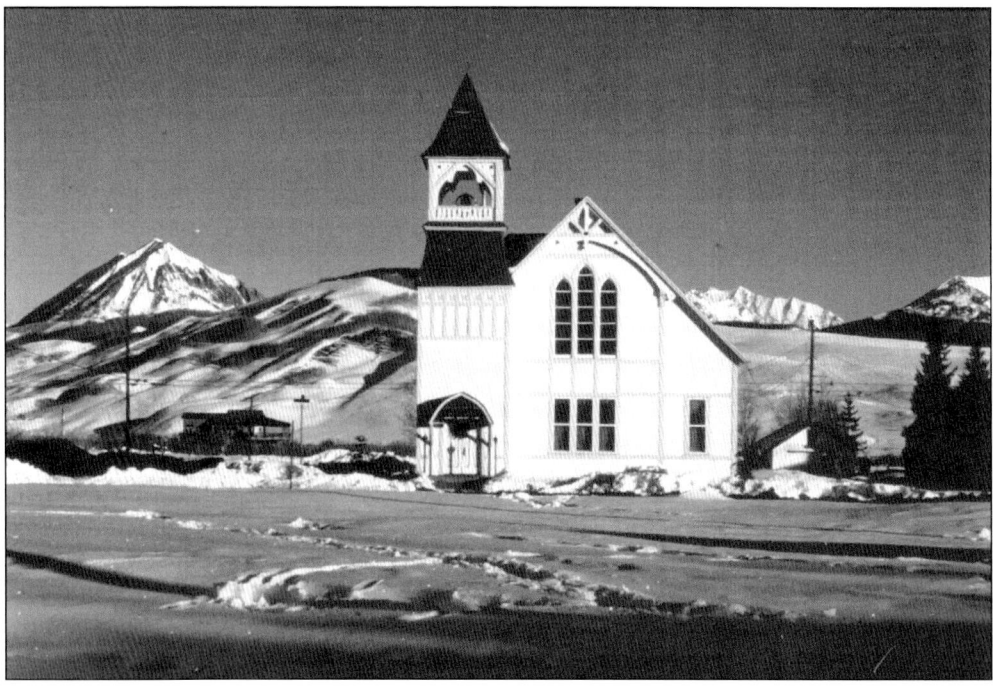

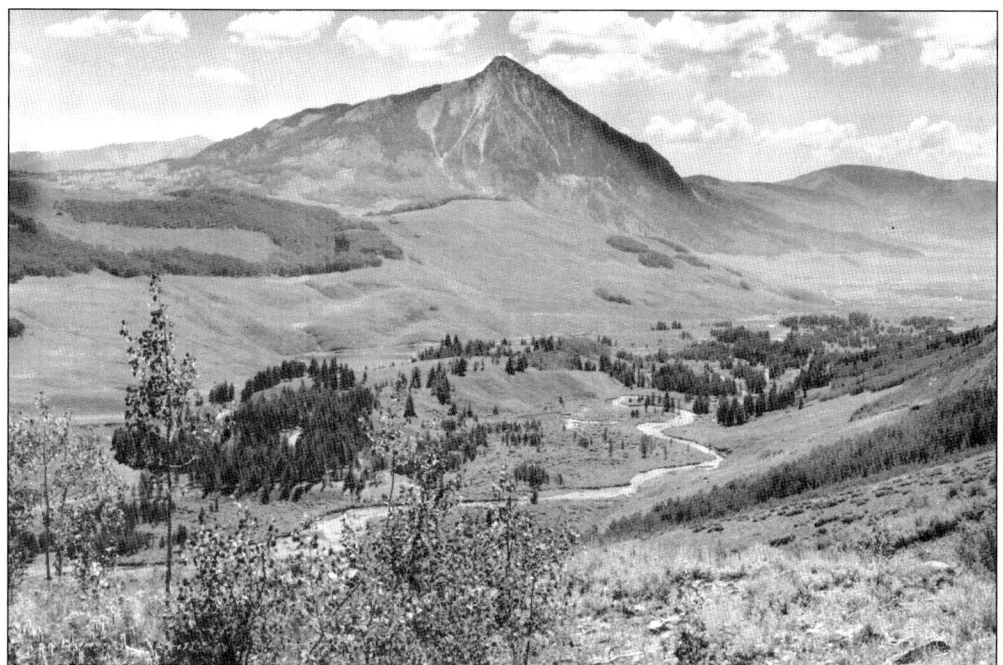

MALENSEK RANCH. Soaring 12,171 feet high, Mount Crested Butte is an isolated sentinel overlooking the East River Valley. Surveyor Ferdinand Hayden named the mountain in the 1870s; he felt it resembled the crest of a Spanish helmet. This photograph shows part of the Malensek Ranch, which became the Crested Butte Ski Area in 1961.

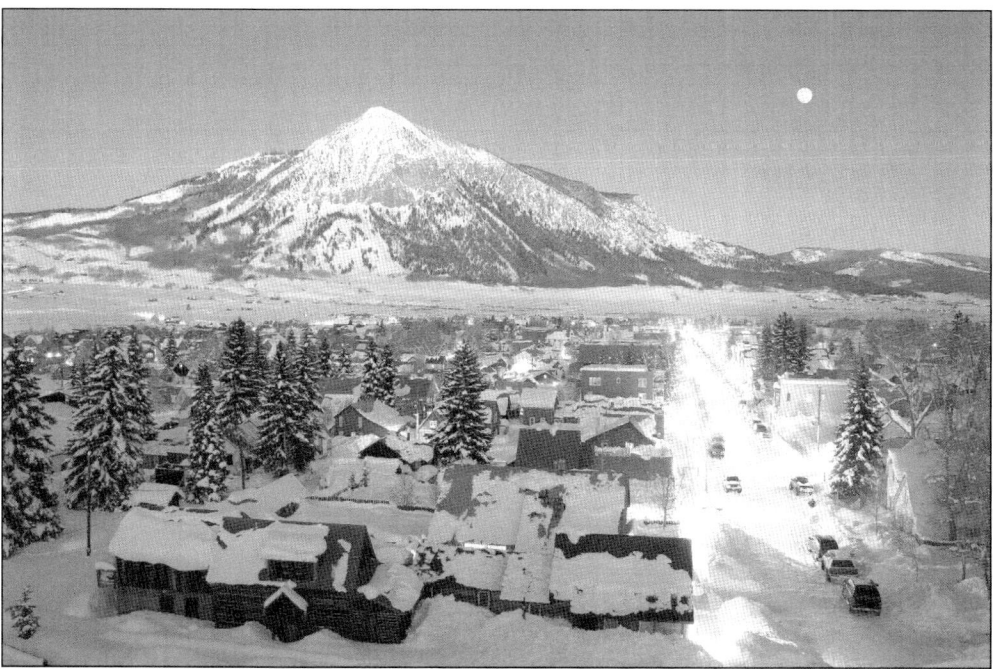

WINTER IN CRESTED BUTTE. This beautiful scene shows Crested Butte in mid-winter. Lights illuminate Elk Avenue under a full moon. After a great day of skiing, both locals and outsiders are involved in après-ski eating, dancing, and drinking. (JCL.)

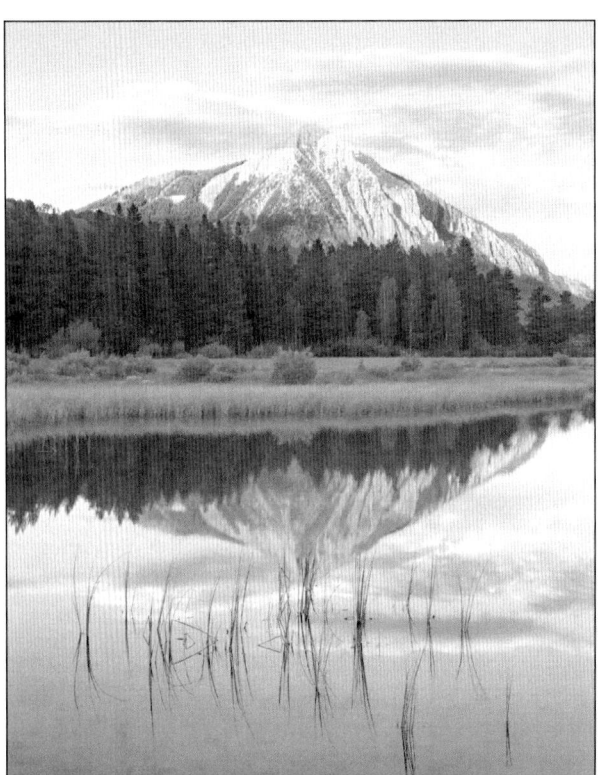

HIGH COUNTRY POND. Mount Crested Butte is reflected in a pond near Peanut Lake. The bodies of water are near the Peanut coal mine, which was one of the major coal producers in Crested Butte's history. (JCL.)

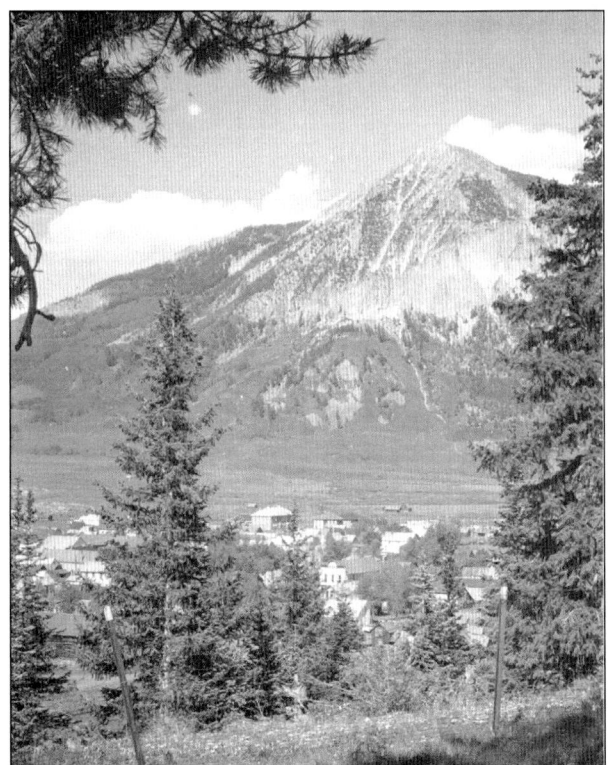

MOUNTAIN SPLENDOR. Resembling a Swiss village, Crested Butte is nestled in a high alpine valley at 8,885 feet. The town of 1,500 is a national historic site and, with Mount Crested Butte as a backdrop, is glorious in its beauty.

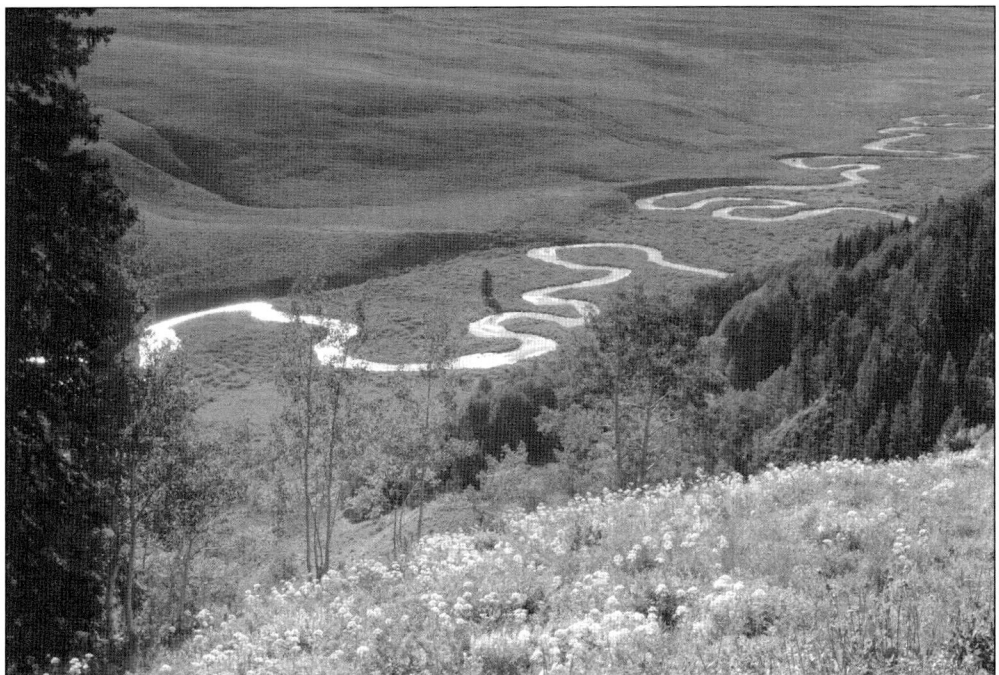

EAST RIVER MEANDERS. The beautiful East River meanders through the valley of the same name. The river heads off 10,007-foot-high Schofield Pass to the north and flows south over 30 miles to a union with the Taylor River at the town of Almont. (TS.)

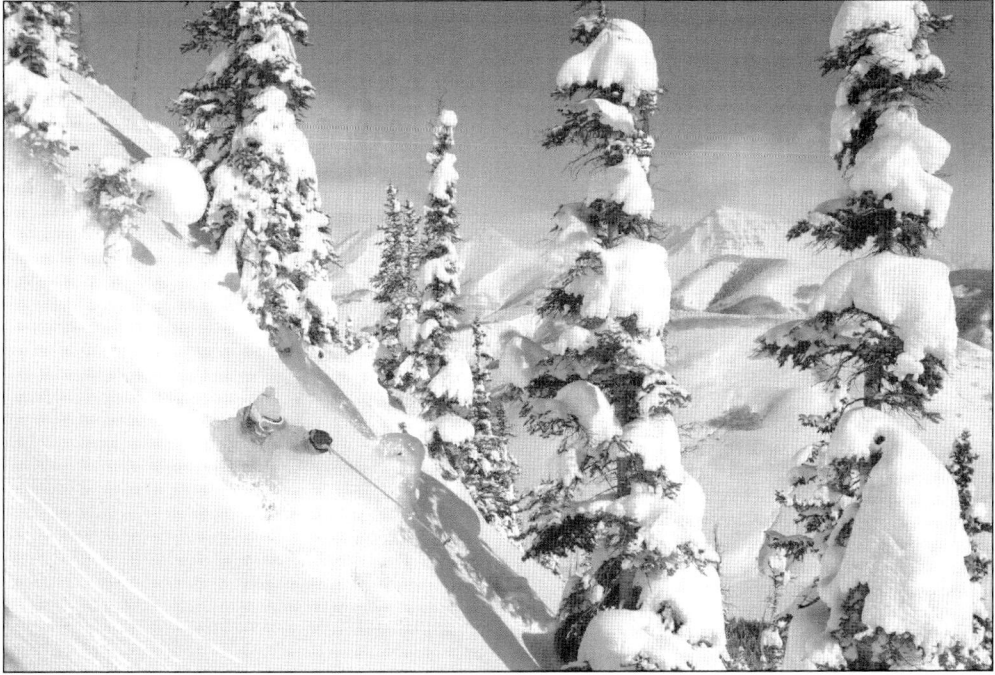

THIRD BOWL. A lone skier is almost buried in deep snow as he skis Crested Butte's famous Third Bowl, with Mount Teocali in the background. The Crested Butte Ski Area is famous for its extreme skiing, featuring such runs as Rambo, Dead Bob's, the Headwall, and Body Bag Chute. (TS.)

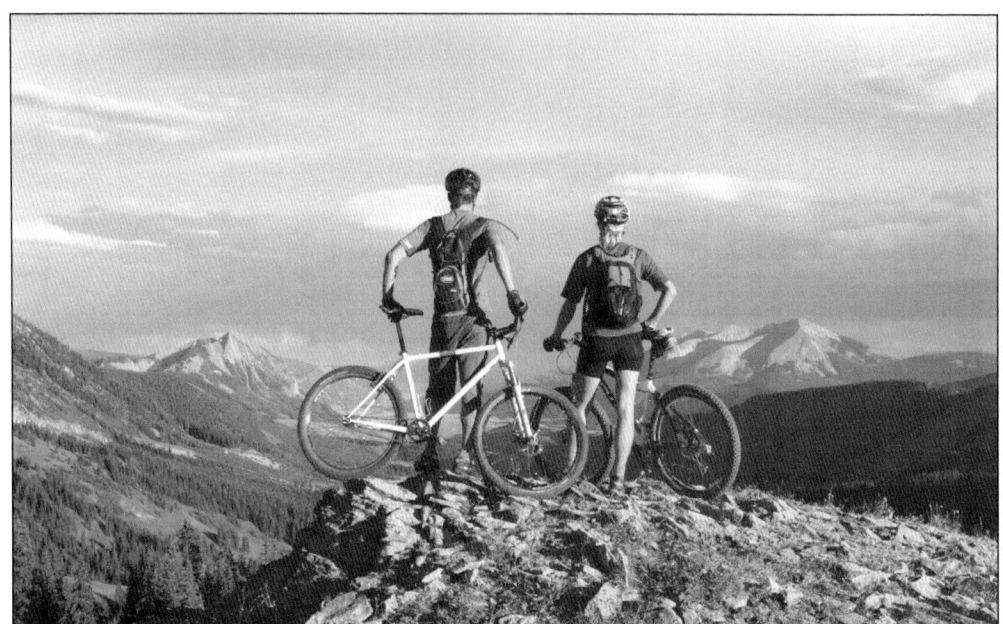

MOUNTAIN BIKING PARADISE. Two mountain bikers gaze south at a stunning panorama highlighted by Crested Butte and Whetstone Mountains. The two riders are near 11,000 feet at the head of Washington Gulch. (JCL.)

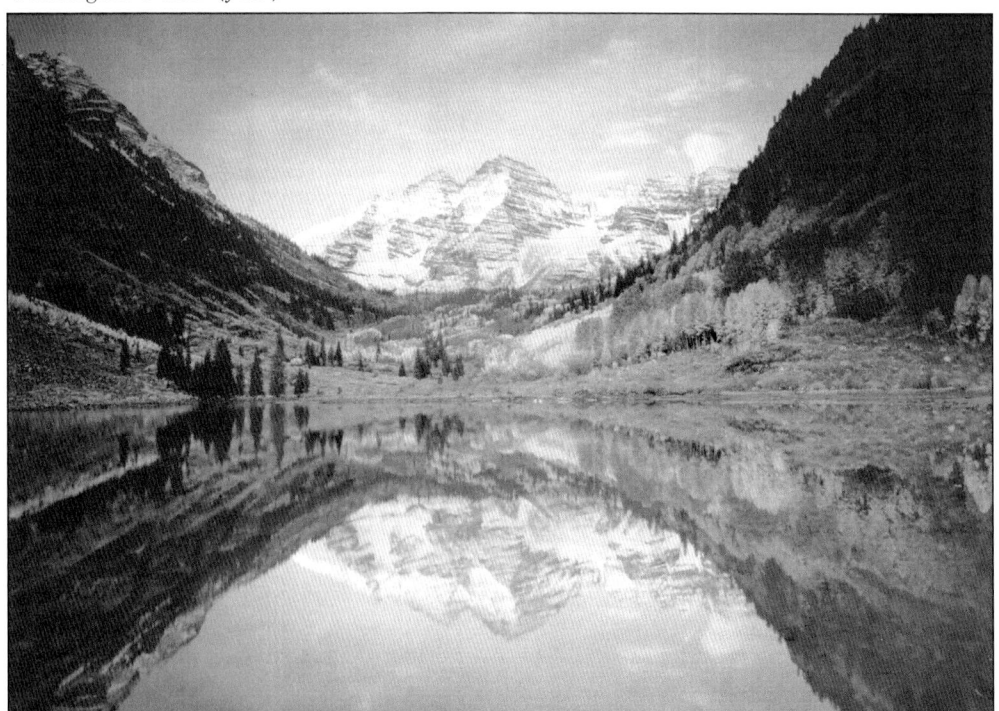

MAROON BELLS. North and South Maroon Bell Mountains highlight this spectacular scene from Maroon Lake above Aspen. In the 1880s, long "jack trains" carried ore from Aspen's great silver mines over 11,800-foot-high East Maroon Pass to the railroad at Crested Butte 30 miles away. (JCL.)

Two
Satellite Camps

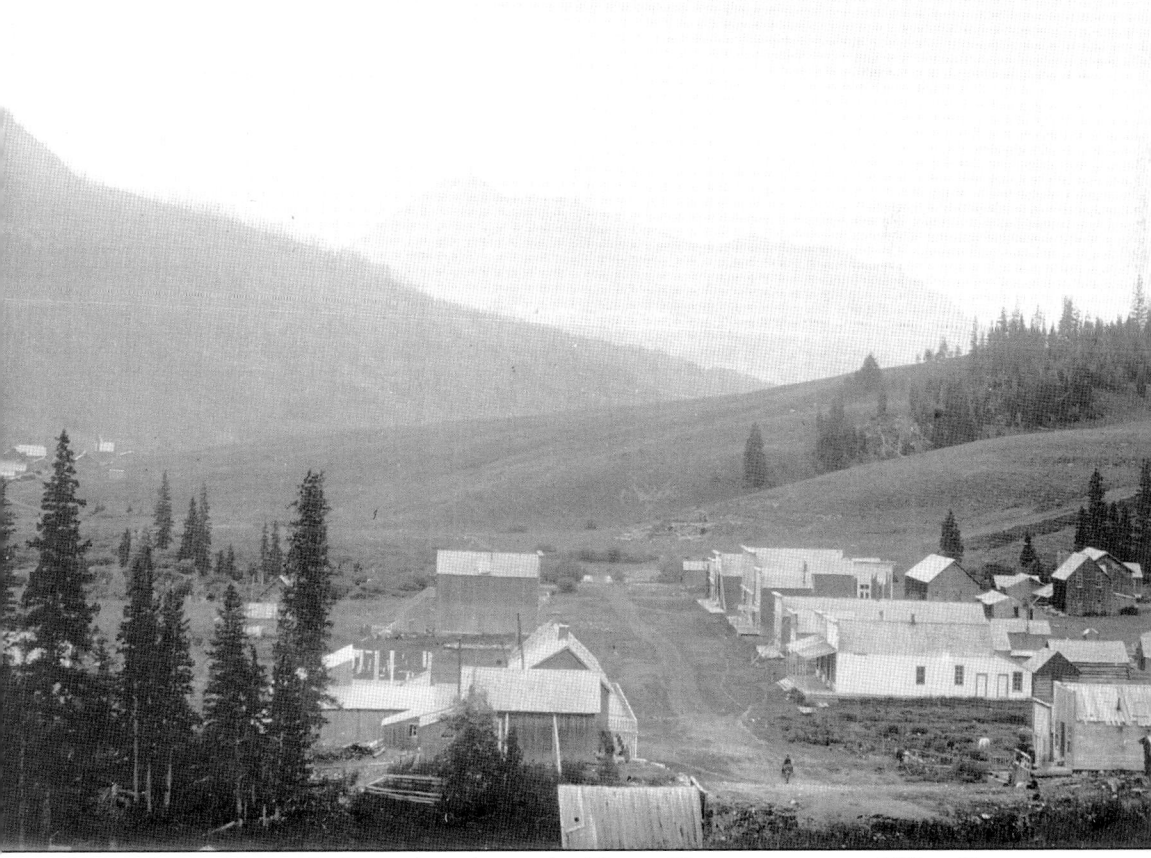

CITY OF SILVER WIRES. Gothic, eight miles north of Crested Butte, sprang up in 1879 and became famous for its wire silver. The silver camp is shown here about 1890, shortly after the mining boom ended. Crested Butte Mountain is in the background. (CHS.)

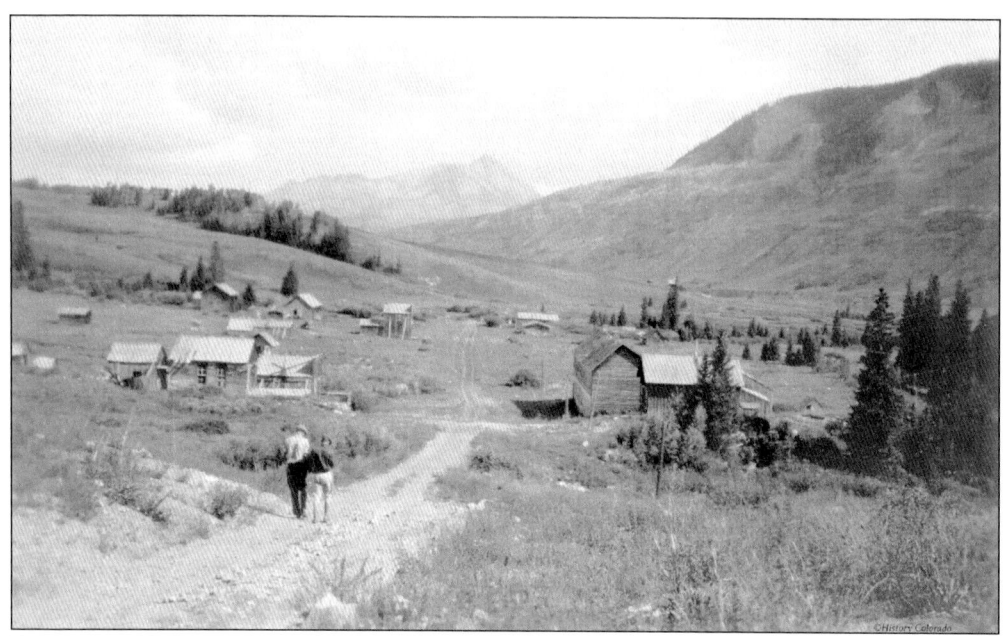

DREAMS OF YESTERYEAR. With Crested Butte Mountain as a backdrop, Gothic is a shell of its former self in the 1930s. In 1928, Dr. John C. Johnson, a former professor at Western State College, started the world famous Rocky Mountain Biological Laboratory in Gothic for the study of plants and animals. (CHS.)

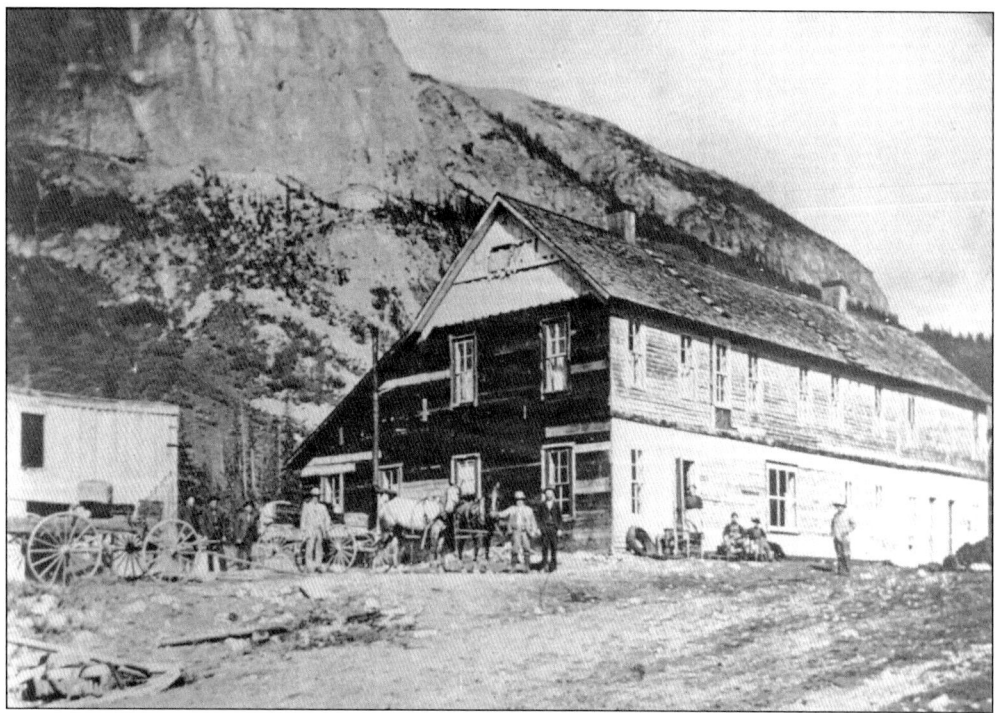

GOTHIC HOTEL. Gothic was a very promising silver camp in 1880, when the mammoth Gothic Hotel was built by Capt. E. Bunn. Three stories high, the hotel was full most of the time as thousands of prospectors flocked into camp during 1880 and 1881.

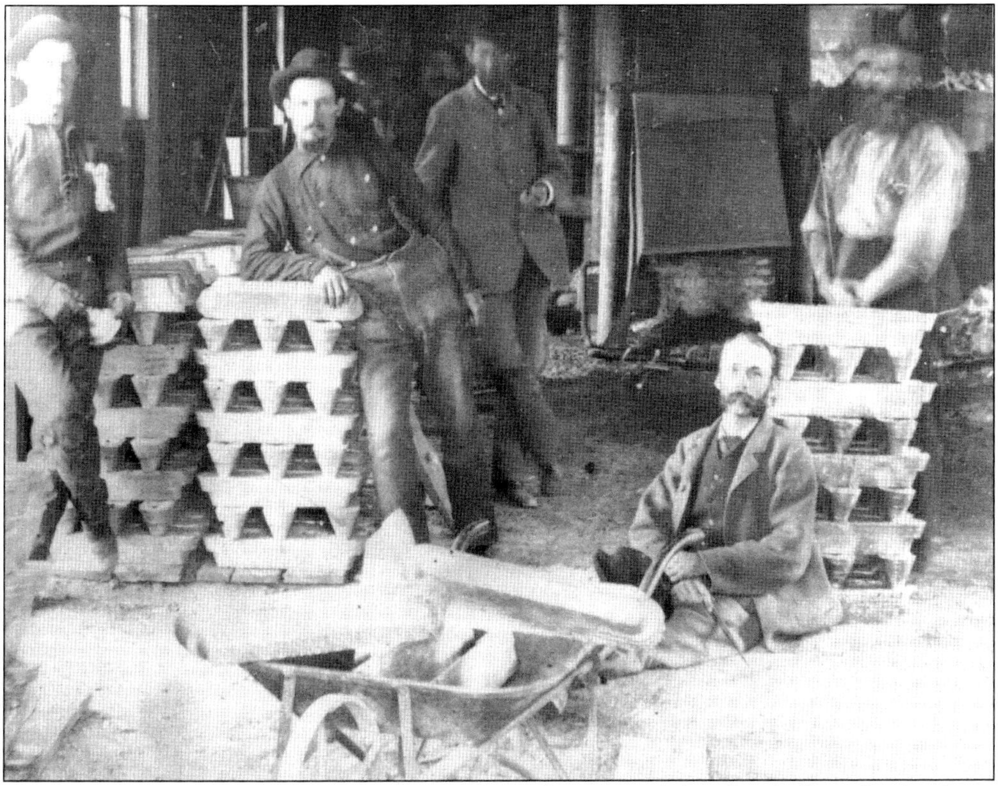

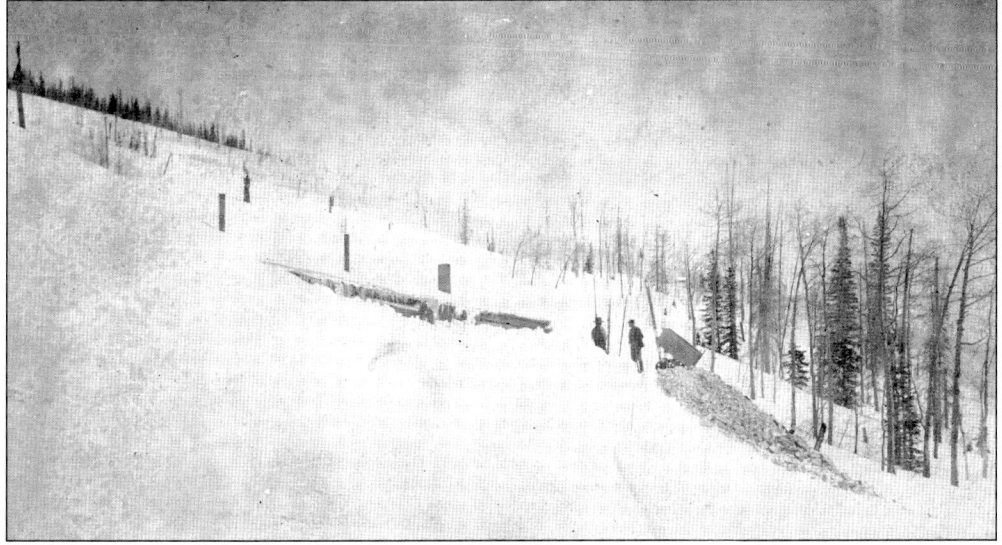

SILVER BULLION. Men in a Gothic smelter in the early 1880s exhibit silver bullion that has been reduced from ore from the many mines around the silver camp. The bullion came from the Jim Blaine, Sylvanite, and Virginius Mines.

THE GREAT SYLVANITE. The Sylvanite Mine, located three miles east of Gothic and high above Copper Creek, was the major mine of the silver camp. During the winter months, miners stockpiled ore. The Sylvanite was sold in 1879 for $200,000; by the time it closed in 1910, it had produced over $1 million.

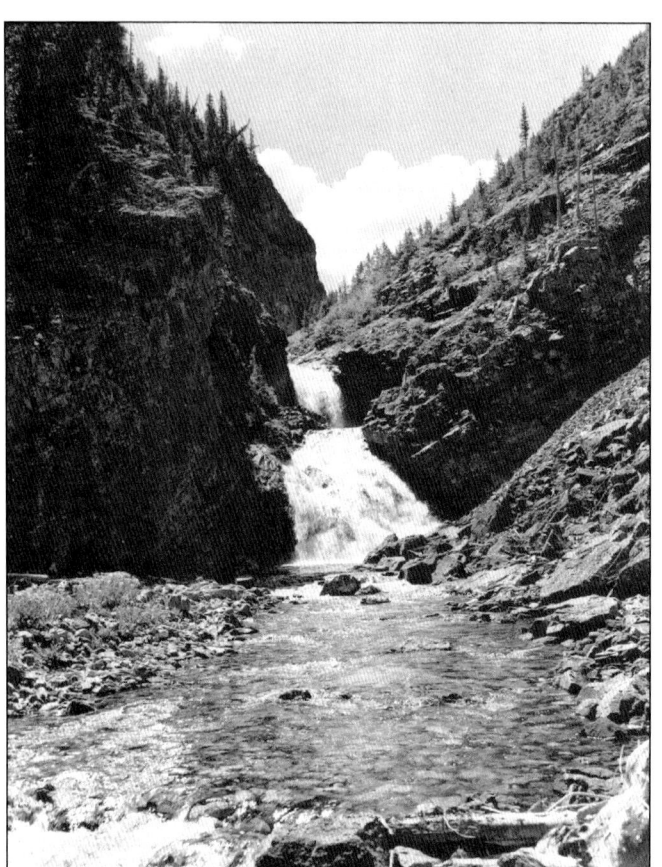

DEVIL'S PUNCHBOWLS. North of Crested Butte, in the treacherous Crystal Canyon, these two waterfalls are close to one of the most feared four-wheel drive roads in Colorado. The route above the waterfall has a 17 percent grade, and nine people died in an accident when their vehicle plunged into the Crystal River in 1971.

SKI PARTY. Ten hardy skiers head uphill above the mining camp of Crystal in the upper Crystal River Valley in 1886. They were prepared to ski down the same route. Two days before, that area was hit with an avalanche. The skiers believed that the same area would not avalanche again.

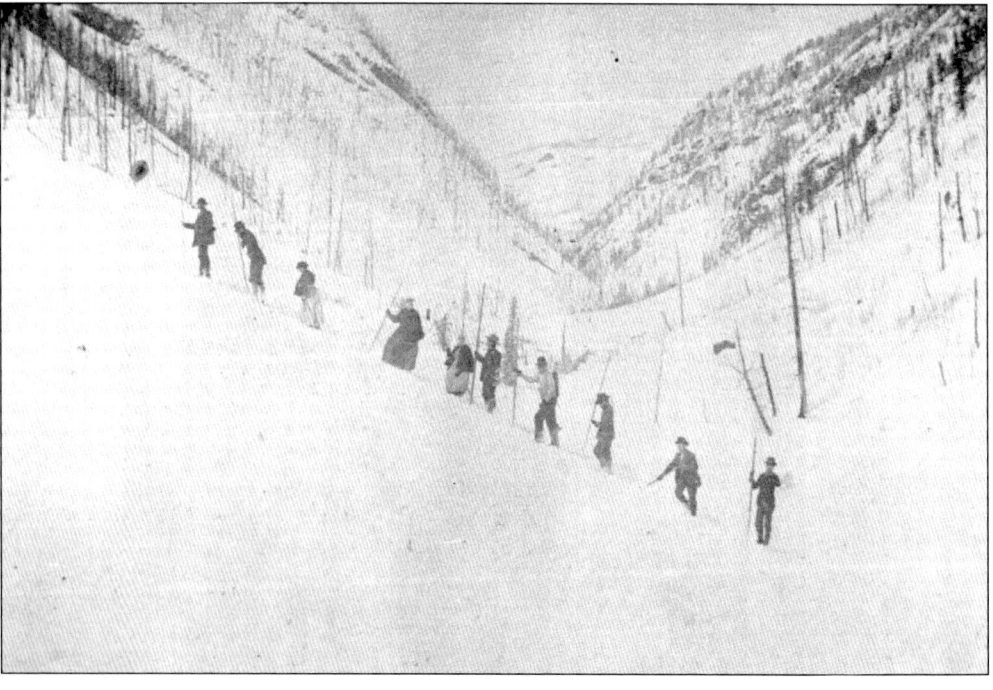

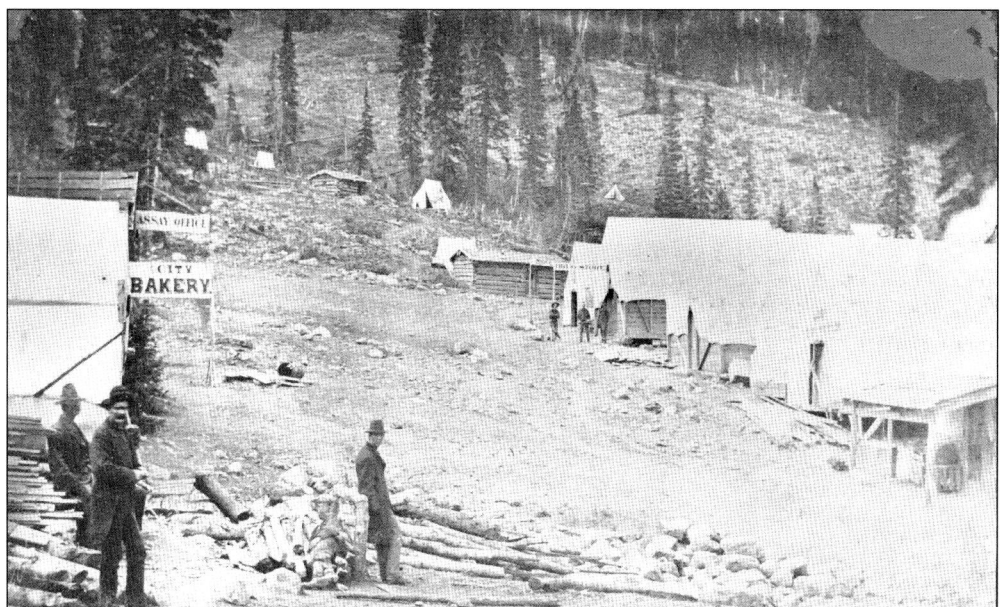

IRWIN. The boom had just begun in Irwin in 1879. Tents and a few cabins served as lodging for excited prospectors. The mining camp was named for Dick Irwin, who had searched for riches in Central City, Creede, Coeur d'Alene, and Nome. Irwin was looking for a new El Dorado in 1879.

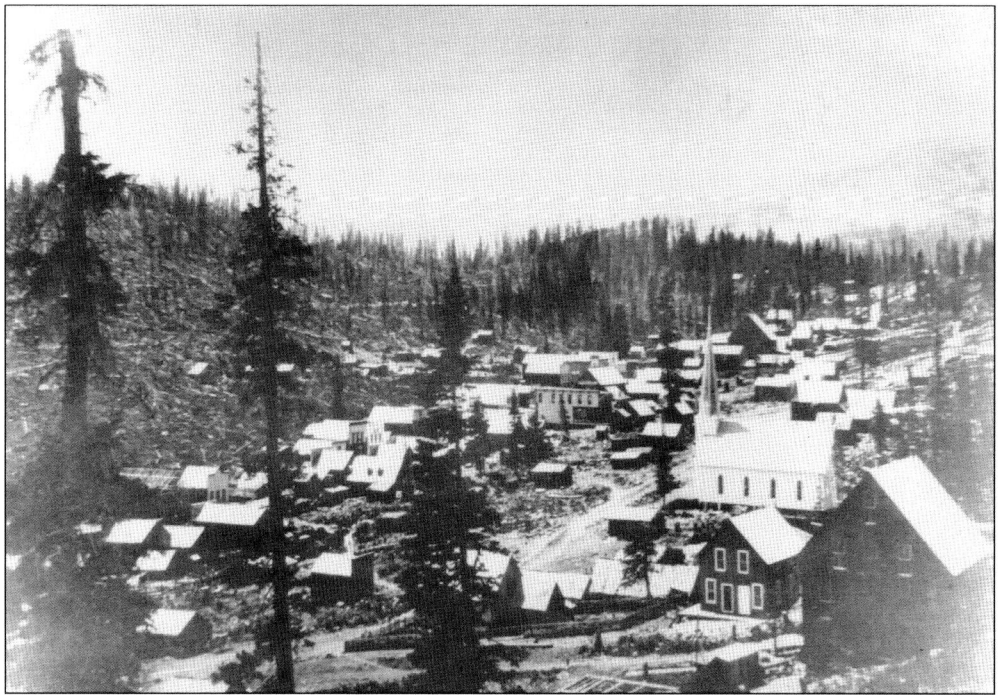

IRWIN AT ITS PEAK. Located 10 miles west of Crested Butte at over 10,000 feet, Irwin became a booming silver camp by 1881. An estimated 4,000 people flocked into the encampment, filling up every nearby gulch. Investors came in from the East, and the Denver South Park Railroad planned to arrive in 1882.

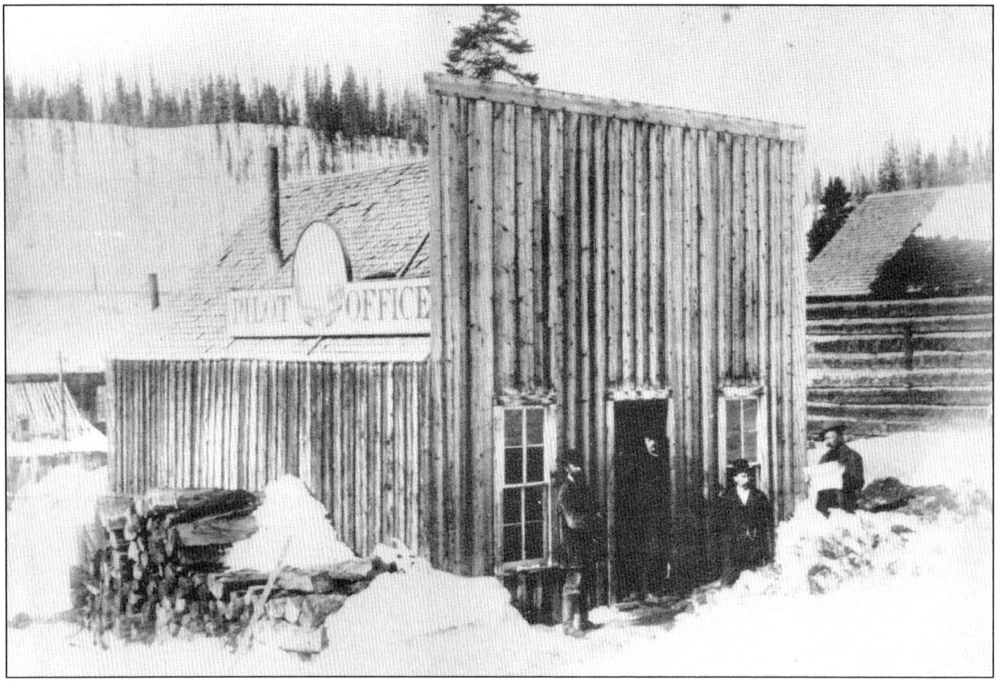

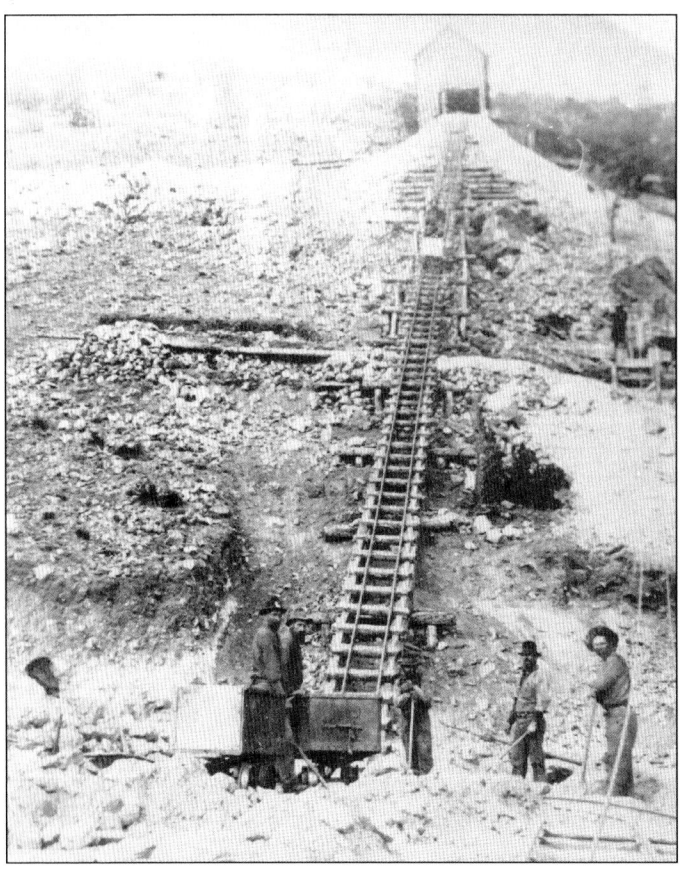

ELK MOUNTAIN PILOT. The *Elk Mountain Pilot* newspaper was started in Irwin in 1880. In this photograph, famed editor John E. Phillips is standing in the doorway. The fading fortunes of Irwin forced Phillips to move the paper to Crested Butte in 1884. The entire newspaper plant was loaded on two bobsleds and hauled over the snow to the neighboring town.

MINE TRAM, 1881. Five miners pose at the bottom of a steep mine tram in Gothic in 1881. Ore cars laden with silver ore descended the tram. The ore was then taken by wagon to nearby smelters.

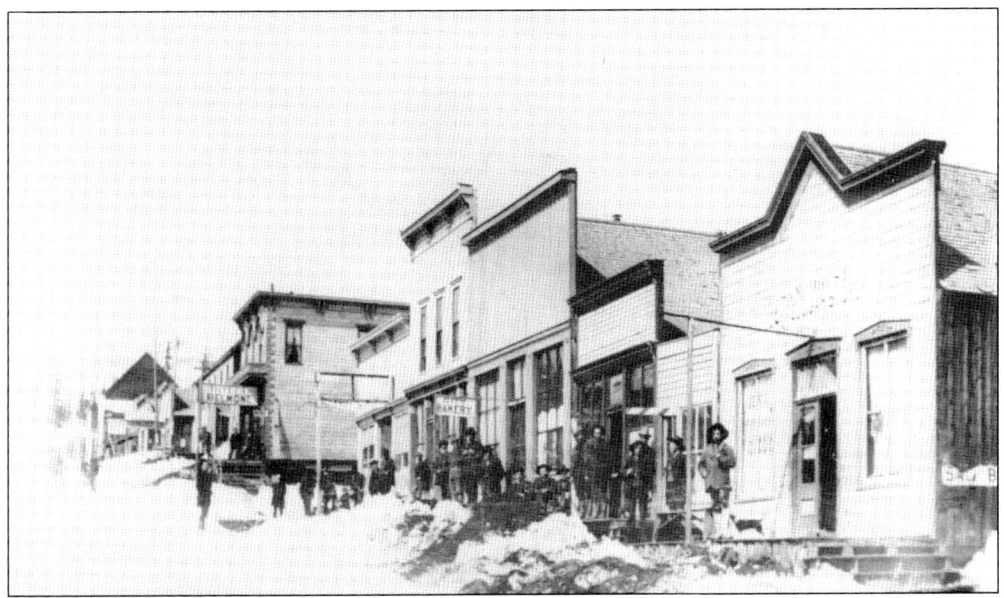

MAIN STREET, IRWIN, 1881. The mining boom in Irwin started in 1879 and lasted through 1881. This picture shows the camp still in the throes of prosperity. The decline and fall of Irwin was caused by weather and lack of a railroad but most of all because of lower-grade ore the deeper men descended into the mines.

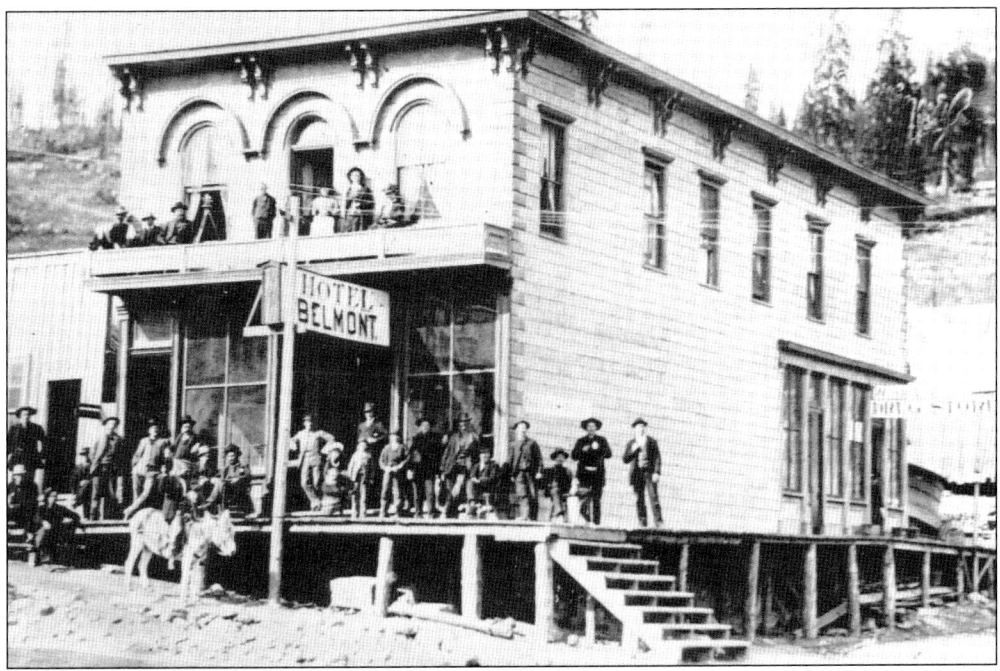

BELMONT HOTEL. One of three hotels in Irwin during its boom in the 1880s, the Belmont was also a place where locals gathered. The hotel had 15 rooms and also included a drugstore in the back. Many distinguished investors and travelers stayed at the Belmont.

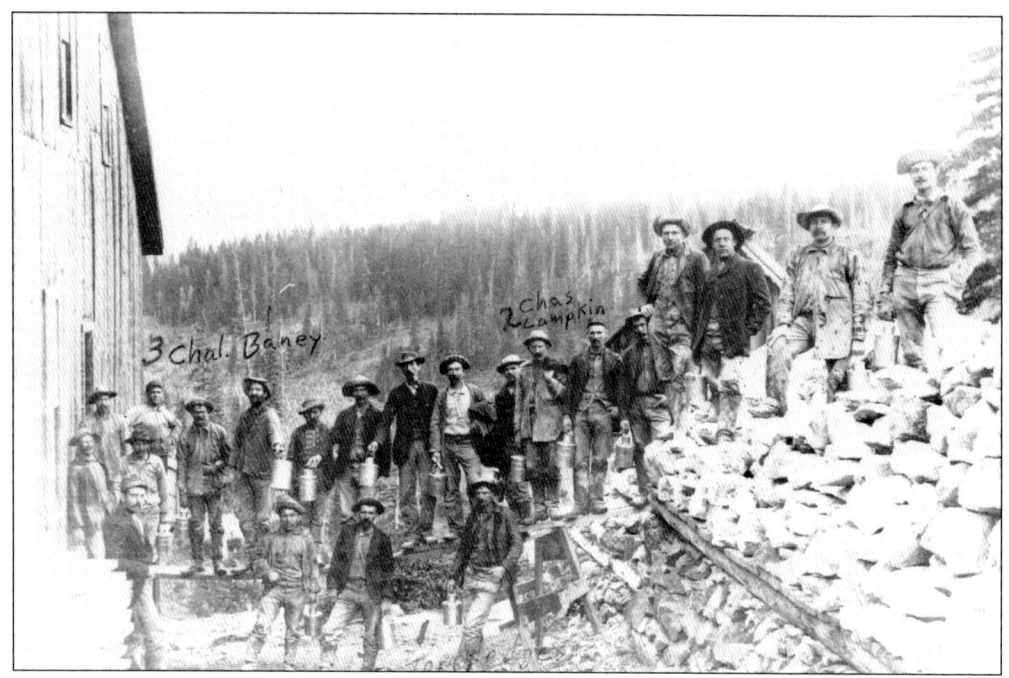

THE FOREST QUEEN. Irwin's greatest mine was the Forest Queen, discovered by William Fisher in 1879. Fisher sold the mine for $40,000 shortly after finding it. The Forest Queen produced over $1 million in silver before closing in the 1890s.

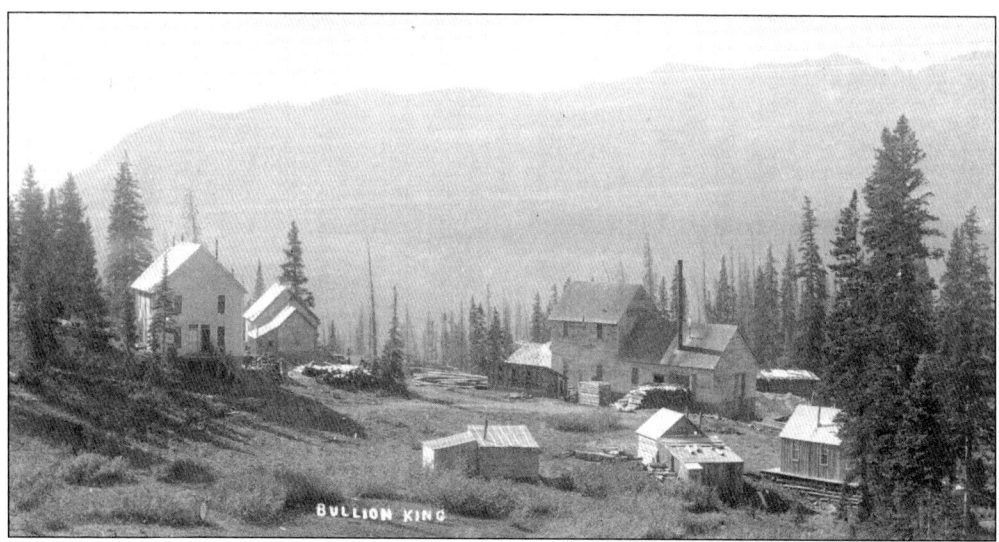

BULLION KING. The Bullion King Mine was one mile northwest of Irwin and one of the camp's top mines. In 1891, a 150-foot-wide avalanche roared down Ruby Peak and smashed into the Bullion King's boardinghouse. Only moments before, miners had left the boarding house and descended into the mine. A man, two women, and a two-year-old baby boy were killed in the avalanche.

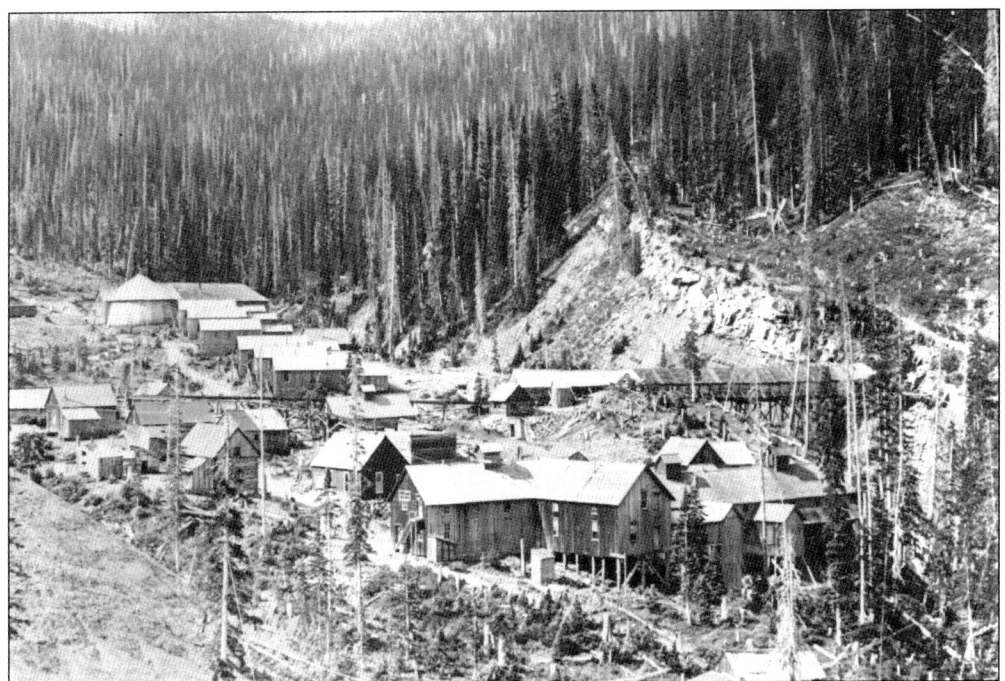

FLORESTA, 1900. Floresta grew rapidly after the arrival of the Denver and Rio Grande Railroad in 1893. The coal camp's population soared to 250, and it had a post office, a large boardinghouse, a sawmill, Colorado Supply Store, and Western Union telegraph service. The coal town was booming.

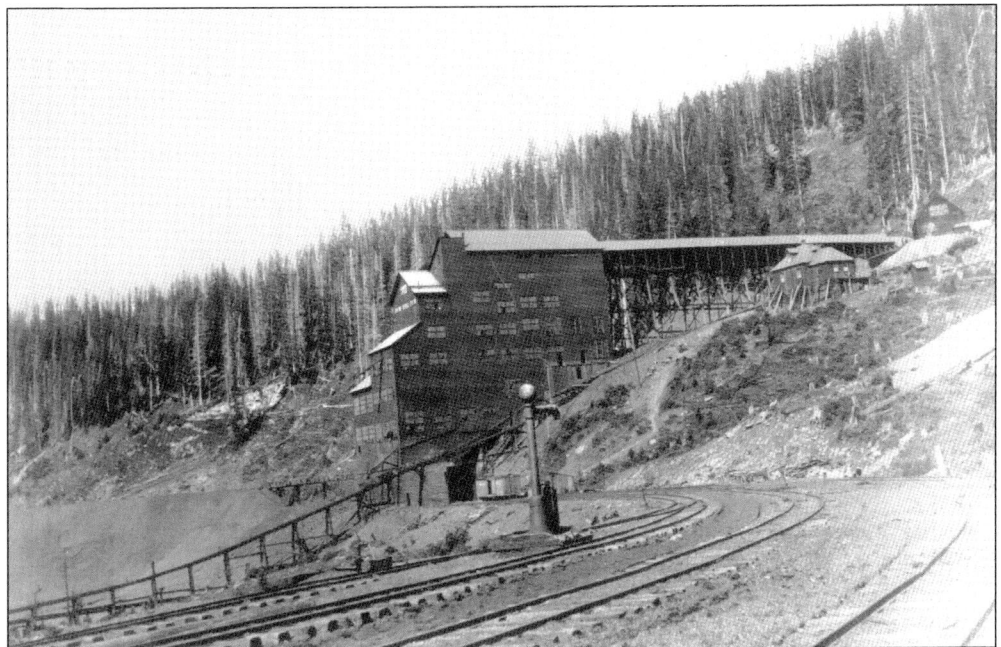

COAL AND THE RIO GRANDE. Denver and Rio Grande Railroad tracks run to the great Floresta coal breaker in 1911. The breaker was 114 feet high, 76 feet wide, and 124 feet long and was capable of handling 2,000 tons of coal every 24 hours. The great anthracite mine employed 100 men.

POST OFFICE IN THE CLOUDS. Floresta got a post office in 1897, one of the highest in the nation at nearly 10,000 feet. Though the coal camp had a population of 250, no more than 10 families stayed there during the brutal, long winters. Coal was only produced from July to January because of the heavy snow, which halted railroad traffic.

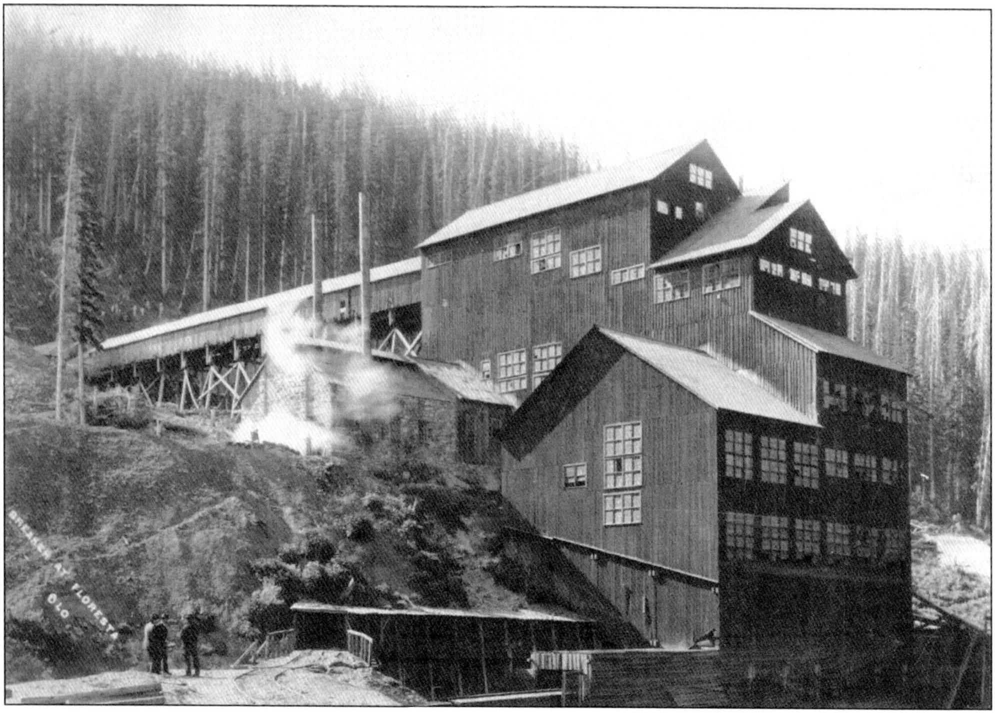

COAL BREAKER. The coal town of Floresta, 11 miles west of Crested Butte, produced anthracite or hard coal. The original name of the town was Ruby-Anthracite but it was changed to Floresta in 1901. This five-story coal breaker broke the coal into five different sizes and was the largest breaker west of Connellsville, Pennsylvania.

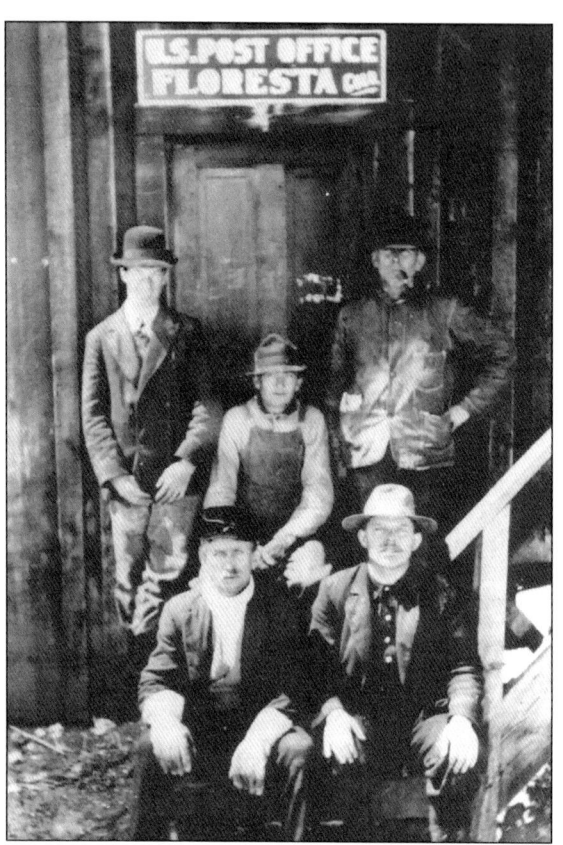

Three
CRESTED BUTTE
EARLY YEARS

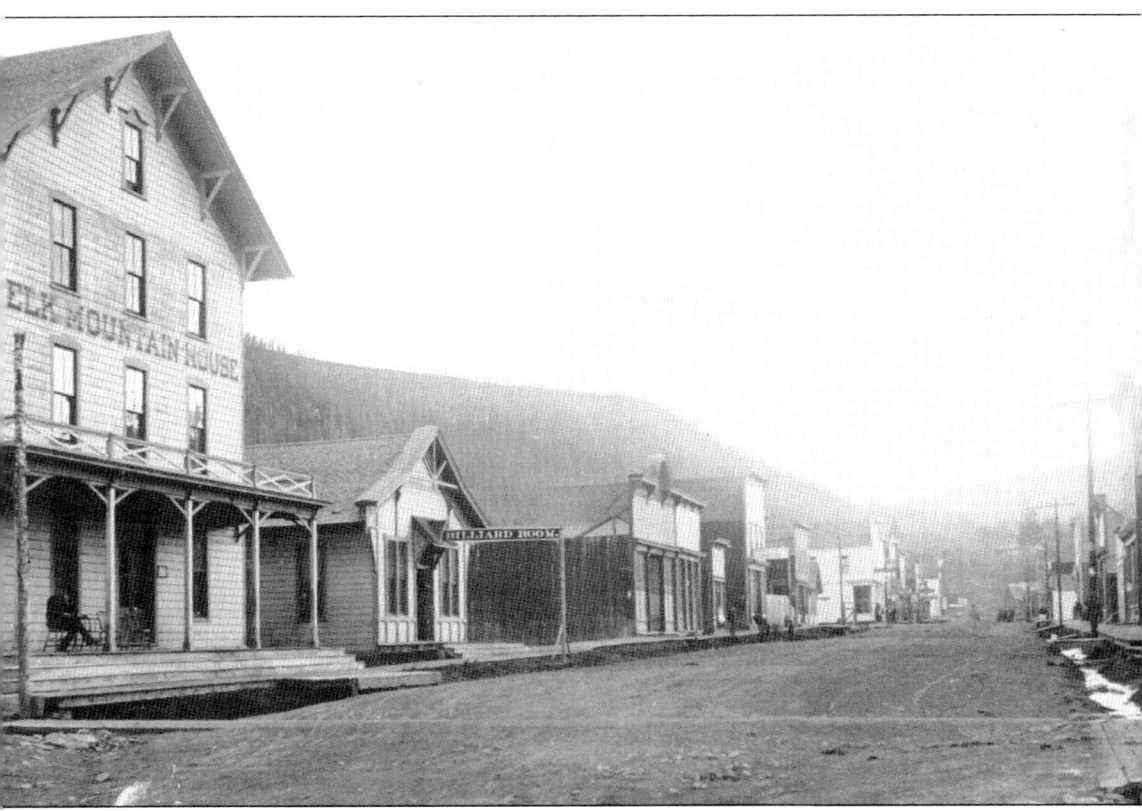

MAIN THOROUGHFARE, CRESTED BUTTE. Elk Avenue is very quiet in this 1884 photograph. The Elk Mountain House and a billiard room are among the establishments on the south side of the avenue. The street is dirt, the sidewalk is made of boards, and water from Coal Creek runs alongside Crested Butte's main street.

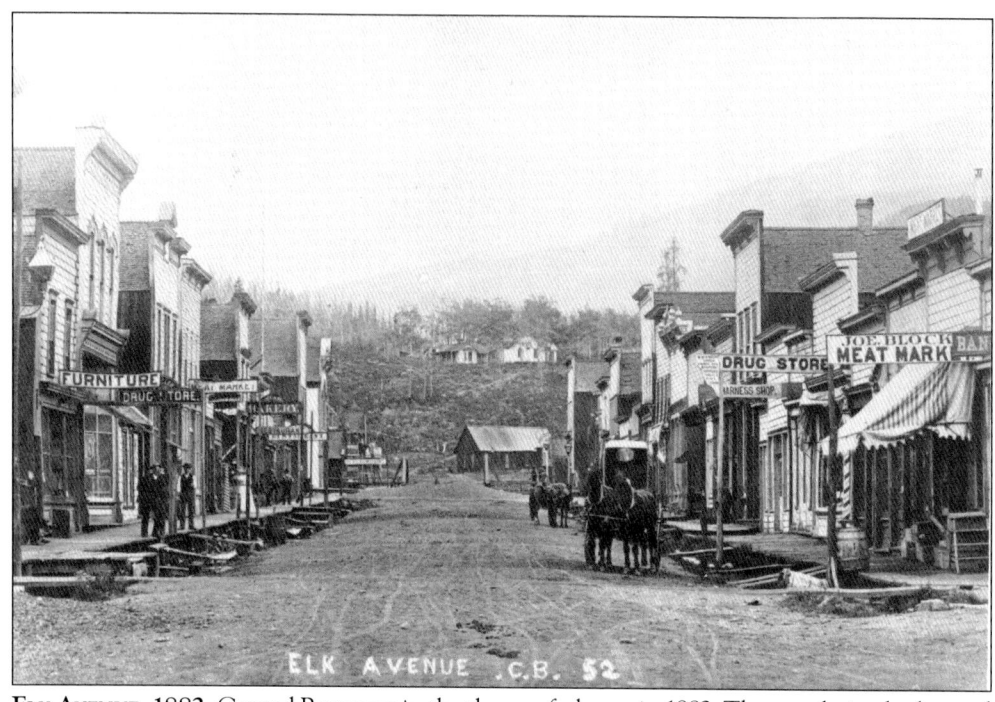

ELK AVENUE, 1882. Crested Butte was in the throes of a boom in 1882. The population had soared to 1,000, and the town now boasted five hotels, a bank, three livery stables, a dozen restaurants, and five nearby sawmills. This picture shows Elk Avenue looking west.

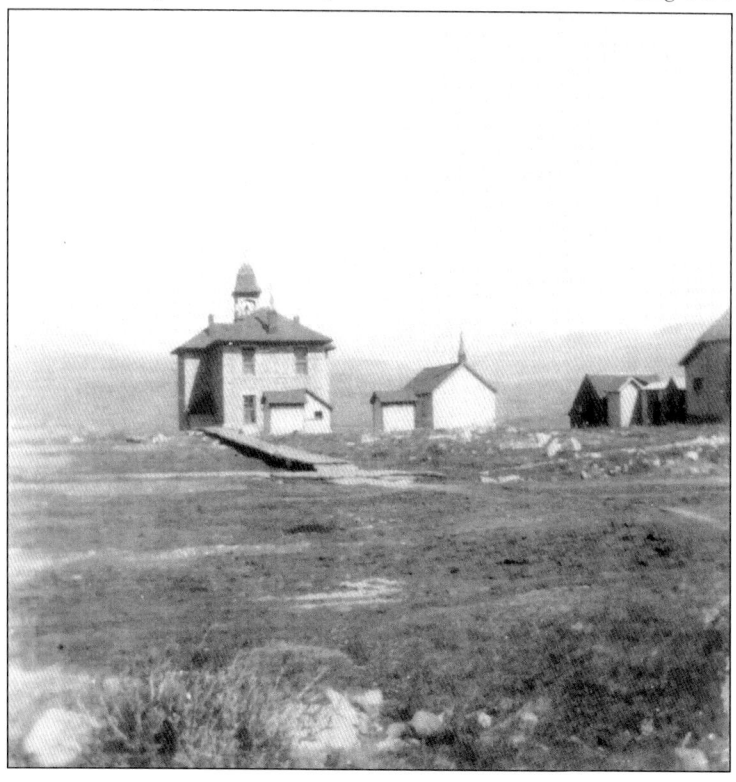

LONE SENTINEL. Crested Butte's famous rock schoolhouse stands nearly alone on the northeast side of town shortly after being built in 1883. The two-story structure housed upper grades. A nearby frame school had been built the previous year to handle lower grades.

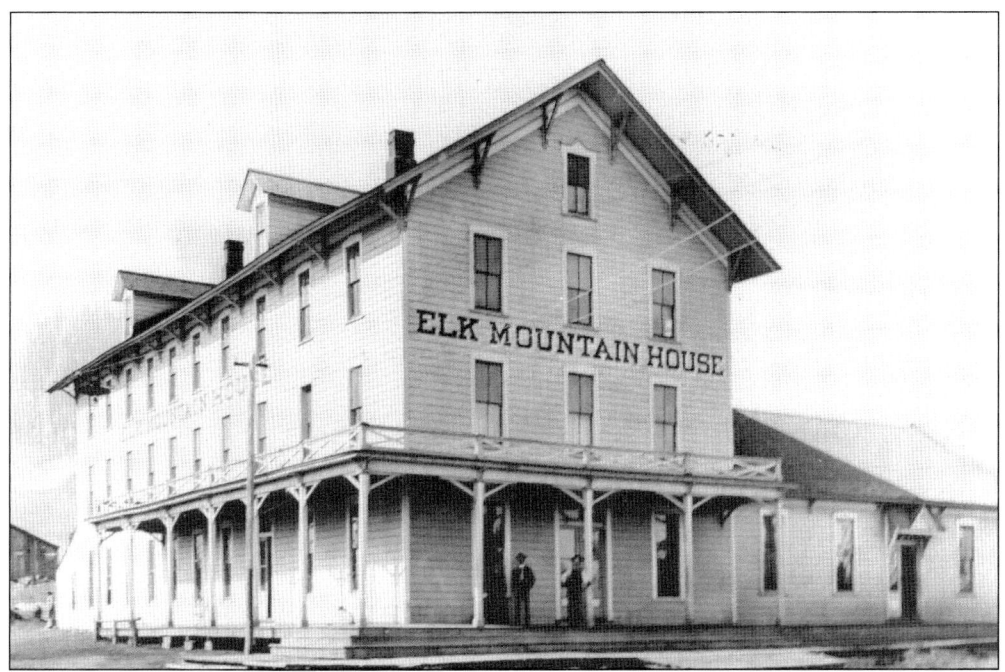

ELK MOUNTAIN HOUSE. The finest and largest hotel in Crested Butte, the Elk Mountain House opened in December 1881 on Elk Avenue. The three-story building was 34 feet by 100 feet, and a huge stove in the center of the main floor provided heat for the floors above through the use of registers.

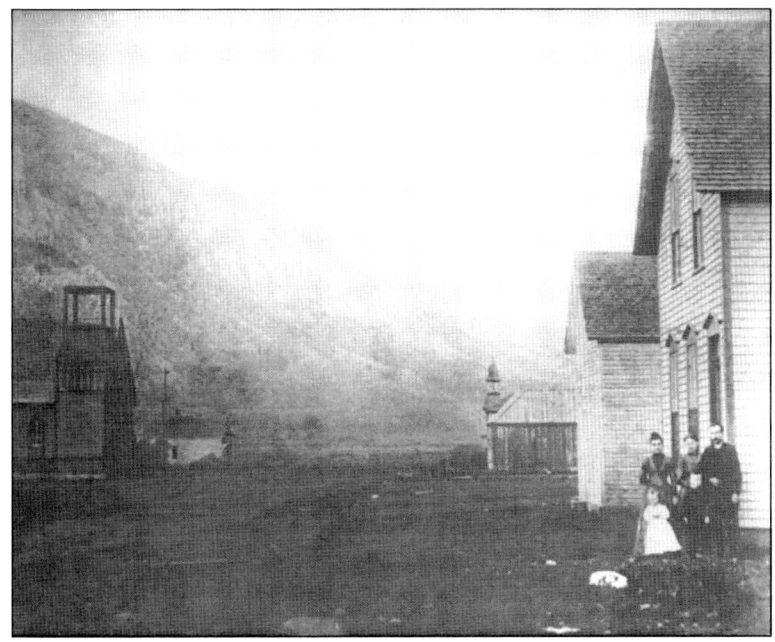

EARLY DAYS IN THE ELK MOUNTAINS. With Crested Butte Mountain in the background, a family poses in Crested Butte not long after the town began. The year is 1880, and the area had high hopes for both precious metal and coal mining.

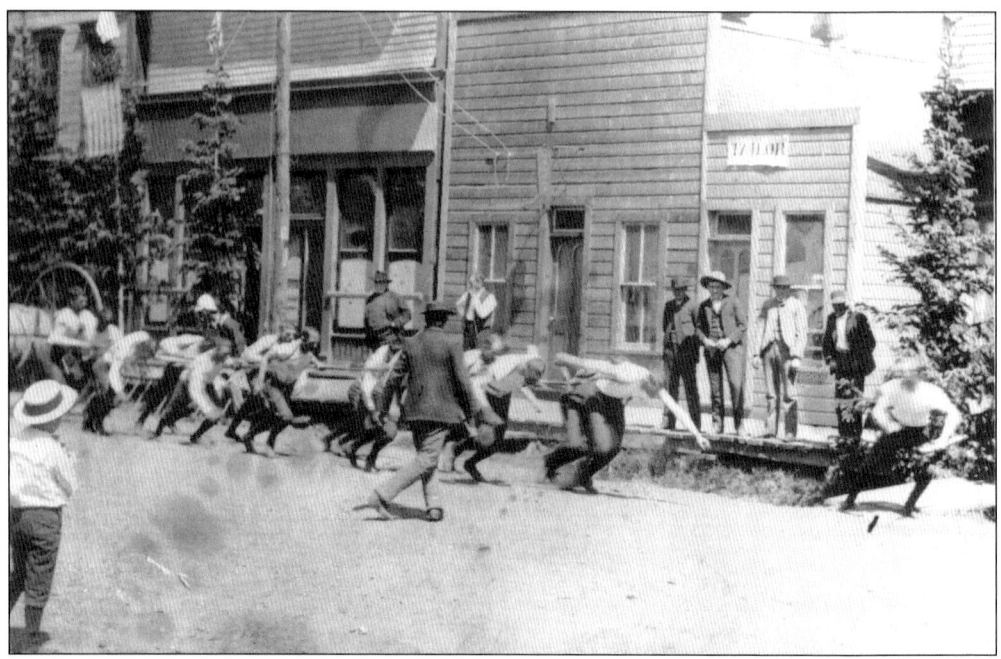

FOURTH OF JULY RACE. One of Crested Butte's fire department teams, the E. Cunningham Hose Squad, is urged on by its captain in this July 4, 1896 photograph. The men are straining as they pull a wheeled vehicle holding many feet of hose. With big prizes and much prestige on the line, different fire companies raced each other every Fourth of July.

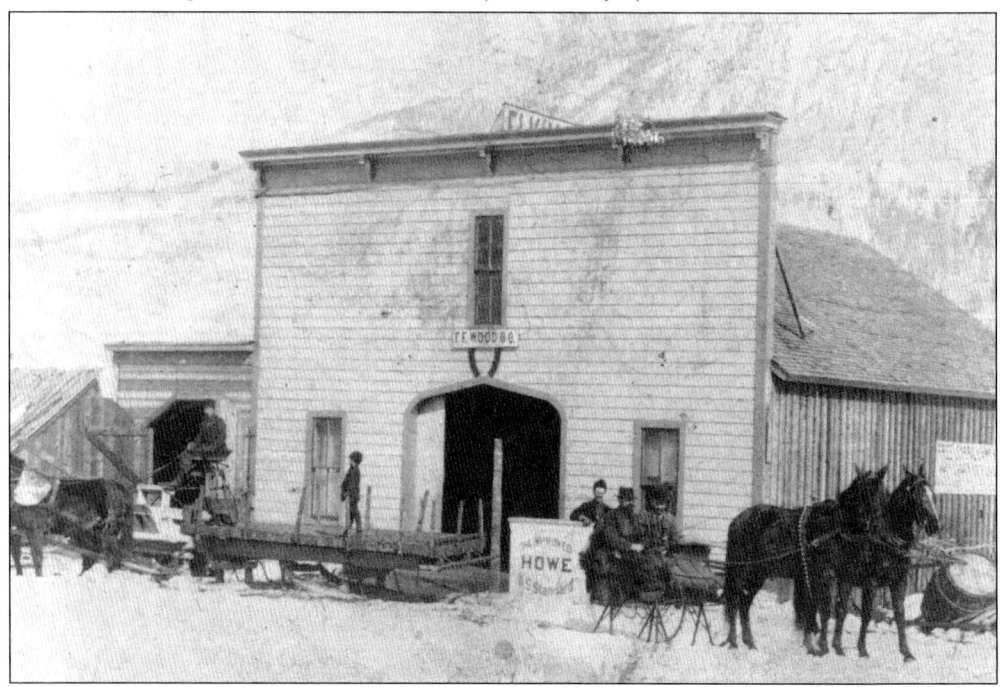

LIVERY STORE, 1883. The F.F. Wood Livery Store has customers early in the morning on the south side of Elk Avenue in Crested Butte. The dray with wooden skids and the sleigh both reflect the only way, outside of skiing, of getting around during winter months.

WAITING FOR THE MAIL. The Crested Butte Post Office in the 1880s was on Elk Avenue inside the general store owned by Holland and Axtell. The mail was brought in daily by rail after the arrival of the Denver and Rio Grande in 1881.

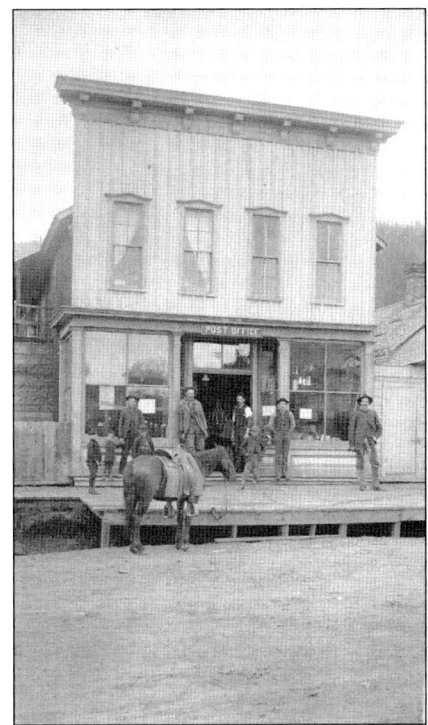

ROZICH'S SALOON. A little girl sits on a rail between two spittoons in one of Crested Butte's popular saloons in the 1890s. Most saloons had gambling and also featured polka dances on Friday and Saturday nights.

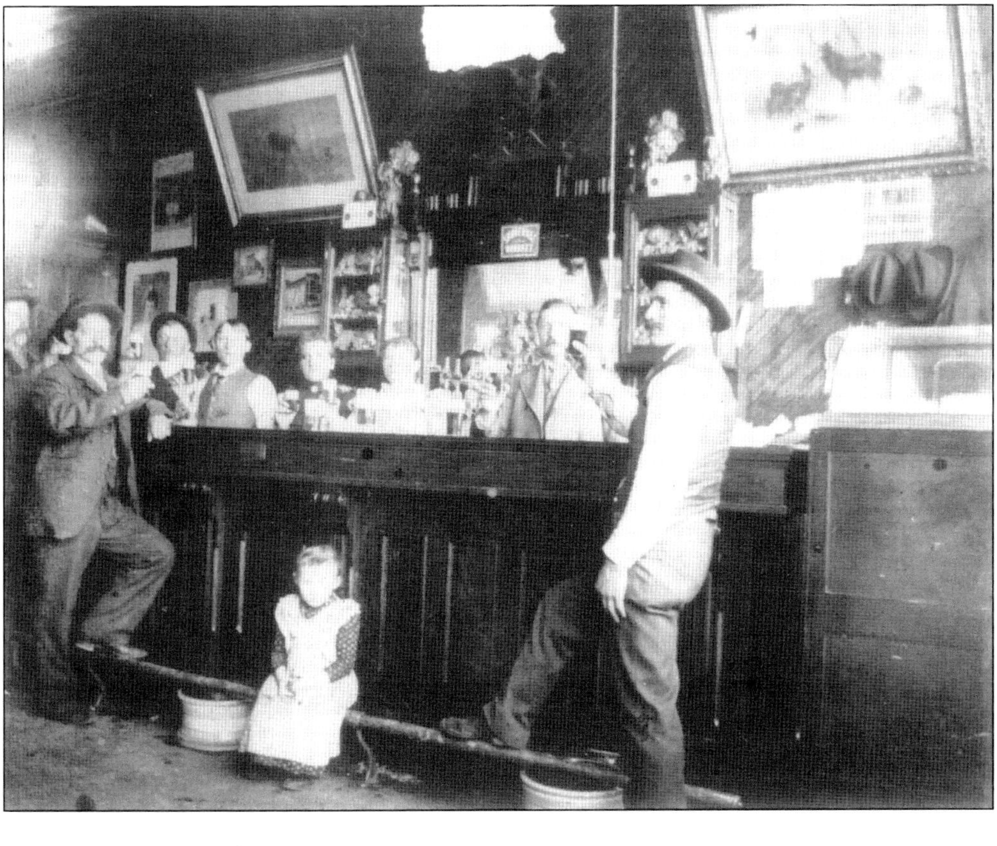

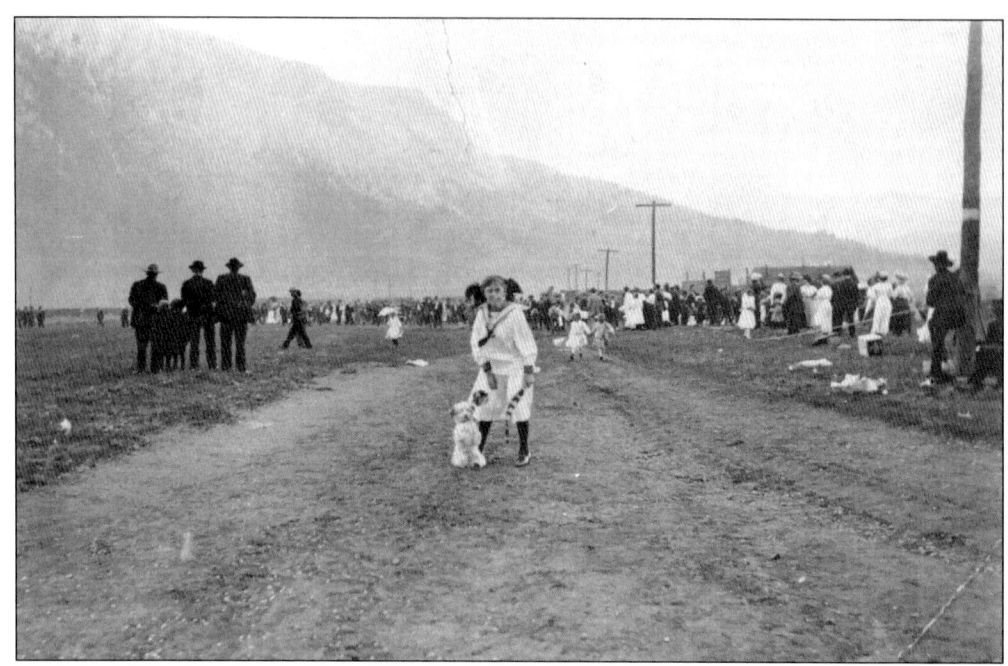

CRESTED BUTTE CELEBRATION. A young girl and her dog pose for a picture on a dirt road in Crested Butte in 1884. A celebration is going on in the background. Crested Butte's festivals were colorful, and most involved lots of cold beer, polka dances, and sporting events such as baseball games.

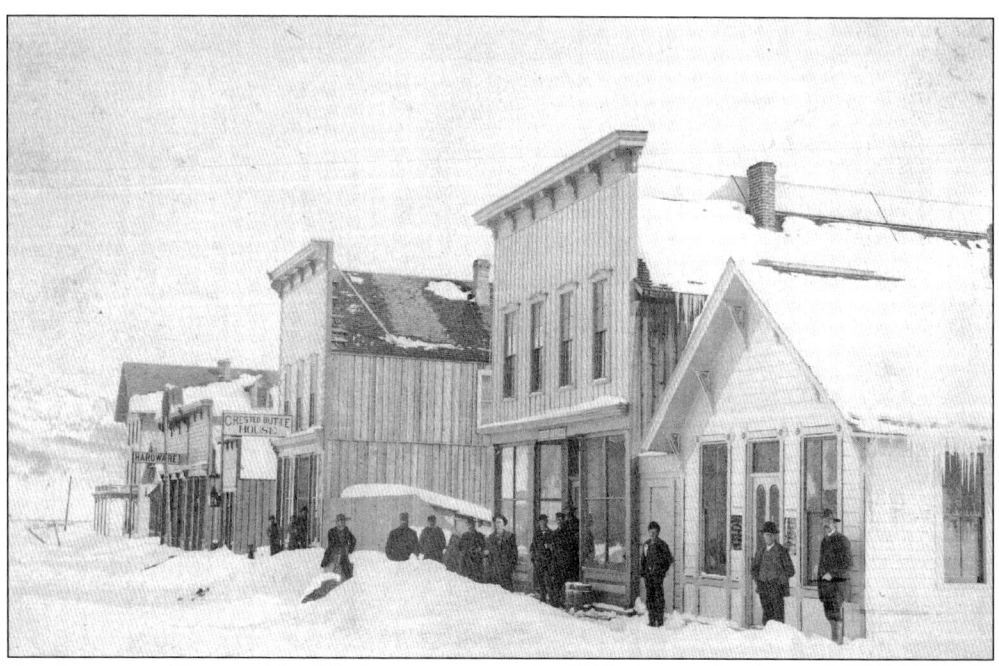

ELK AVENUE IN WINTER. This Elk Avenue scene in the 1880s shows a hardware store, the Crested Butte House, and the post office on Elk Avenue during an early winter. The only effective means of personal transportation then was via skis.

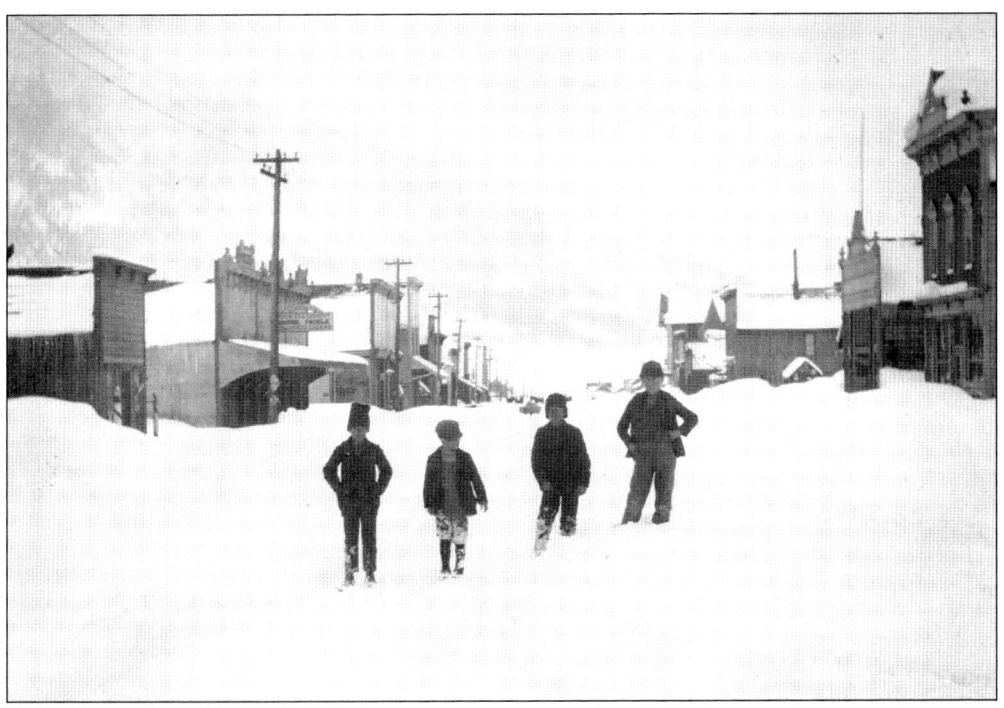

BIG WINTER. Four Crested Butte boys pose in the middle of Elk Avenue during the winter of 1895–1896. The photograph looks east toward Crested Butte Mountain. More than 400 inches of snow fell that winter—one of the biggest snowfalls in the history of the town.

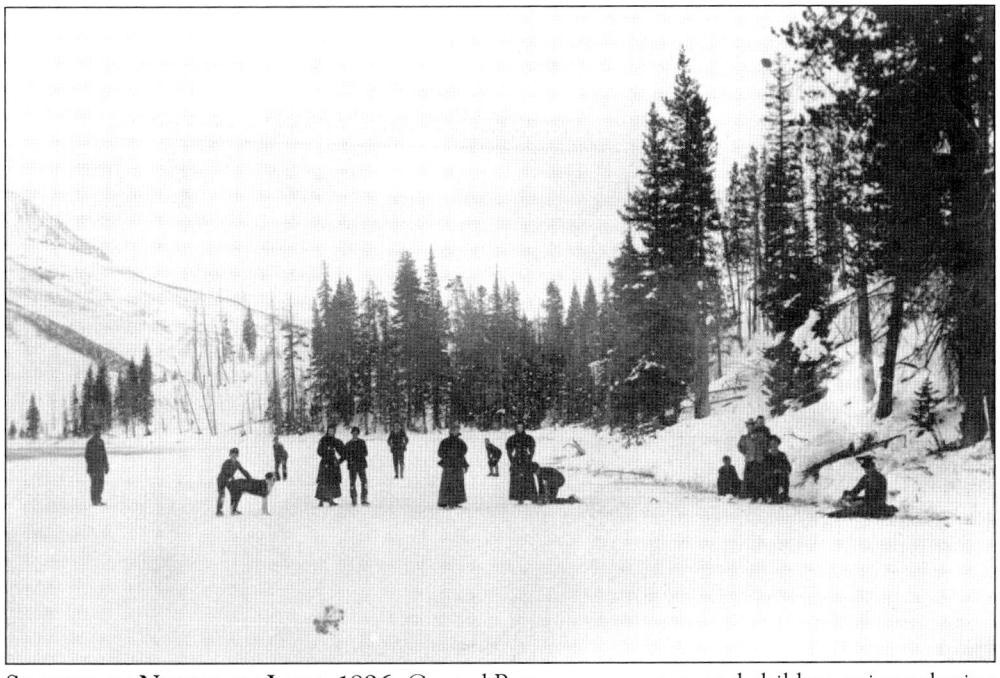

SKATING ON NICHOLSON LAKE, 1896. Crested Butte men, women, and children enjoy a skating party on Nicholson Lake on Christmas Day. The lake is located about three miles north of town and was the scene of many gathering throughout the year.

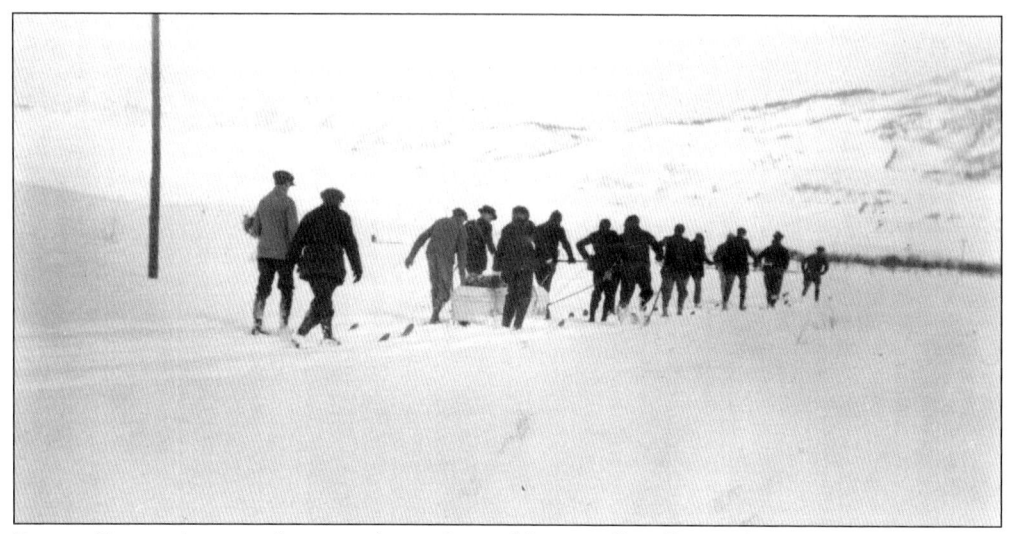

BURIAL PARTY. A group of men on skis in Crested Butte pull Tuffie Hugh's coffin to a blockhouse during the winter of 1921. The coffin would not be lowered into the ground in the Crested Butte cemetery until spring when the thaw came.

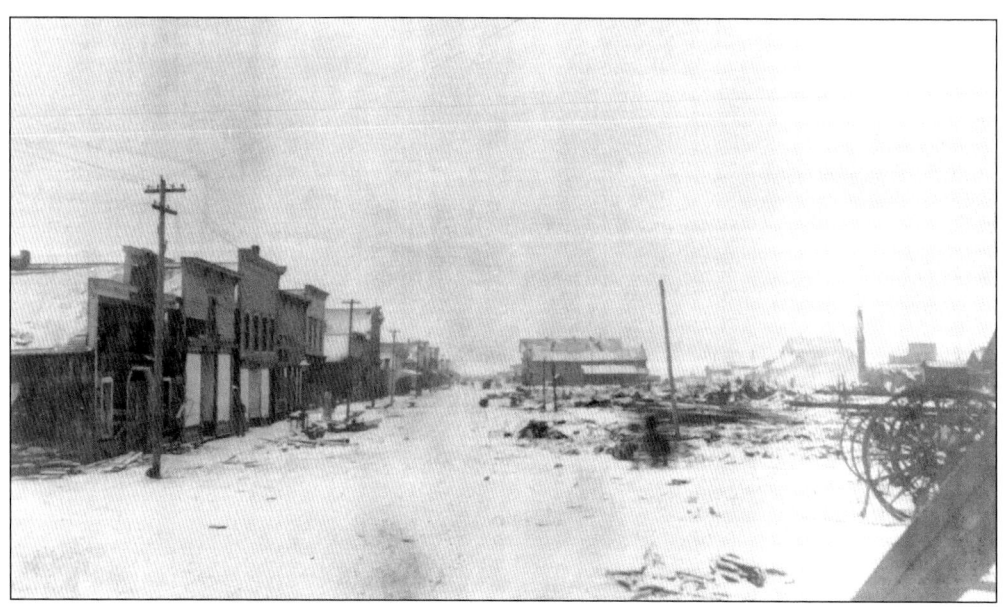

DAMAGING FIRE. The first major fire in Crested Butte's history occurred on January 25, 1890. The blaze was caused by an overheated stove on the north side of Elk Avenue and destroyed 15 businesses at a cost of $50,000. High winds fanned the flames, making it very dangerous.

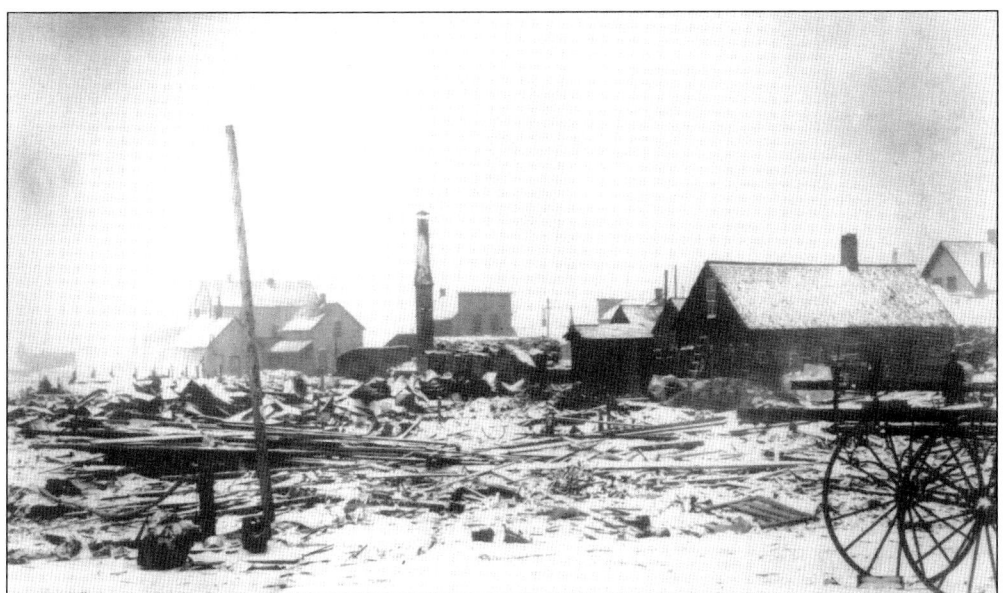

DEVASTATION OF 1893. Tremendous devastation can be seen on Elk Avenue in Crested Butte after a disastrous fire on January 9, 1893. The fire began in the Carlisle and Tetand Market and quickly raged out of control. Frozen water lines contributed to the destruction of nearly all of Crested Butte's major street.

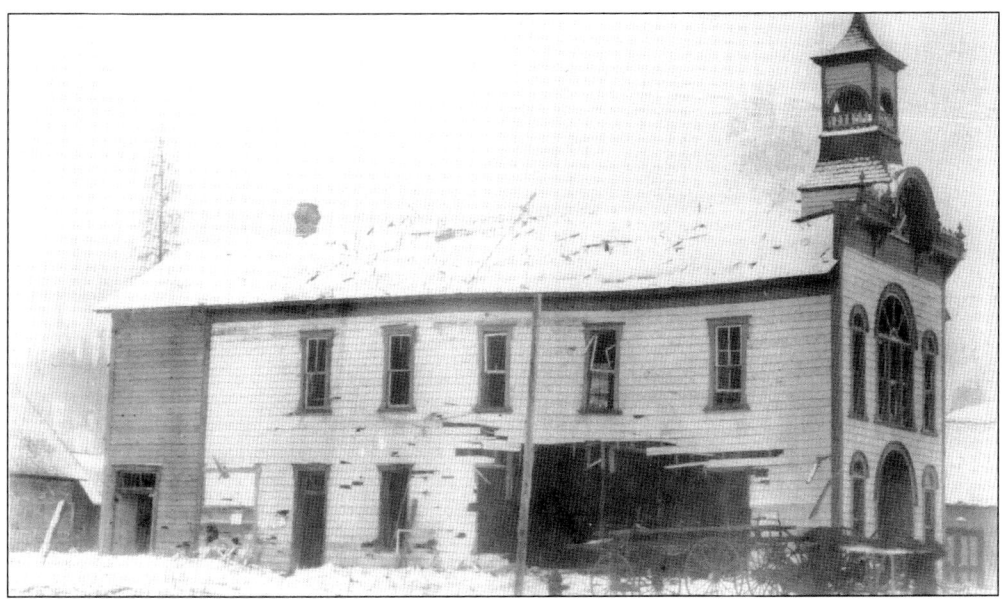

CITY HALL DISASTER. In a desperate attempt to stop the January 9, 1893, fire in Crested Butte, firemen deliberately blew up A.E. Miller's furniture store. The 150 pounds of explosives, however, was too much. The blast tore a gaping hole in the city hall, and broke nearly every window in town.

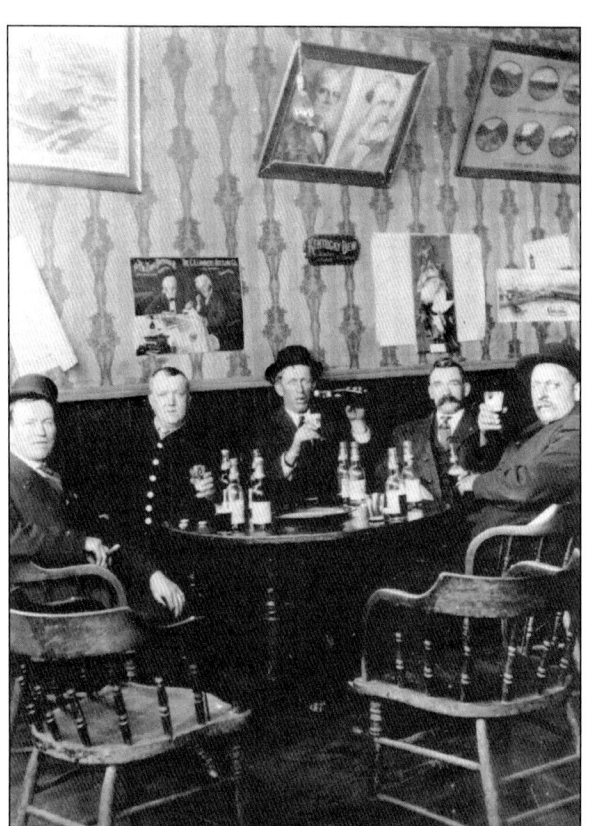

CRESTED BUTTE SALOON. Five locals enjoy a cold beer at the end of a hot summer day before 1900 at Rozich's Saloon on Elk Avenue in Crested Butte. The saloons were a favorite gathering spot for miners and other men after the day's work was completed.

A BEAUTIFUL ELK MOUNTAIN LAKE. A young lady is fly-fishing on spectacular Long's Lake, a few miles north of Crested Butte in the 1880s. The lake was a favorite recreation spot for the people of Crested Butte. Fishing and boating were popular, as was swinging out on a rope and jumping into the lake.

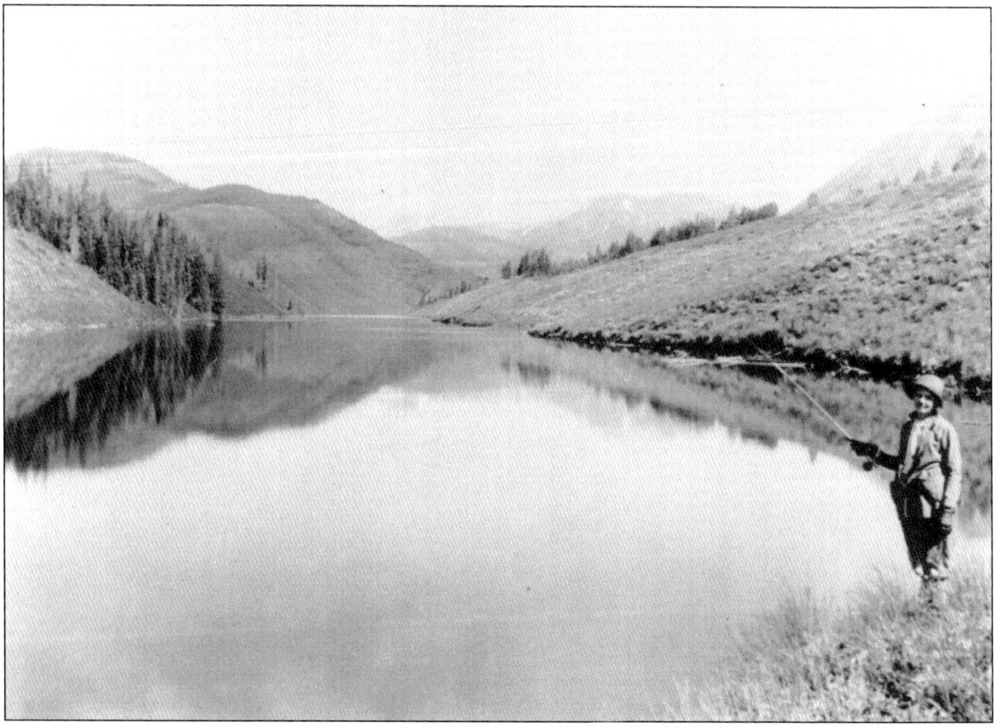

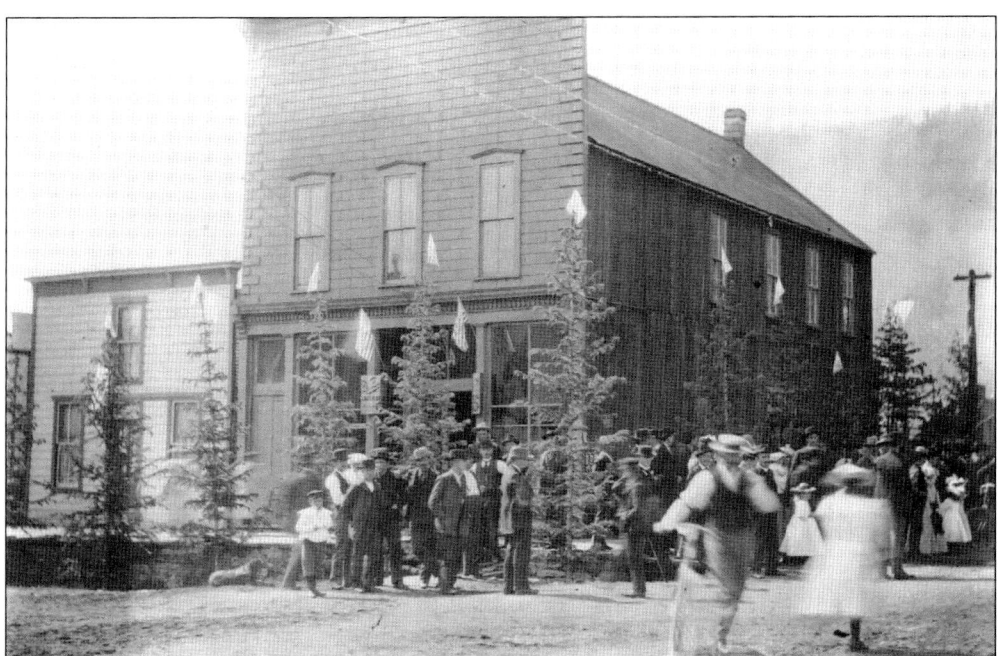

ROZICH'S SALOON. John Rozich's saloon was the top drinking establishment in Crested Butte before 1900. The building originally stood on the north side of Elk Avenue but was moved by men and horses to the south side, with the only damage being one cracked window.

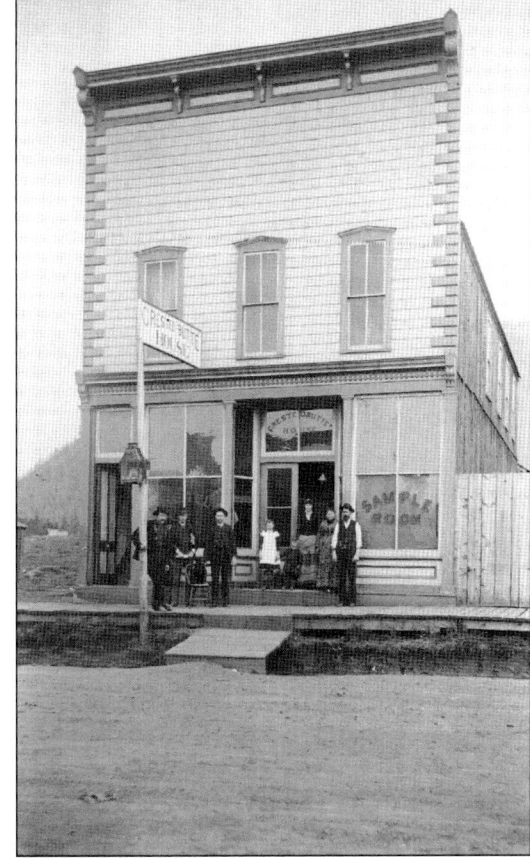

CRESTED BUTTE HOUSE. An unidentified little girl and her younger brother stand at the entrance to the Crested Butte House in the 1880s. The establishment was a hotel with 20 rooms that was located on Elk Avenue. The main desk and parlor room were in the front of the building.

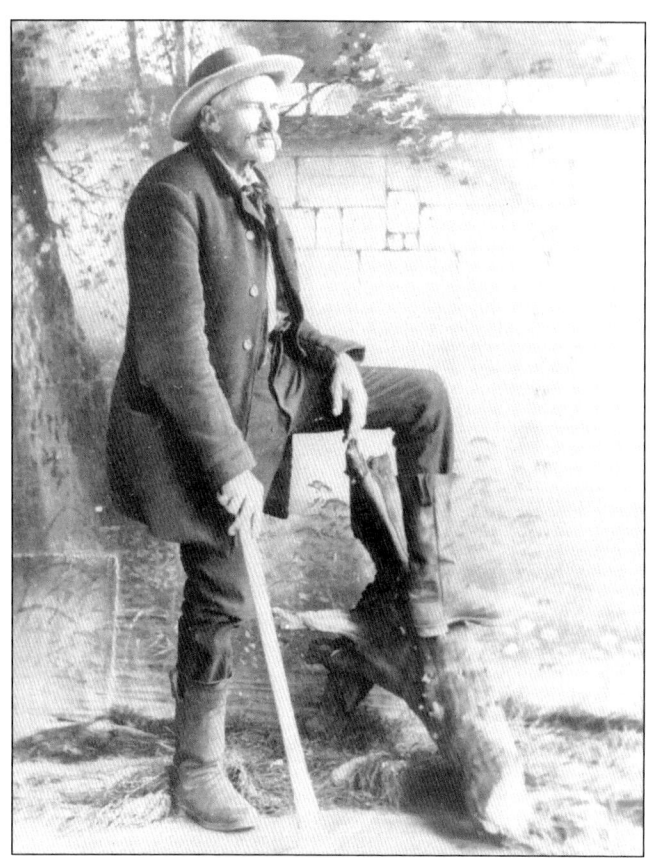

YANK BAXTER. Yank Baxter was one of the most colorful characters in Crested Butte's early history. He was part of the California Gold Rush, a Pony Express rider, and finally came to Poverty Gulch north of Crested Butte to mine for silver in 1879. Baxter's voice was reportedly so loud that one miner referred to it as a "dividend paying institution."

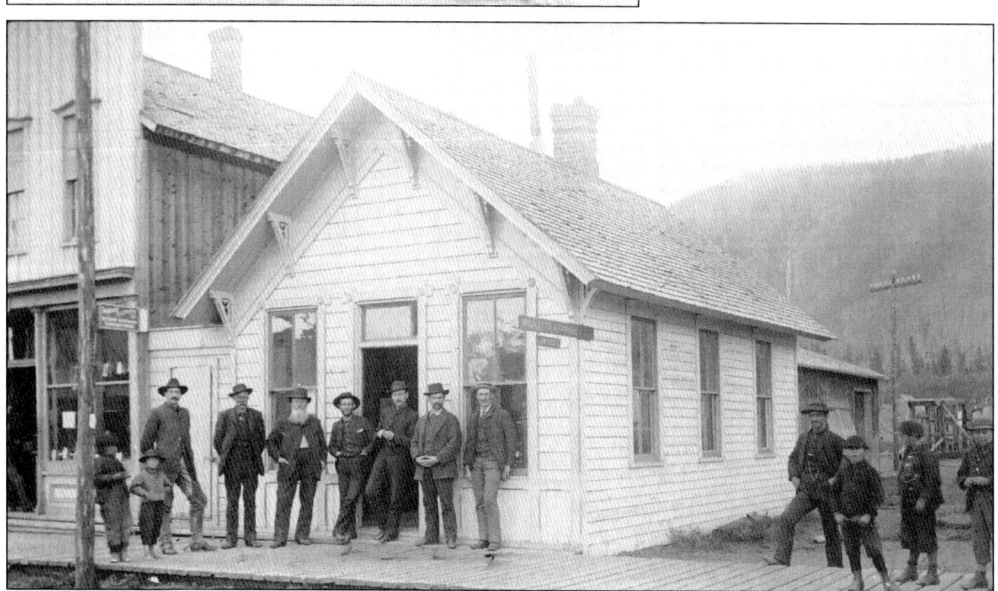

CRESTED BUTTE LAW OFFICE. This frame building on the south side of Elk Avenue housed one of the many law offices of the town. In the early 1880s, Crested Butte harbored hopes of becoming a great silver town. With mines close to each other with intersecting veins, litigation was common, and lawyers thrived.

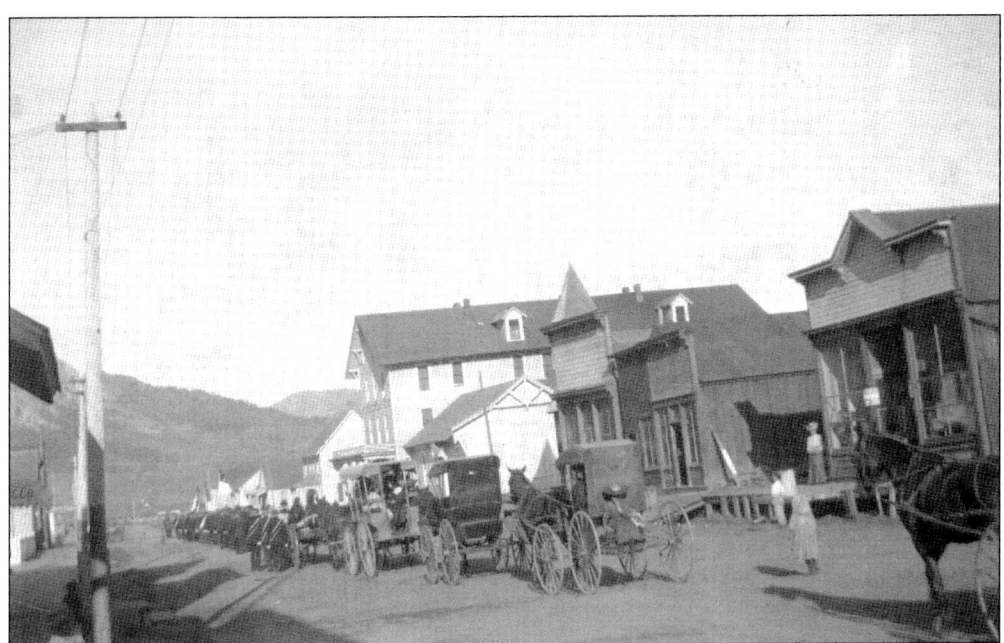

ELK AVENUE FUNERAL. A solemn funeral procession led by one of Crested Butte's fraternal orders passes down Elk Avenue in the 1880s. The many fraternal orders in town were important social, political, and economic aids to the many different ethnic groups.

PLACER MINING. The 1860s were a placer mining decade in the Slate and East River Valleys and in Washington Gulch, near today's Crested Butte. Famed missionary John F. Dyer preached to 250 placer miners near the head of Washington Gulch in 1861. The men here, in nearby Taylor Park, are attempting to find gold through the use of a sluice box. (DPL.)

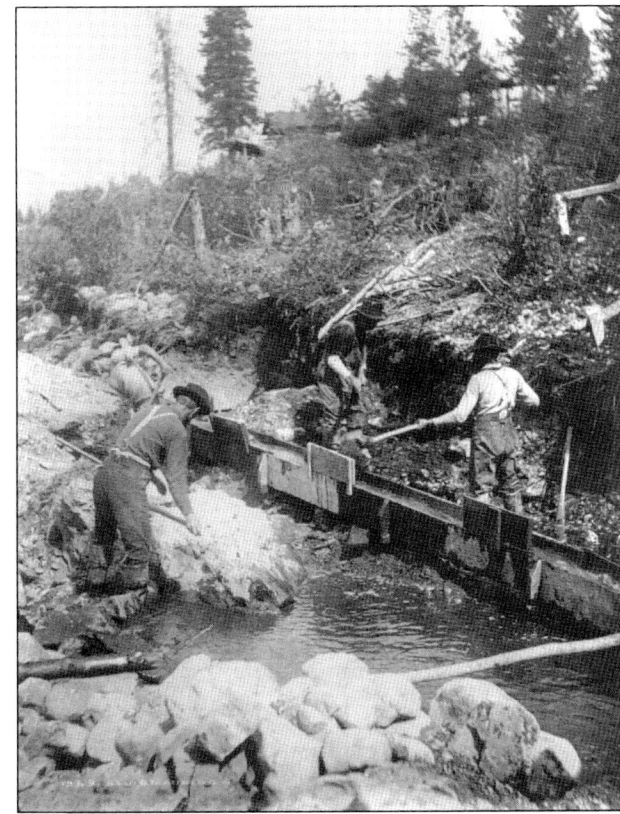

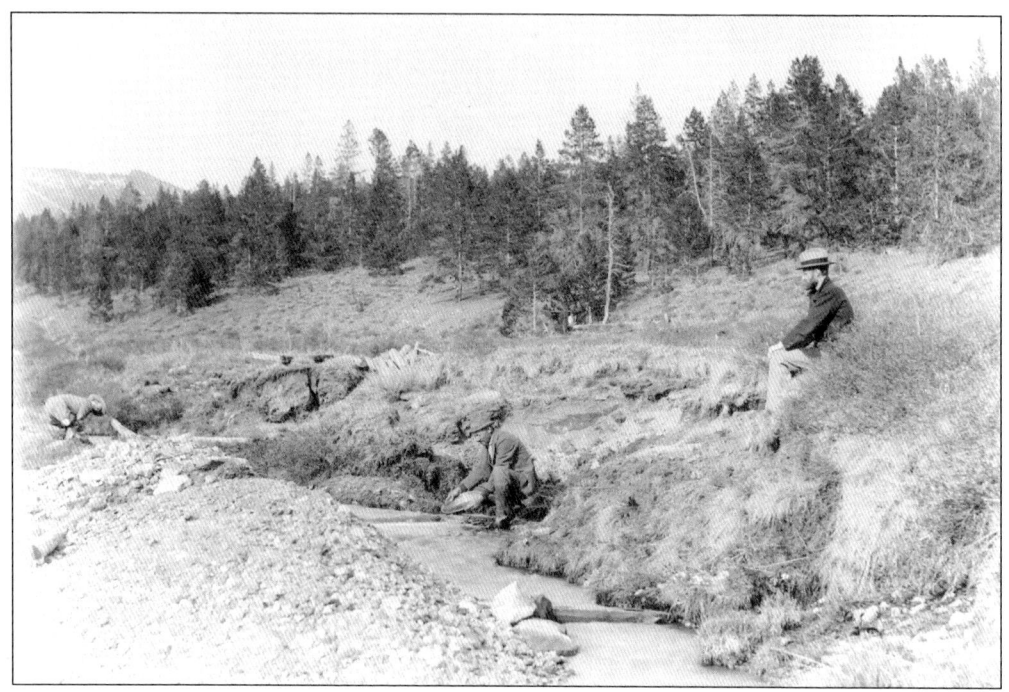

GOLD PANNING. Men with gold pans search for gold in the early 1870s on a branch of Willow Creek in Taylor Park, southeast of today's Crested Butte. Hundreds were in the park in a quest for gold following initial discoveries by Jim Taylor and Fred Lottis in 1861.

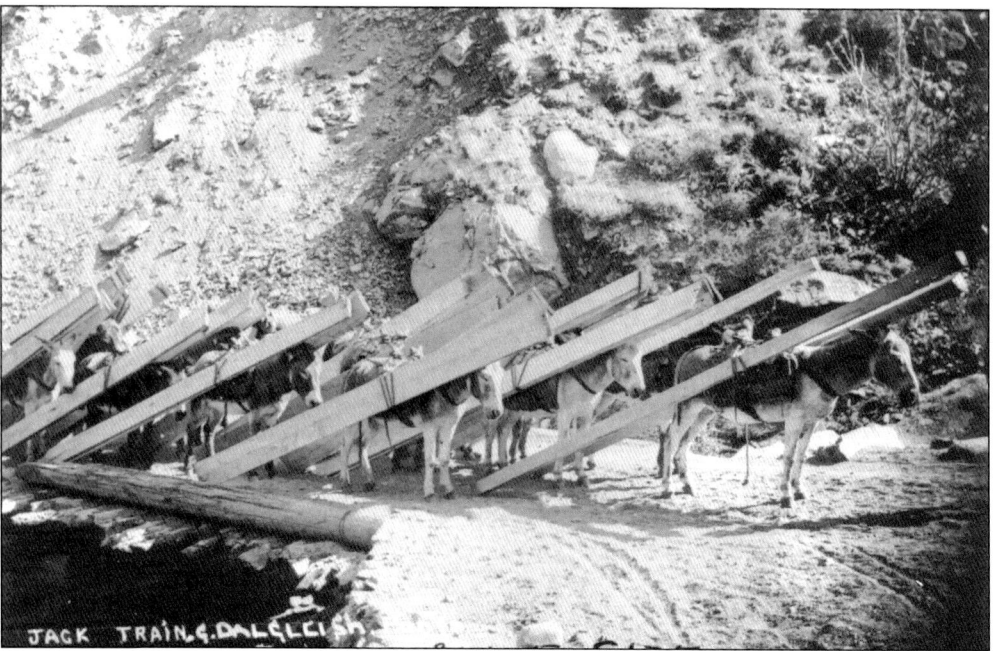

ROCKY MOUNTAIN CANARIES. Burros, better known as Rocky Mountain canaries, are transporting cut lumber to a mill at high elevation in the 1880s. These "jack trains" were essential in the Elk Mountains around Crested Butte. They carried needed supplies up to isolated mining camps and carried ore down to smelters on the return trip. (DPL.)

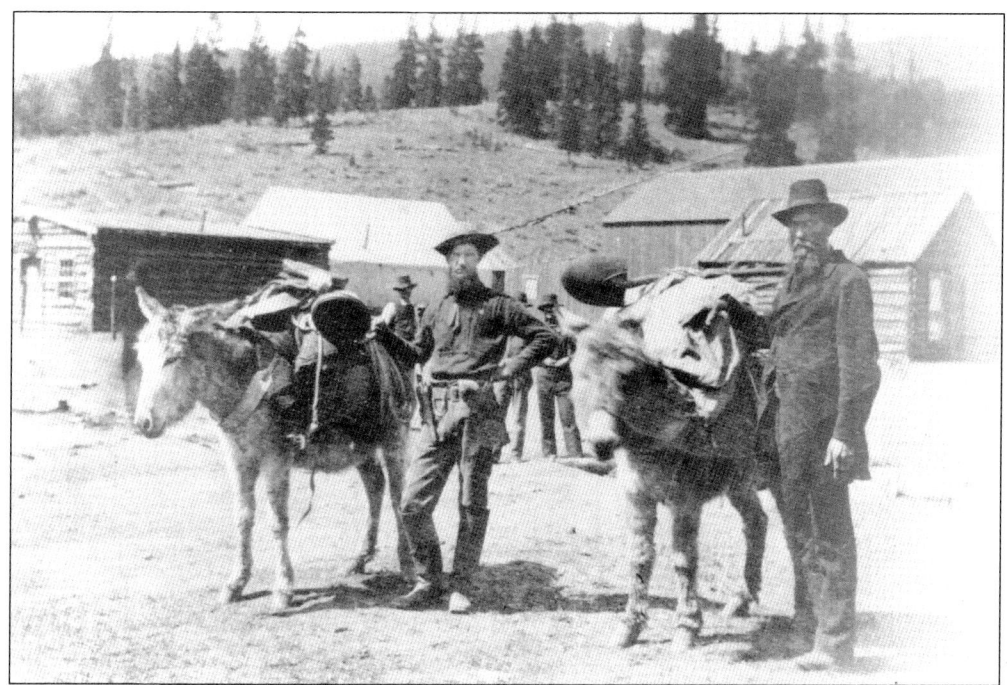

HEADING FOR THE HILLS. These two veteran miners have purchased all their supplies and are ready to head to their placer diggings. The year is 1881, and the placers are located on Lottis Creek at the edge of Union Park southeast of Crested Butte.

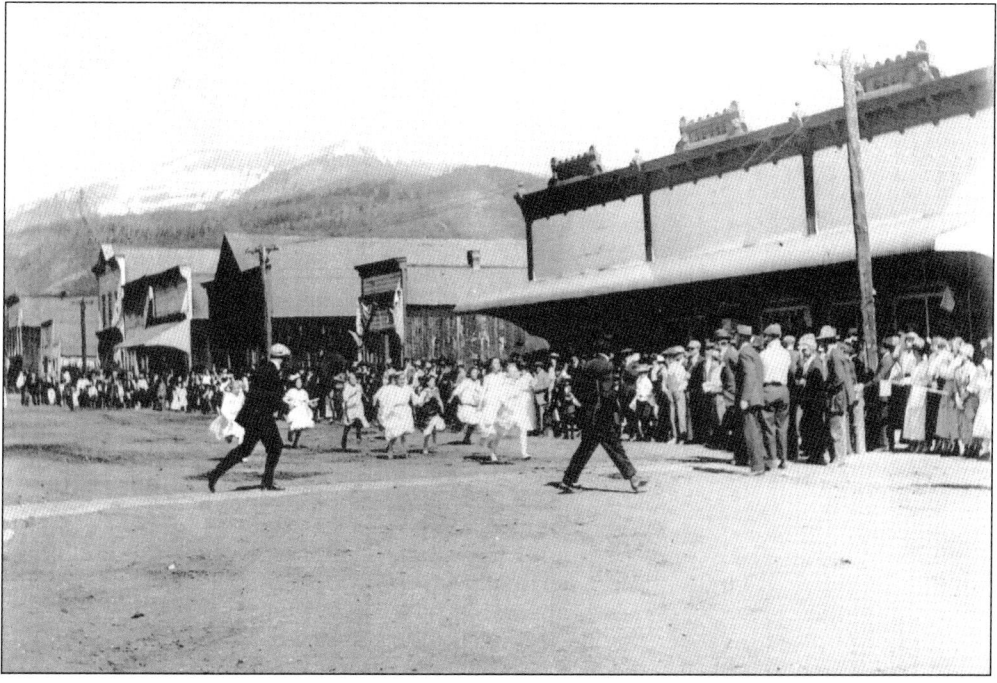

100 YARD DASH. A huge crowd is gathered in Crested Butte on a Fourth of July in the 1930s to watch Crested Butte girls run a 100 yard dash. Fourth of July celebrations were filled with races, drilling contests, tug-of-wars, baseball games, and sawing contests—all creating great excitement.

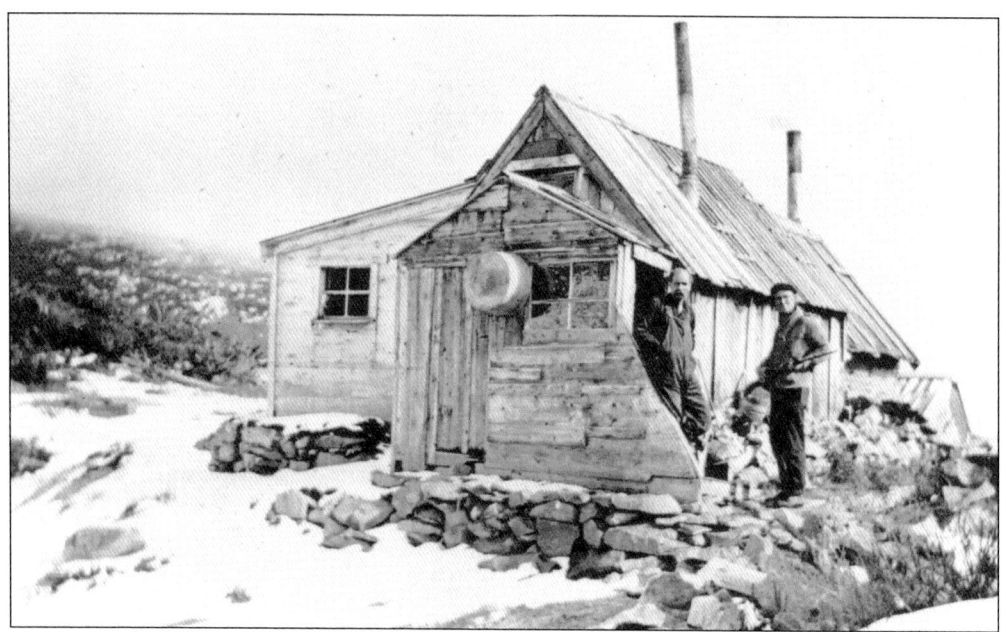

WASHINGTON GULCH. High above Crested Butte, 12 miles to the north near Paradise Divide, Yule Pass, and Treasury Peak, two grizzled silver miners pose in front of their rustic cabin. Their mine was far above timberline, and getting supplies in and ore out was a tremendously difficult task.

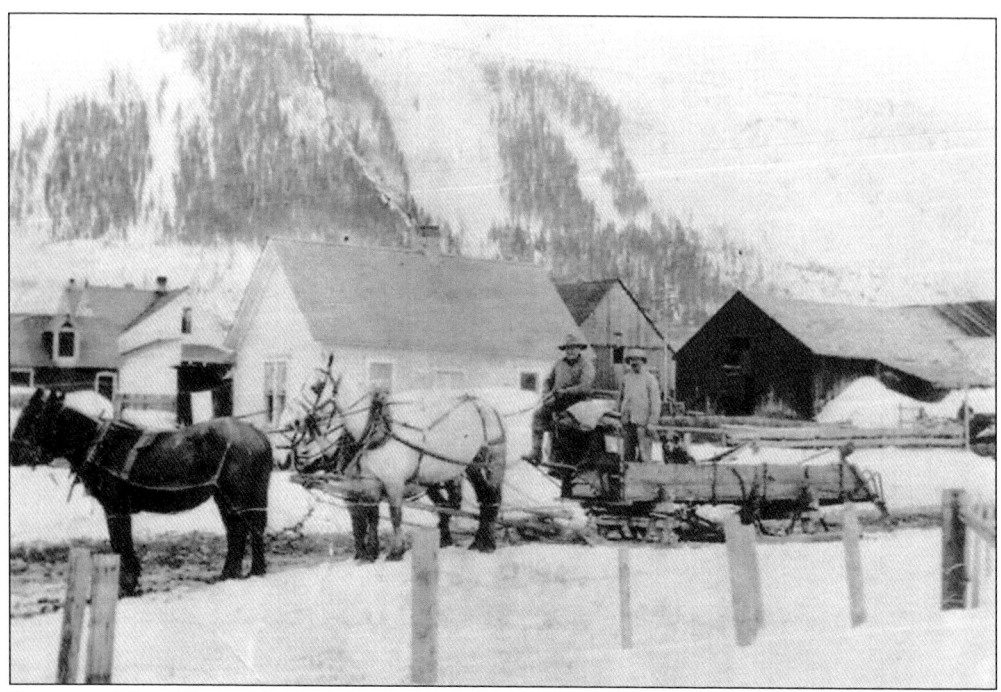

DELIVERY MEN. With Gibson Ridge in the background, Oliver Thomas, a hired man, and a dog make deliveries of supplies in early Crested Butte. The horses are pulling a sleigh through the snow, which will get much higher deep into the winter months.

Four
CRESTED BUTTE
Later Years

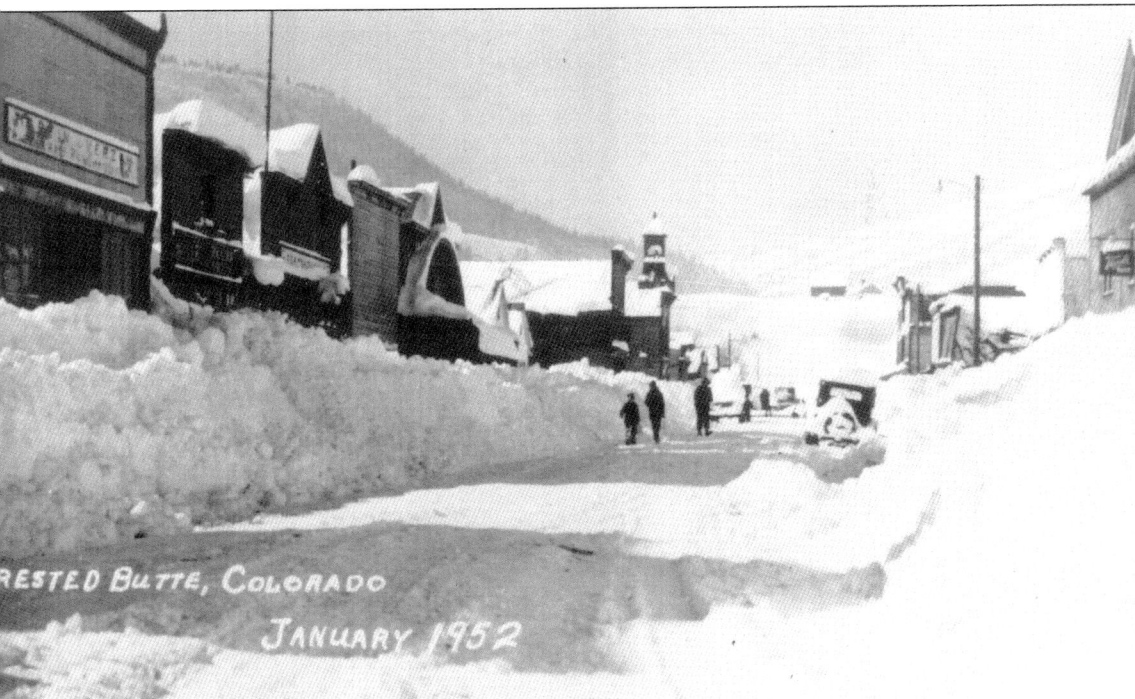

ELK AVENUE WONDERLAND. The winter of 1951–1952 was one of the toughest of the 20th century. The snow was so heavy that customers had to walk through tunnels to get to businesses. Elk Avenue is dotted with only a few cars, and they had trouble getting around.

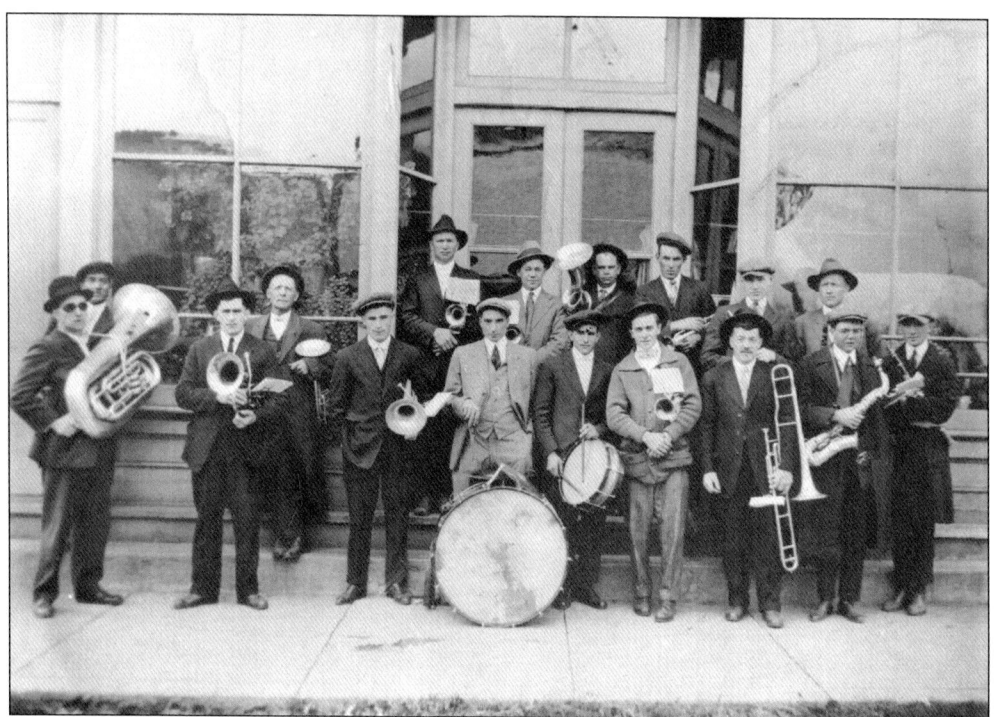

CRESTED BUTTE TOWN BAND, 1900. The Crested Butte town band poses on Elk Avenue before playing at a Memorial Day celebration. Crested Butte was well known for its great musicians. Many had come from European countries like Italy, Austria, Croatia, and Slovenia, where music had been a big part of everyone's life.

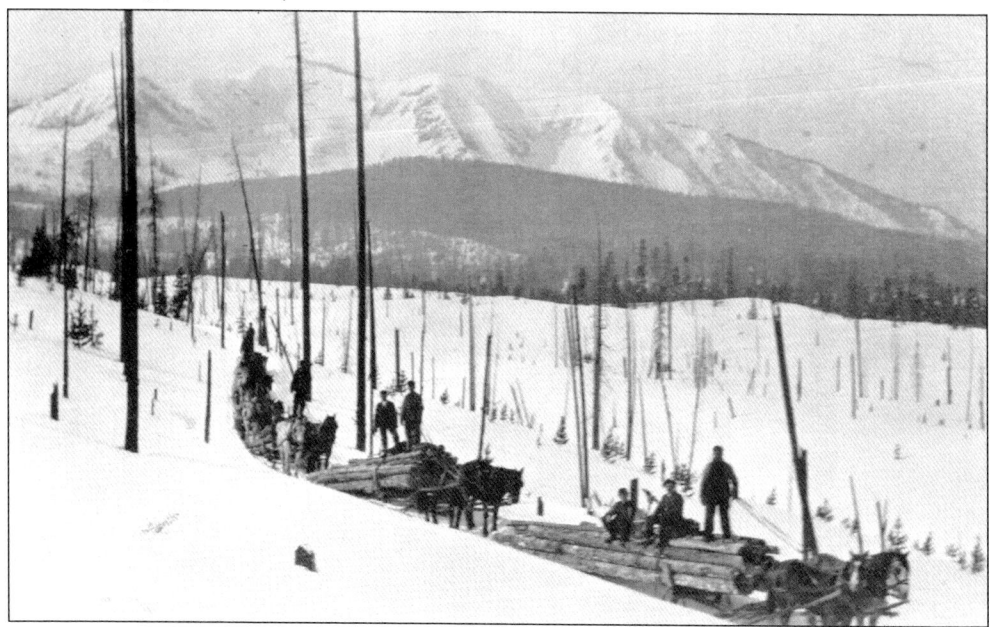

HAULING LOGS NEAR CRESTED BUTTE. Joseph Archer and his men are hauling logs to the Colorado Fuel and Iron Company's sawmill in 1908. The timber was cut near Kebler Pass, west of Crested Butte, and taken by horse teams to the mill for use as mine props or in buildings.

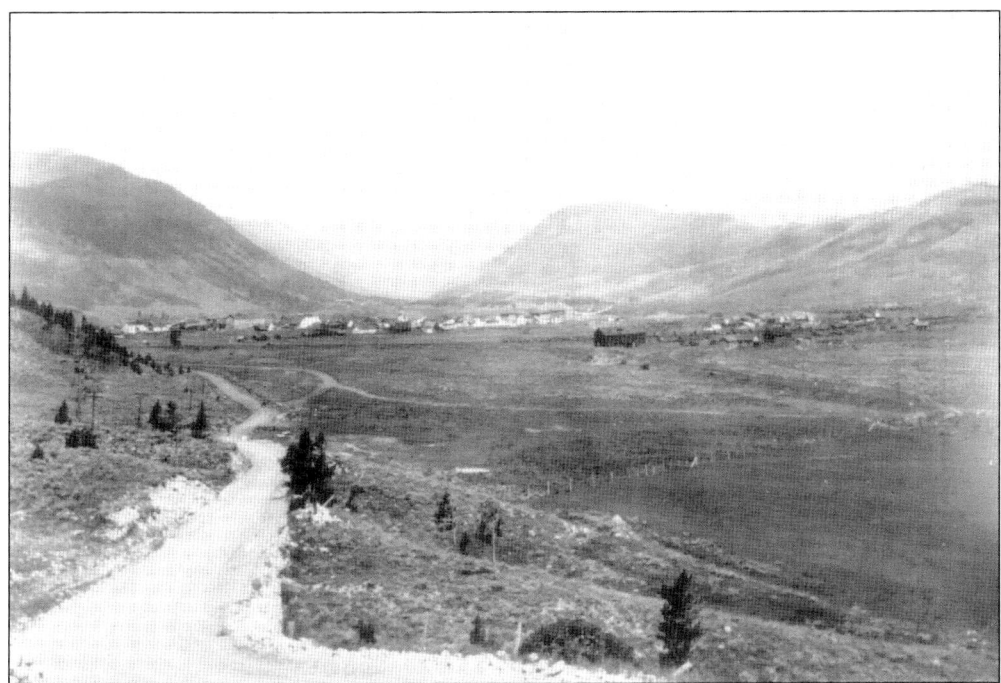

HIGHWAY 135. This photograph shows Crested Butte from Highway 135 around 1915. The dirt road ran 28 miles from Gunnison to Crested Butte and was a horror for travelers. The highway was usually closed in the winter because of snow and during the spring because of mud. The rest of the year it was dusty and bumpy.

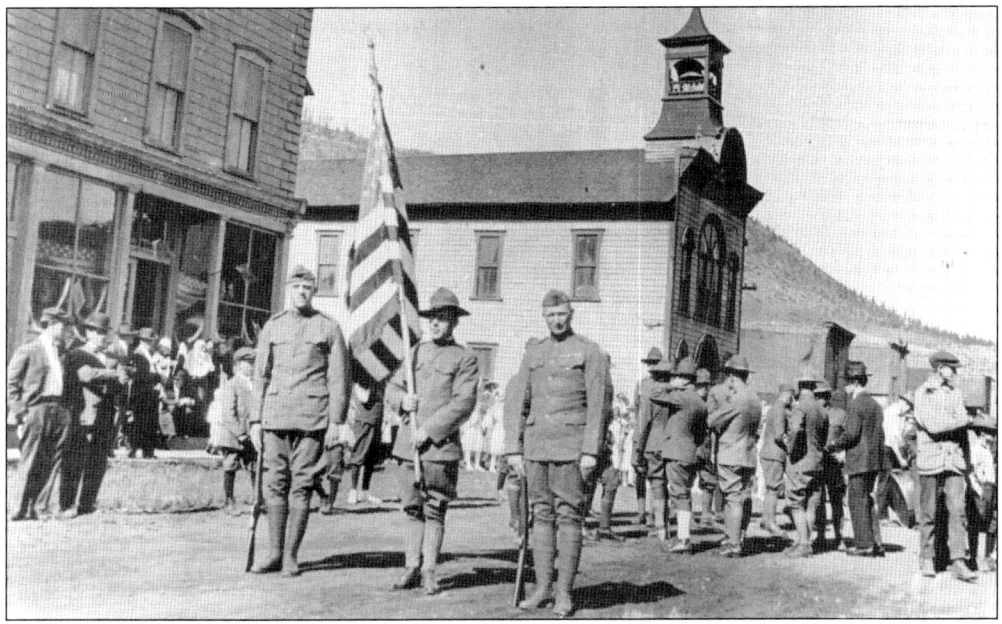

ARMISTICE DAY. With many of their comrades in the background, three World War I veterans stand at attention on November 11, 1919, one year after the end of the war, on Elk Avenue in Crested Butte. Armistice Day was always a gala celebration in town because of the high percentage of young men who served in the military.

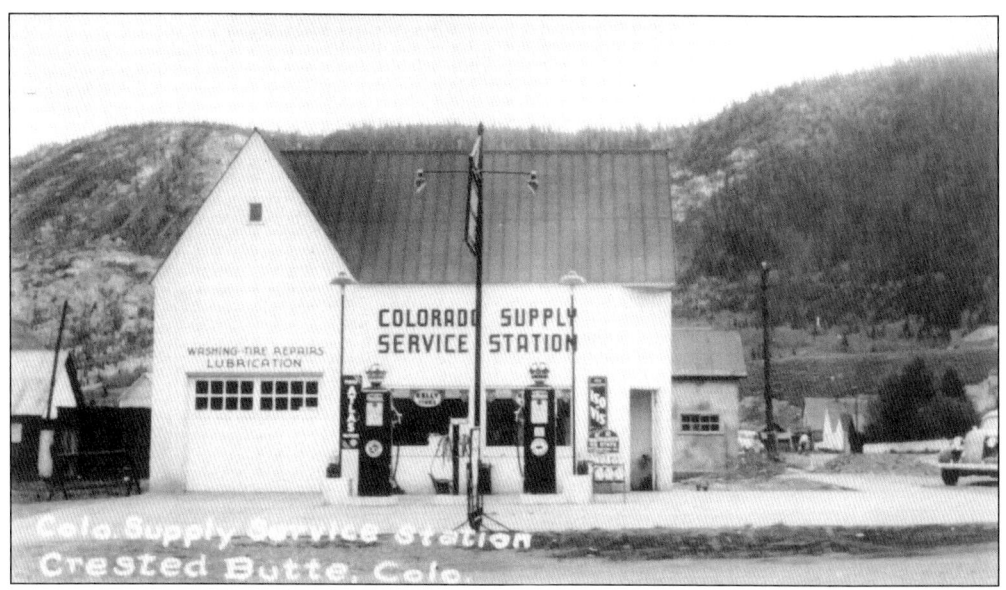

SERVICE STATION. The Colorado Supply Service Station was one of few gas stations in Crested Butte in the 1930s. Located on Elk Avenue, the station provided full service, including tire repair, oil and grease, washing vehicles, and selling gas for under 20¢ a gallon.

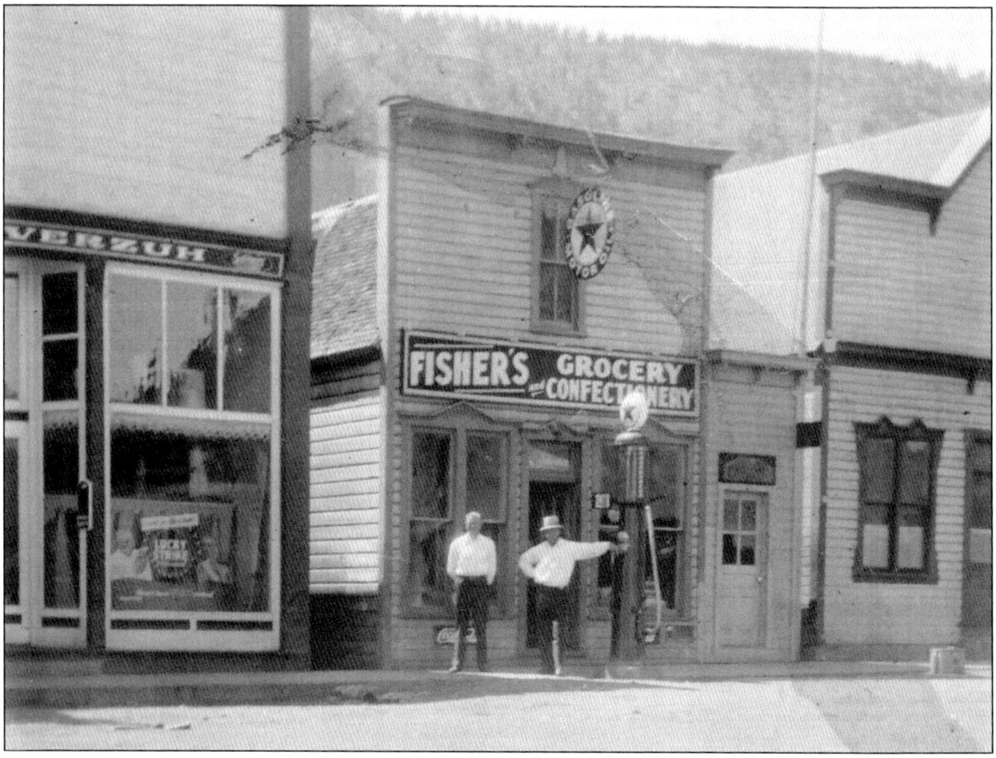

GROCERY STORE, ELK AVENUE. Mike Fisher (left) and an unidentified friend stand next to a gas pump in front of Fisher's Grocery and Confectionery Store around 1920. The grocery part of the store was downstairs; upstairs, Fisher had a small bottling plant that produced soda that he sold to dance halls.

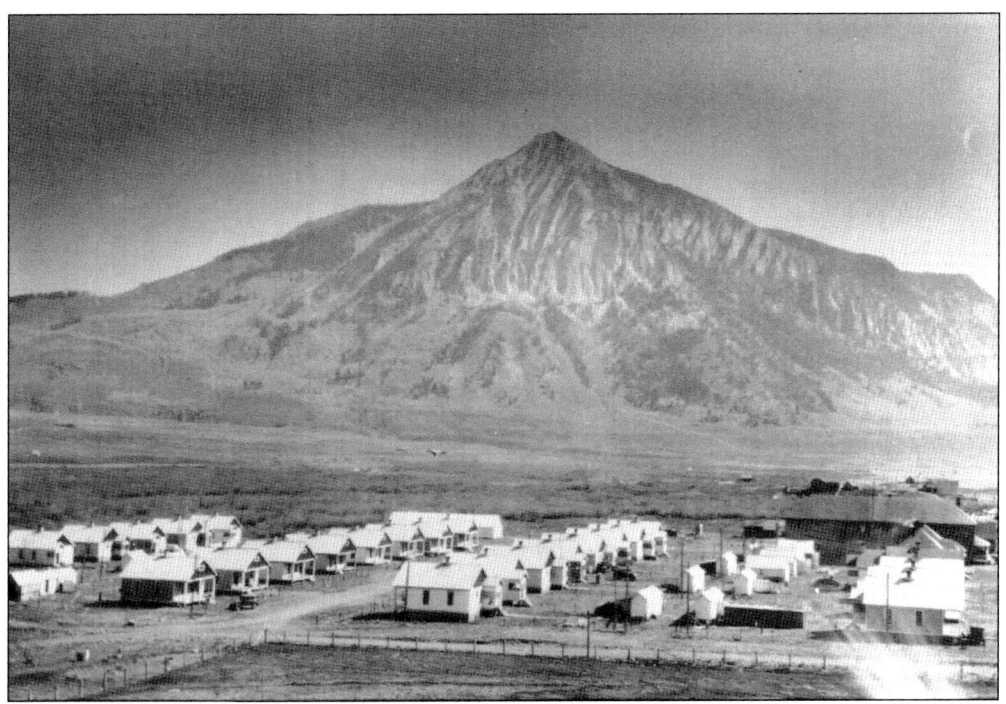

COMPANY HOUSES. The Colorado Fuel and Iron Company built 30 company houses for its workers and their families on the east end of Crested Butte. The homes were kept in immaculate condition by the miners and their families and were within walking distance of the Big Mine.

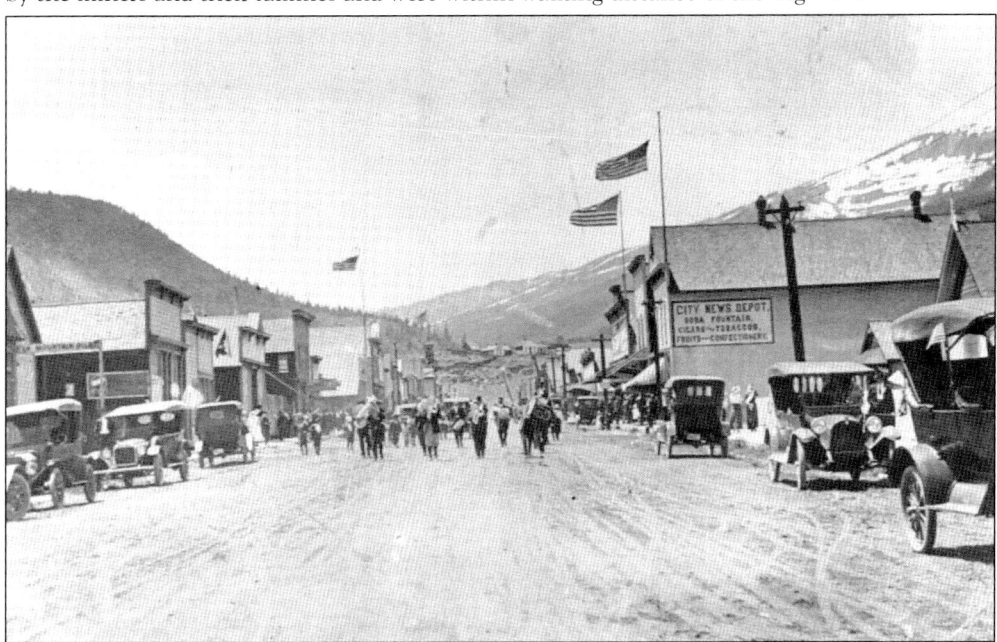

INDEPENDENCE DAY. On July 4, 1918, flags are flying as Crested Butte celebrates America's independence. A small band leads the parade with a small crowd in attendance. No one could know it then, but World War I was nearly at an end, and soon many Crested Butte boys would be returning.

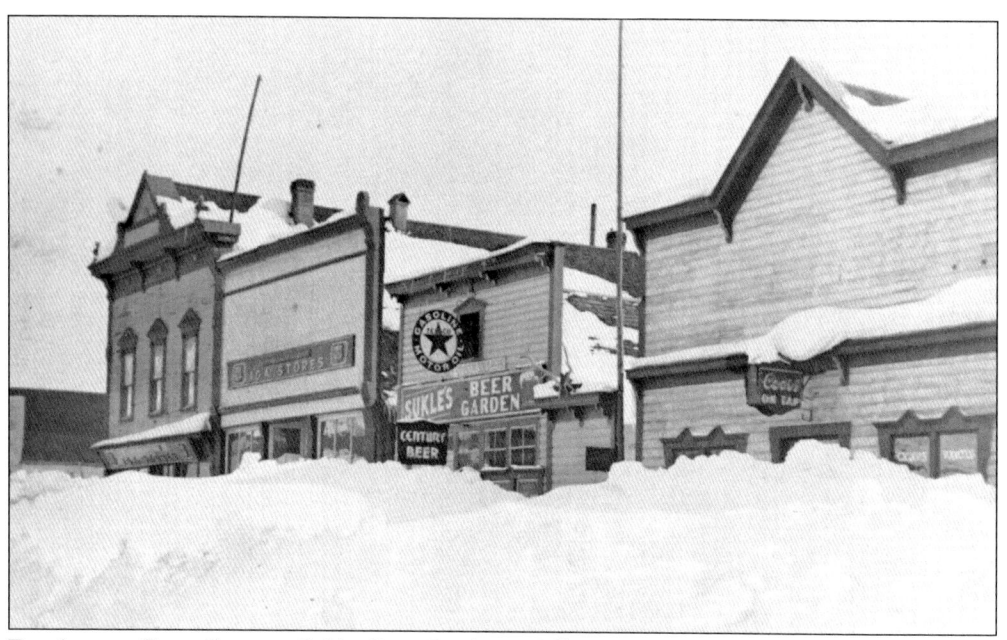

ELK AVENUE BEER GARDEN. Sukles Beer Garden on Elk Avenue in Crested Butte is inundated by snow during a tough winter in the 1930s. Crested Butte was known for its many taverns, which were patronized by coal miners in need of a cold beer after a tough shift in the mines.

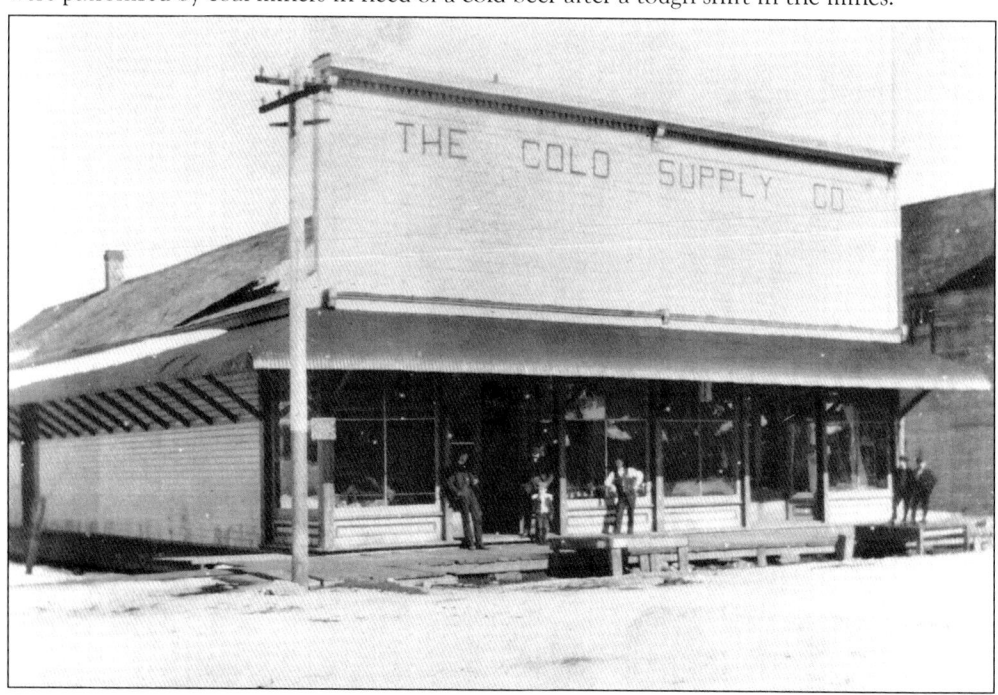

COMPANY STORE. The Colorado Supply Company on Elk Avenue in Crested Butte was the Colorado Fuel and Iron Company's store. The building seen in this photograph was destroyed by a fire in 1937 and replaced by the stucco building that stands on the same corner in 2011. The closing of the CF&I's Big Mine in 1952 marked the end of the company store as the coal company's supplier.

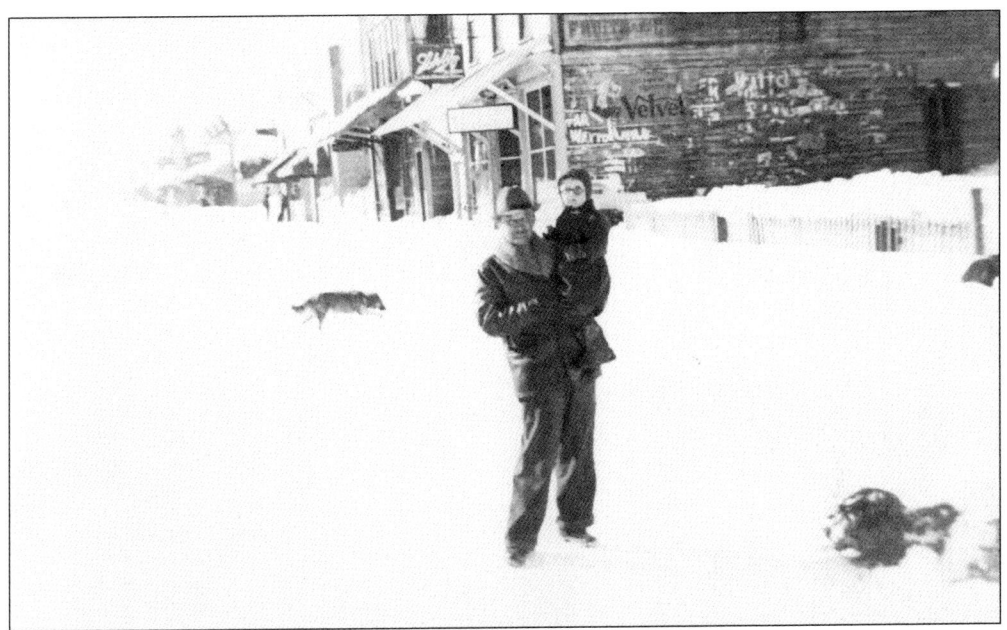

BLIZZARD CONDITIONS. Crested Butte businessman Joe Skoff holds his young son on Elk Avenue during a blizzard in the 1930s. All cars were put on blocks during the winter because roads were not plowed. The only transportation into or out of Crested Butte was on skis or by rail.

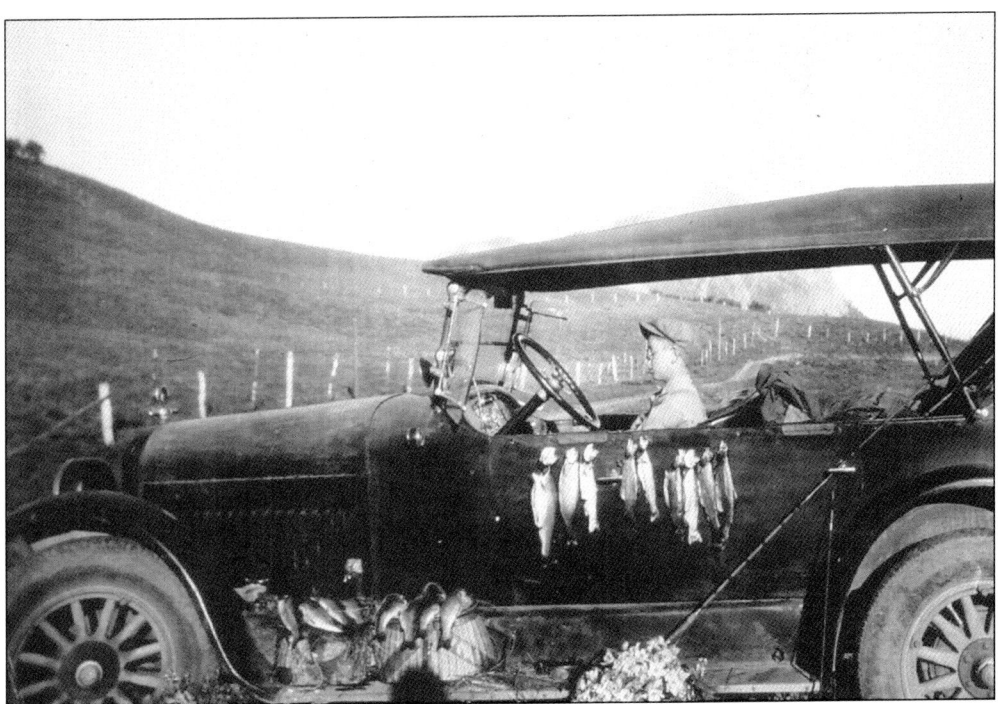

"GONE FISHIN'." Young Mac McGraw sits in his father's automobile after a successful fishing trip in the 1930s. The big fish were caught in the East River between Gothic and Crested Butte, and obviously there was no limit. Crested Butte Mountain towers in the background.

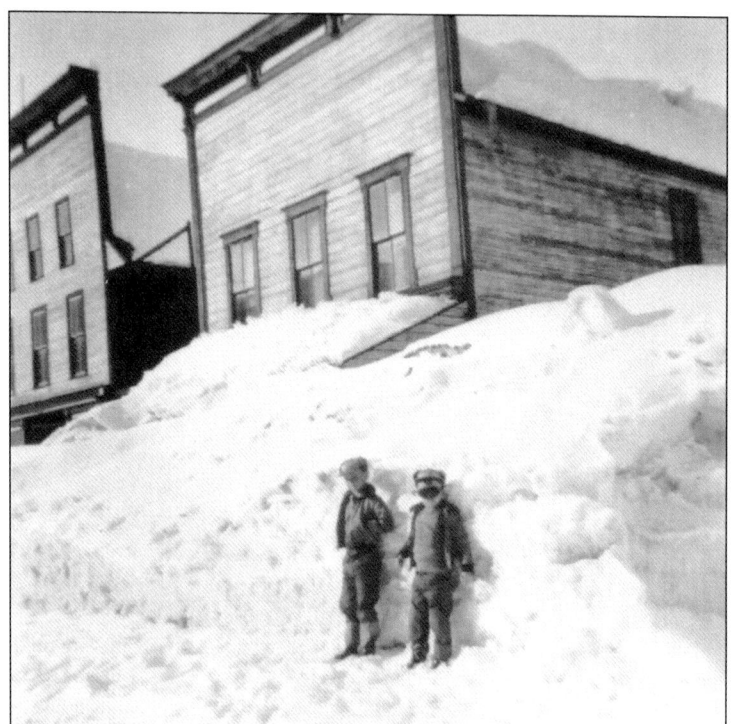

ROOFTOP SNOW. Two young boys pose on Elk Avenue in Crested Butte in the 1950s. Snow has piled so high that the entrances to businesses were completely blocked until tunnels were shoveled out. This was a regular winter occurrence in town.

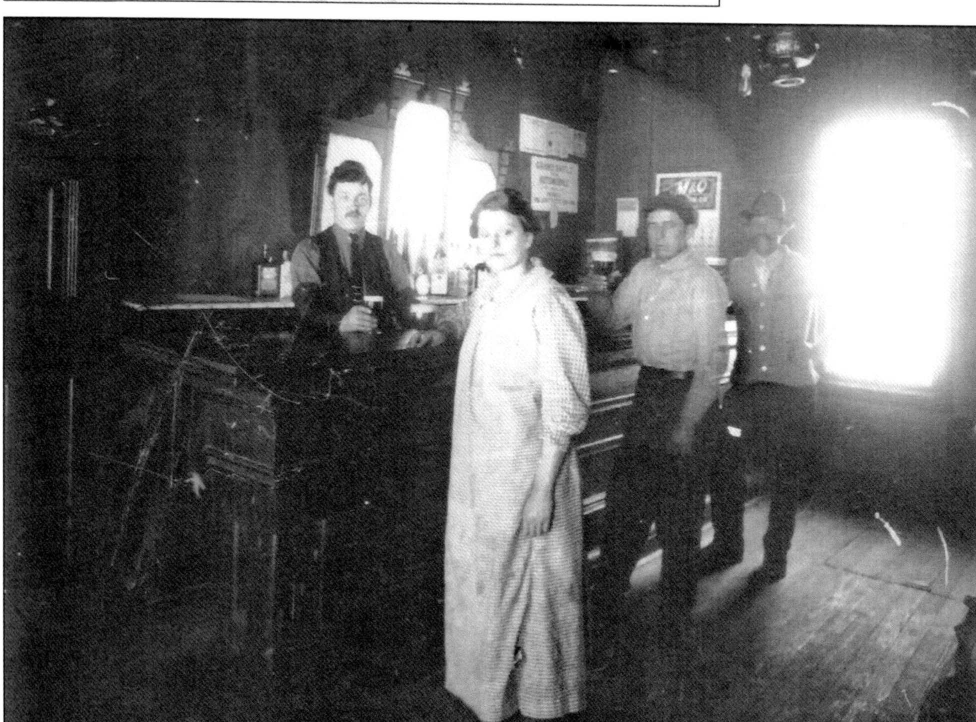

LOCAL SALOON. By the summer of 1882, Crested Butte already had 12 saloons. The saloon was one of the major social gathering spots of the town. Here, a person could have a cold beer, gamble, and catch up on all the local news.

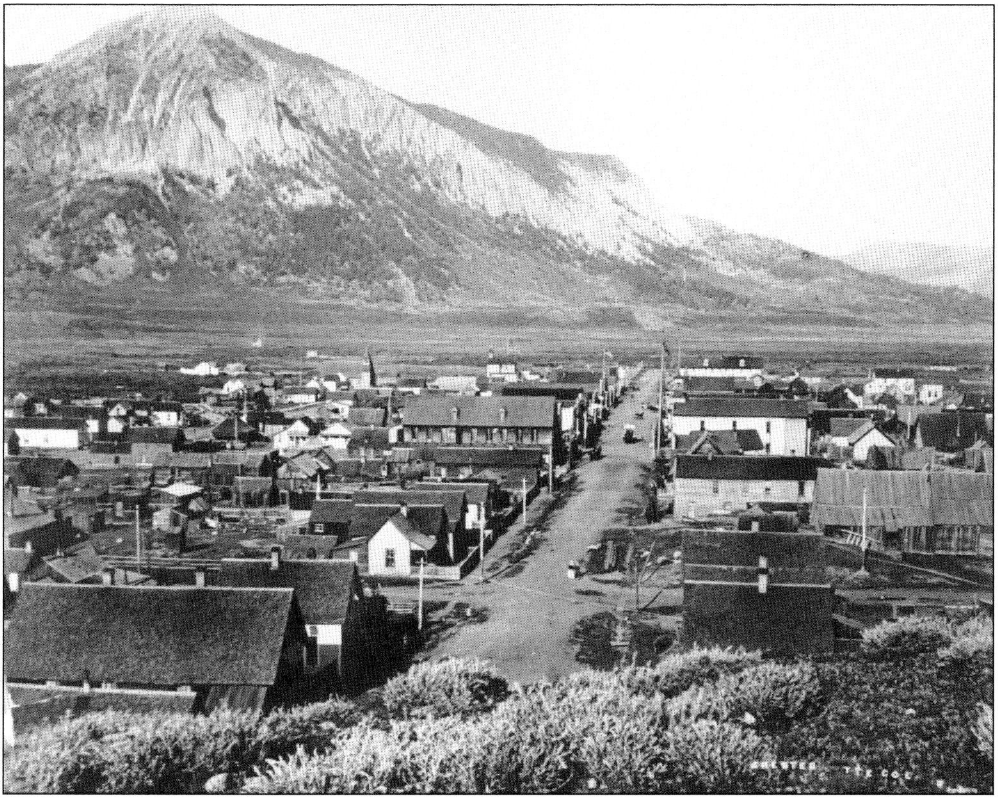

EARLY CRESTED BUTTE. Taken from the hill just west of town, this picture captures Elk Avenue and Crested Butte in 1912. Wagons and horses are on the street and the Elk Mountain House in white can be seen at the end of Elk Avenue.

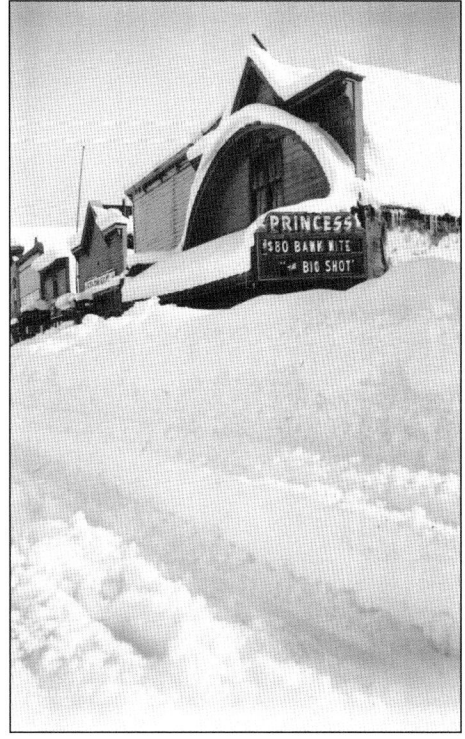

BANK NIGHT IN CRESTED BUTTE. The snow is piled high on Elk avenue in the late 1930s in Crested Butte, and it is Bank Night. To get people to come to movies during the Depression, one night of the week was designated as Bank Night. All movie tickets were put into a hat and the winner was drawn during intermission. The amount paid to the winner was based on the number of tickets sold.

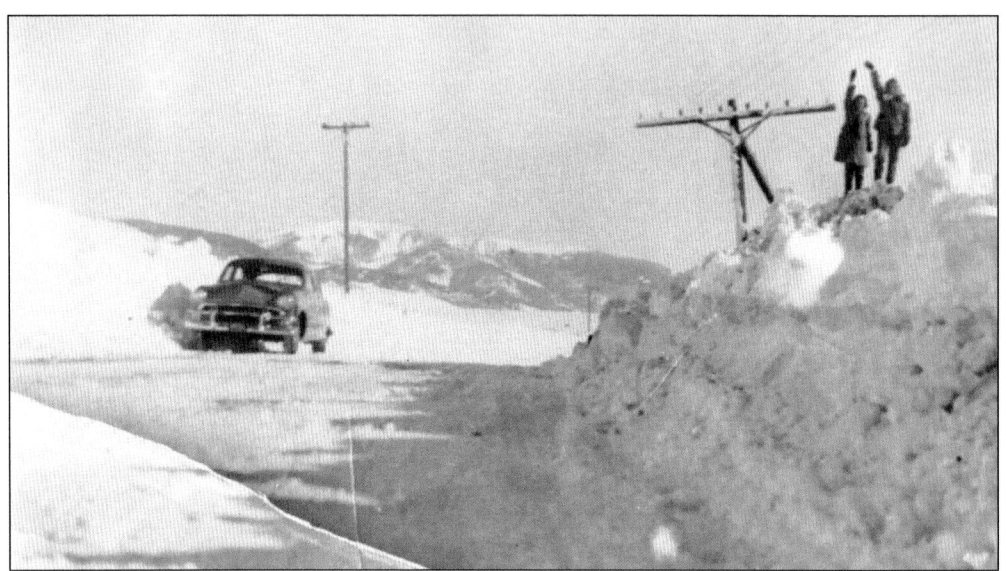

WINTER OF BIG SNOW. Two young children, Marilyn Gibson (right) and Anna Chapell, stand on a snow bank on the side of Highway 135 in the late 1950s with their hands almost touching the power lines. The snow created a "four-wire winter," meaning that it covered all four wires of the fences on cattle ranches from Jack's Cabin to Crested Butte.

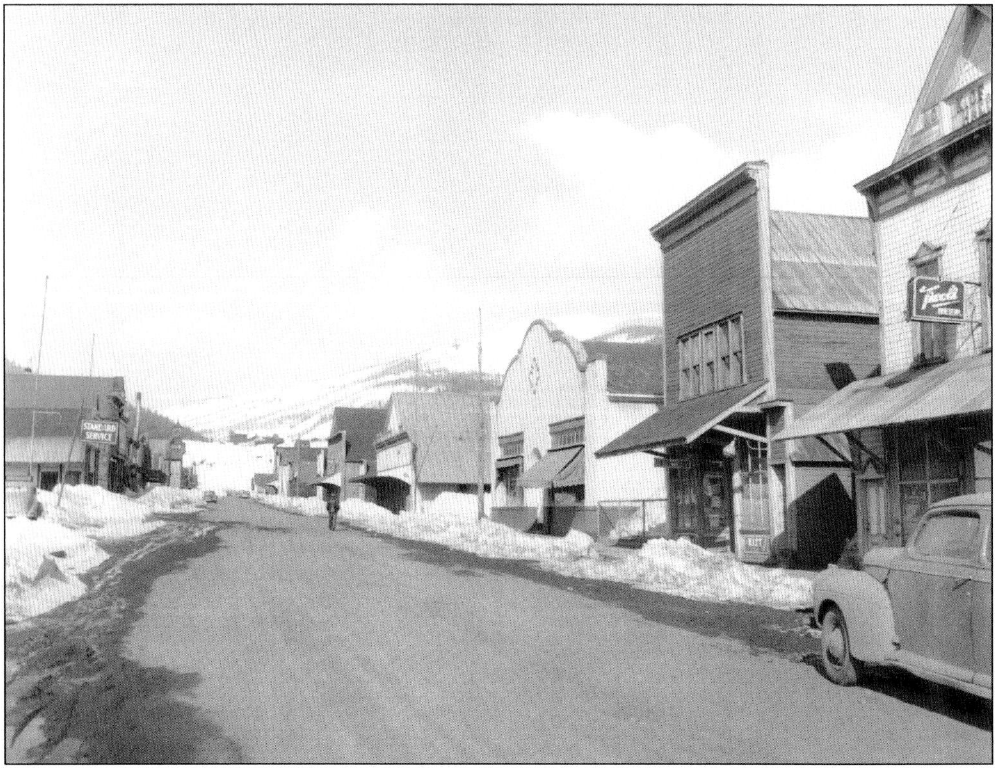

ELK AVENUE, 1940s. It is a beautiful clear day in the spring of the year in Crested Butte in the 1940s. Automobiles, which have been on blocks throughout the winter, are now appearing on Crested Butte's main thoroughfare. Mount Emmons and Red Lady Basin tower off in the distance.

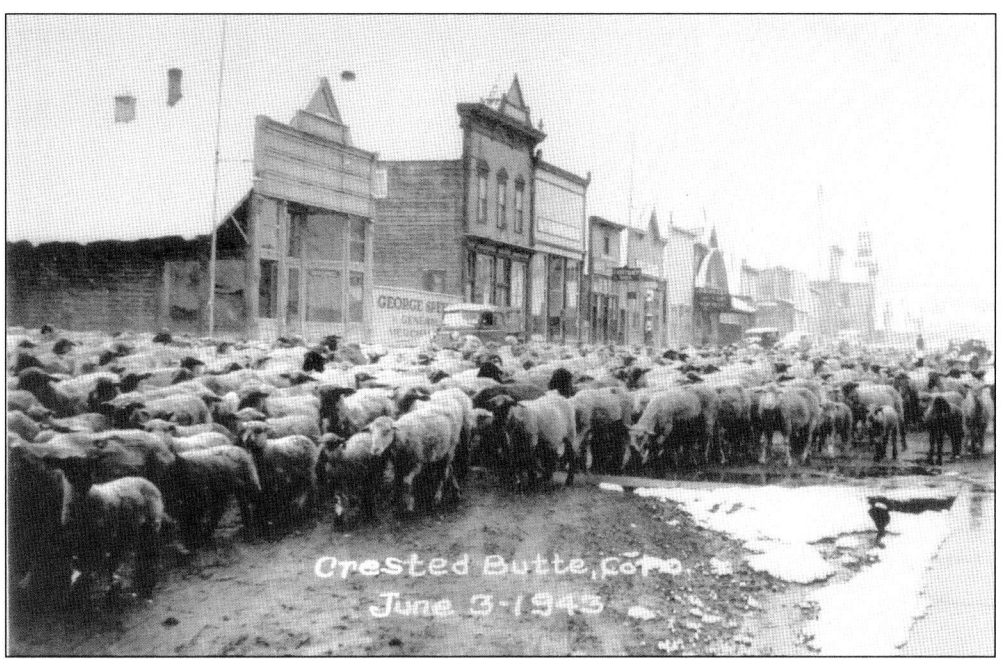

SHEEP DRIVE. A herd of sheep is being driven along Elk Avenue through Crested Butte on June 3, 1943. A late-season snowstorm has hit as the sheep head for rich grazing land nearby.

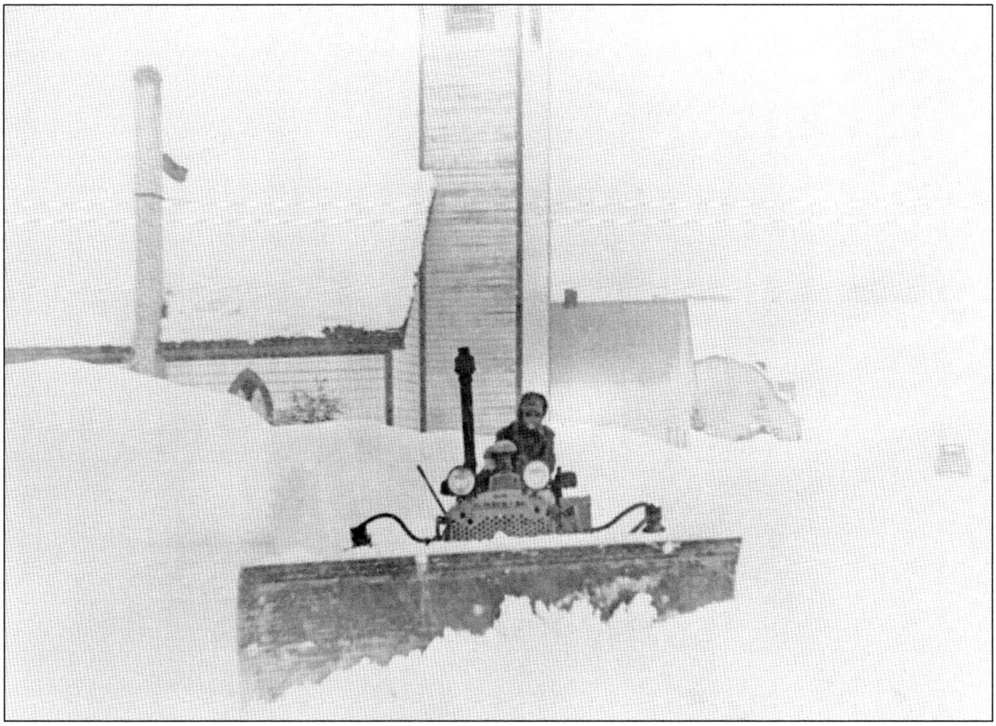

HEAVY SNOW, MAROON AVENUE. With St. Patrick's Church in the background, a snowplow clears snow on Maroon Avenue in February 1962. Crested Butte was annually hit with prodigious amounts of snow, sometimes making travel impossible.

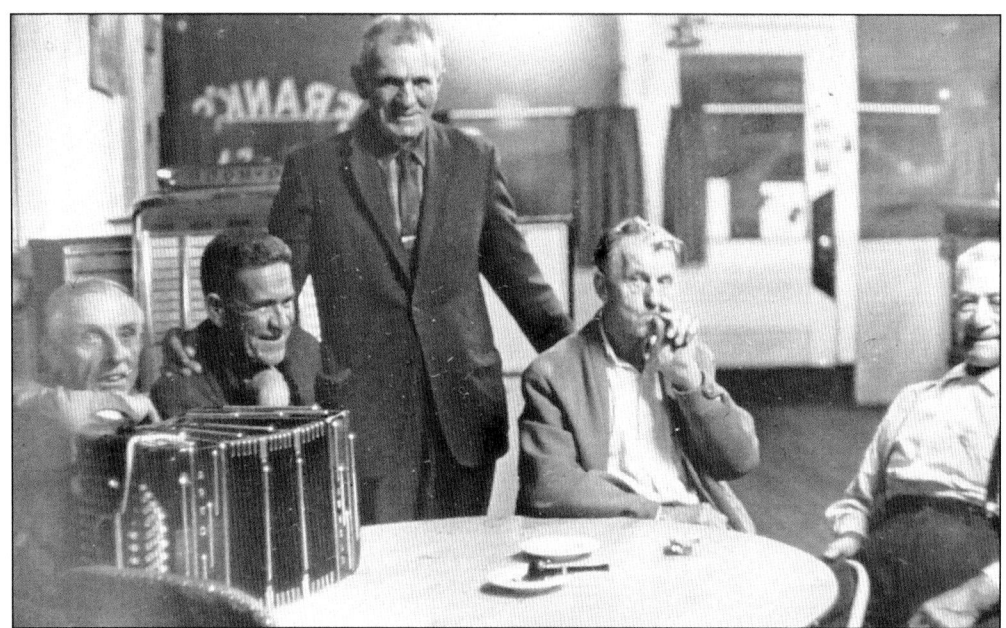

ARMISTICE DAY, 1967. In historic Frank and Gal's Bar in Crested Butte, five old-timers get ready for some beer, music, and war stories on Armistice Day 1967, forty-nine years after the end of World War I. All served in different armies during the war. The men are, from left to right, Emil Lunk (Germany), Frank Hodgson (England), Tony Danni (USA), John Panion (Austro-Hungary), and Ralph Falselto (Italy). (SC.)

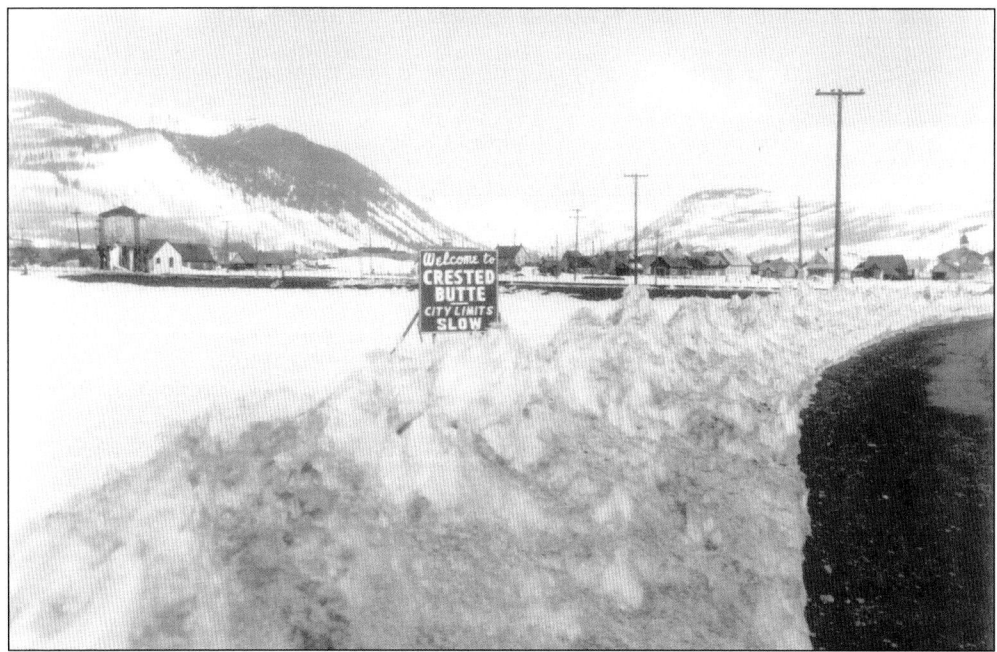

CRESTED BUTTE ENTRY. Crested Butte had hit on hard times by the time of this 1960 photograph. The major coal mine had shut down, the Denver and Rio Grande Railroad had pulled up its tracks, and only 300 people remained in town. The sign says "City Limits," but Crested Butte at that time was little more than a village.

Keystone Miner. Following the close of the Colorado Fuel and Iron Company's Big Mine, which had produced coal for nearly 60 years, the old Keystone silver mine was reopened just west of town on the side of Mount Emmons in the early 1950s. The American Smelting and Refining Company built an $800,000 mill. Here, a miner heads out of the mine at the end of a shift.

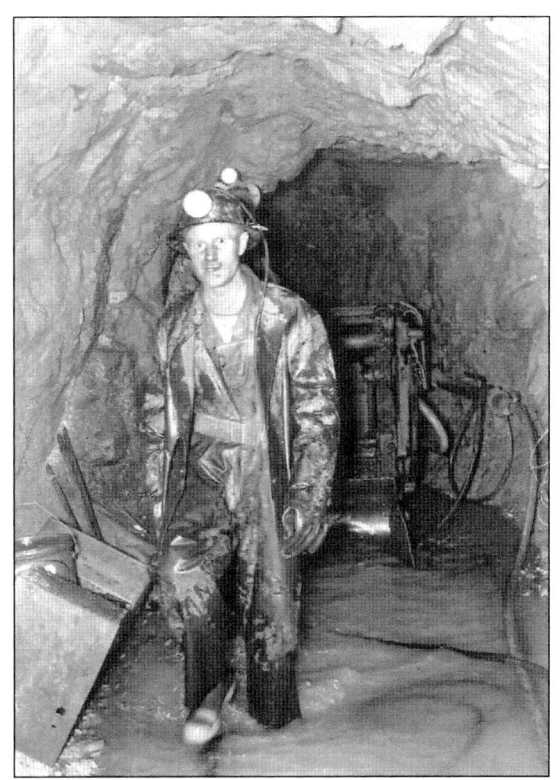

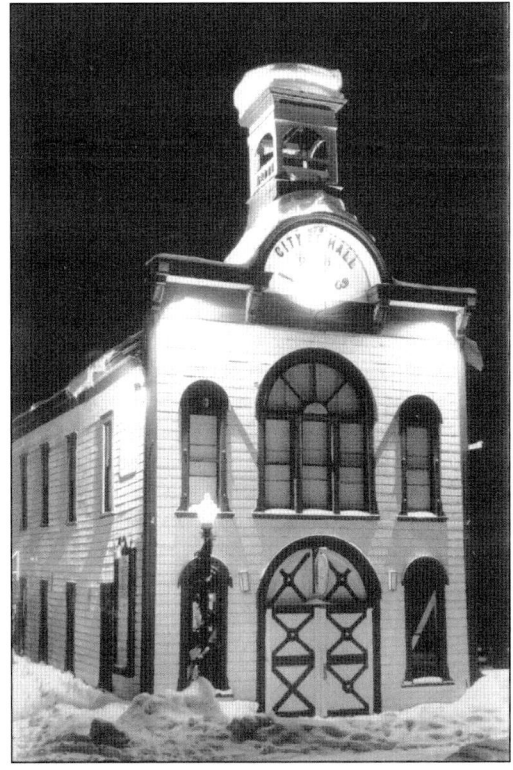

City Hall, Crested Butte. Built in 1883 and one of the oldest buildings in town, Crested Butte City Hall is pictured on a cold winter night in 1970. The lower floor housed the early fire department, and the upper floor was used for dances, church, and public meetings and also served as headquarters for town trustees.

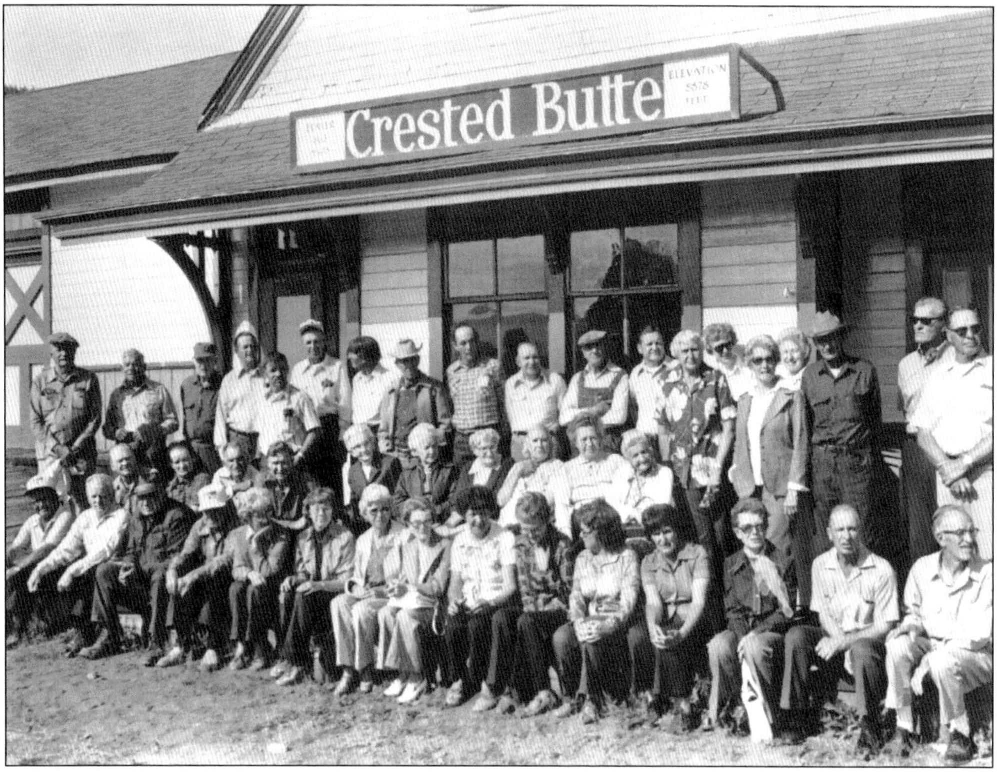

OLD TIME GATHERING. Forty-four Crested Butte old-timers pose in front of the old Denver and Rio Grande Railroad station in 1980. The photographer worked for the AMAX Molybdenum Mining Company, which was interested in mining a rich body of the metal (molybdenum) on nearby Mount Emmons. Most of the men in the photograph were ex-miners.

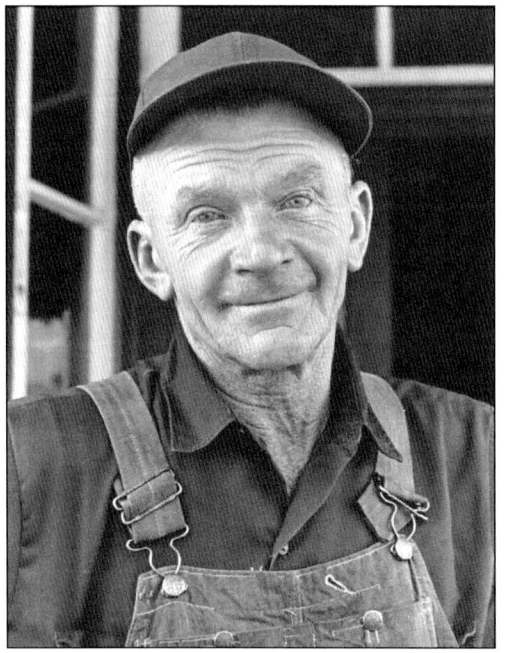

TONY. Tony Mihelich ran Tony's Conoco and a hardware store on Elk Avenue from 1939 until his death on Christmas Day, 1996. His station was the longest-operating independently owned Conoco dealership ever. Tony was a beloved figure in Crested Butte, and when former president Jimmy Carter came to the ski area, he and Tony would have an hour's private conversation in front of the 100-year-old potbellied stove that sat in the middle of the hardware store. (SC)

Five

WHEN COAL WAS KING

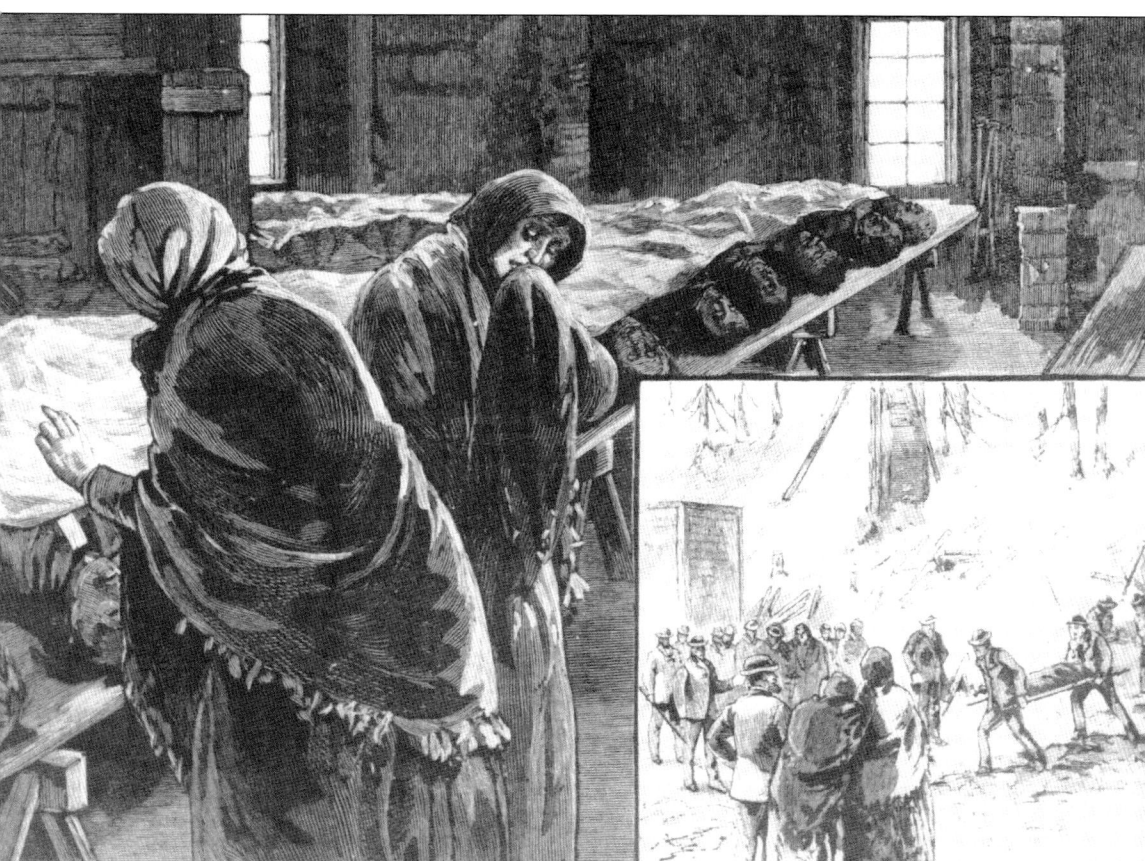

JOKERVILLE EXPLOSION. The national publication *Harper's Weekly* covered the disastrous Jokerville coal mine explosion of January 24, 1884. The blast, caused by methane gas, killed 60 men, one of the worst mining disasters in Colorado history. This drawing shows dead men and grieving widows. Forty-six of the miners were buried in a common grave in the Crested Butte cemetery.

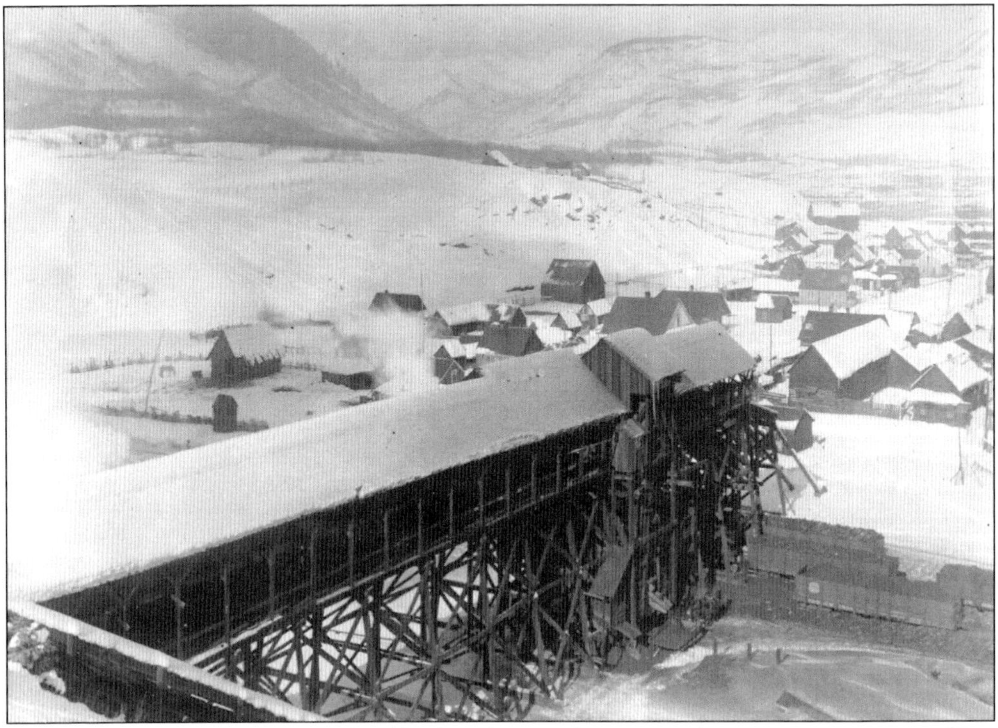

LOADING THE COAL. Heavy snow has blanketed Crested Butte in February 1907. Denver and Rio Grande Railroad cars have just been loaded with coal from the Colorado Fuel and Iron Company Big Mine and will soon depart on a long journey to the company's steel mills in Pueblo. (BHS.)

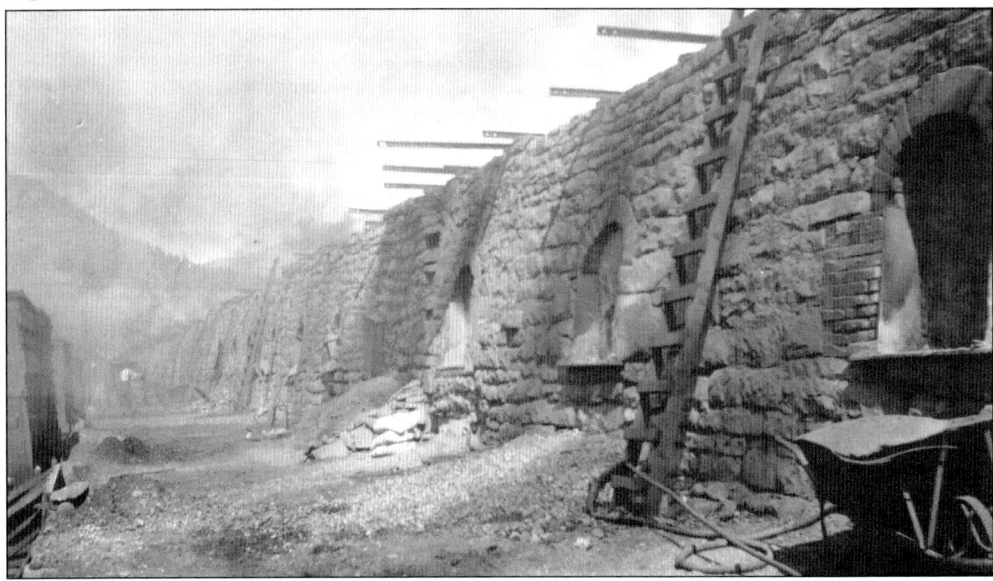

COKING COAL. Below Crested Butte's Big Mine and Gibson Ridge were the town's famous beehive coke ovens, which produced high-quality coke used in the production of steel. The ovens were heated red-hot before coal was dumped in. The coal was baked for 48 hours and then loaded by fork onto waiting railroad cars and taken to the Colorado Fuel and Iron Company's mill in Pueblo, where it was used in the production of steel.

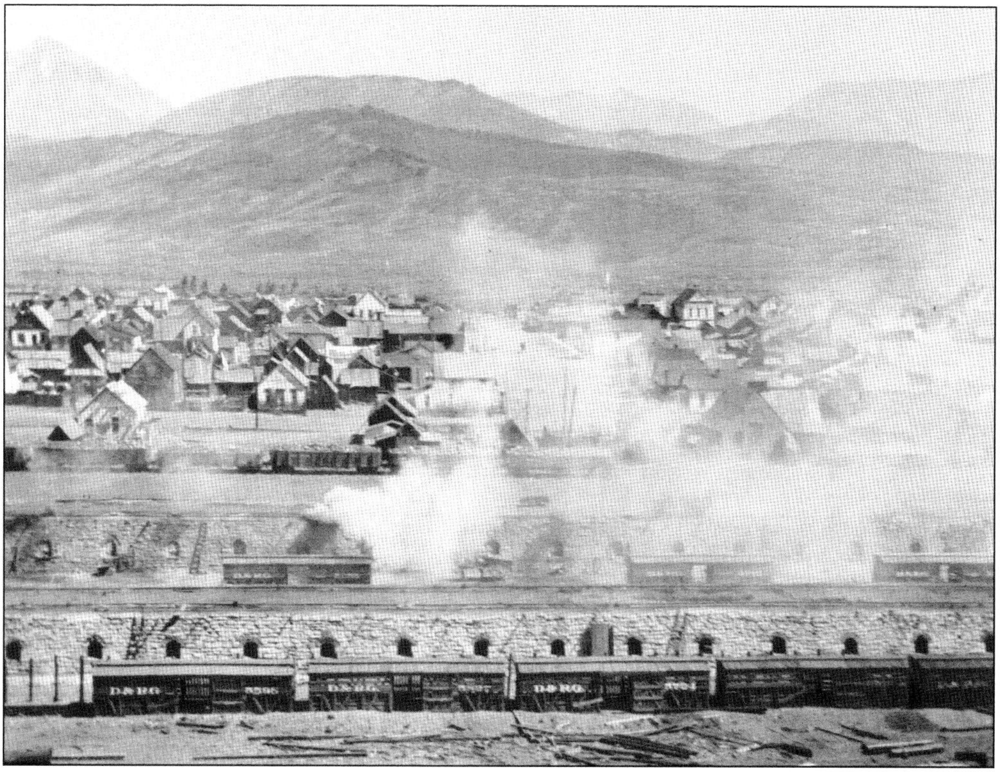

COKE OVENS. Denver and Rio Grande Railroad cars sit next to some of Crested Butte's famous coke ovens on the southeastern end of town. The ovens were built in 1884 and made of firebrick and encased with stone. The brick structures were connected by a large track, which ran next to the oven openings and allowed the coal to be drawn to them by mule.

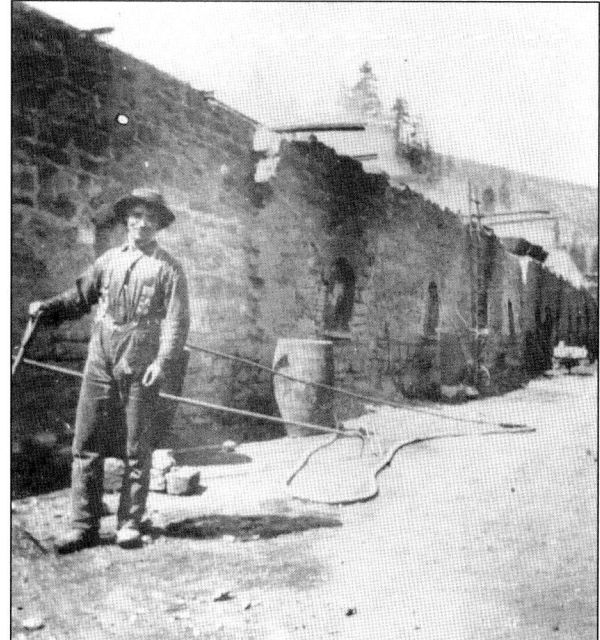

HOTTEST JOB IN TOWN. A worker for the Colorado Fuel and Iron Company's Big Mine stands near the famous coke ovens in Crested Butte. The ovens produced coke, essential in steel production. The intense heat and dangerous fumes made the oven tender's job one of the least desirable in the coal industry.

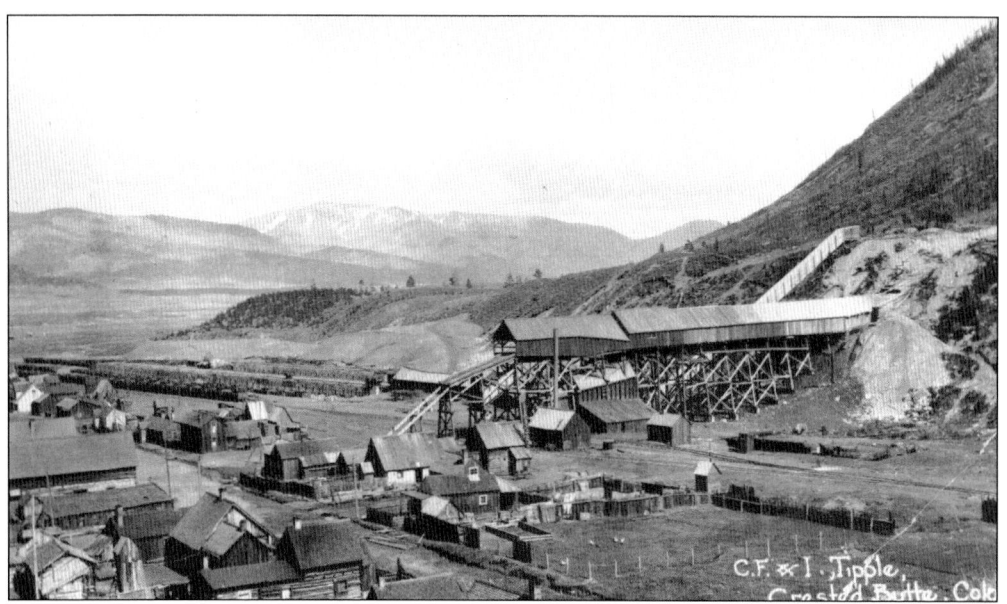

BIG MINE PANORAMA. The long tipple of the CF&I Big Mine at Crested Butte carried cars of coal along tracks before they were dumped into waiting railroad cars below. The company's coke ovens are visible on the left. Many of the buildings below the tipple were private residences on the south side of town.

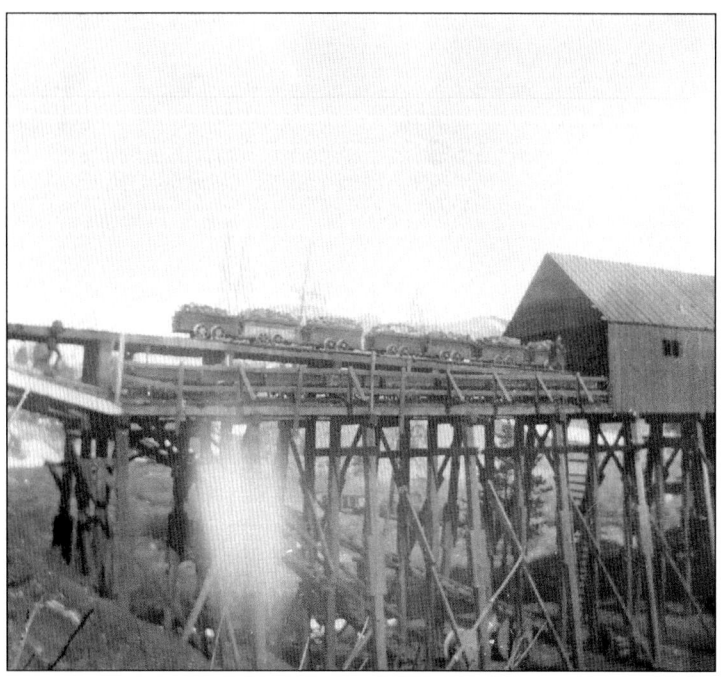

COLORADO'S THIRD-LARGEST COAL MINE. The Crested Butte Big Mine tipple is shown here with loaded coal cars. The Big Mine produced 1,000 tons of coal a day and employed 400 men. Tracks in the mine totaled more than six miles, and 70 mules were used to haul the coal from the vein to waiting Denver and Rio Grande railroad cars.

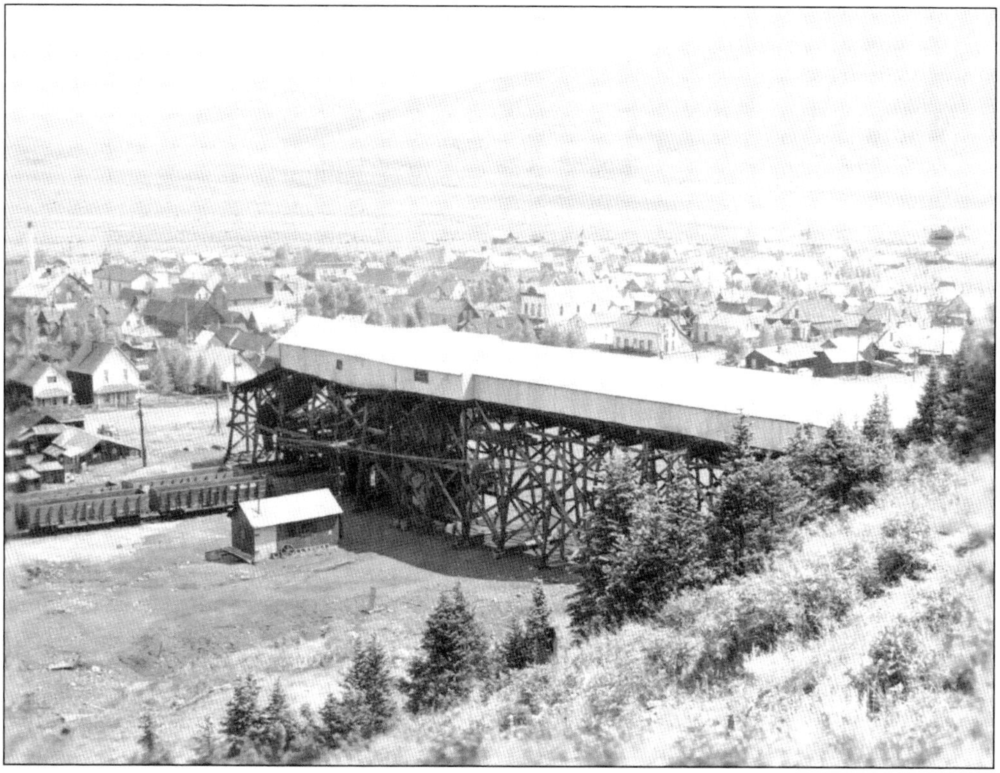

CF&I Tipple. The Colorado Fuel and Iron Company's Big Mine opened in Crested Butte in 1894, tapping a huge vein of coal 10 to 20 feet thick. The mine was one of the biggest producers in Colorado. This photograph shows the covered tipple with a Denver and Rio Grande train under it preparing to receive its load of coal. (BHS.)

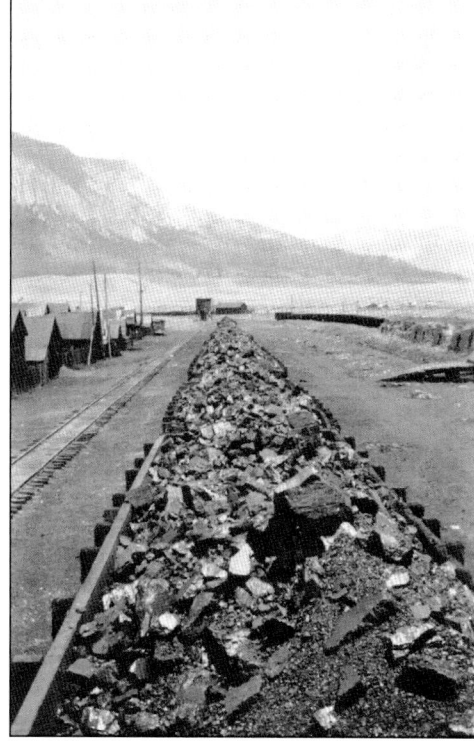

Coal Cars Ready. A long line of coal cars sits on the tracks below the Big Mine in Crested Butte in 1902. Every day, long coal trains left Crested Butte and passed through the East River Valley, Gunnison, the Tomichi Valley, and then over Marshall Pass en route to the steel mills in Pueblo.

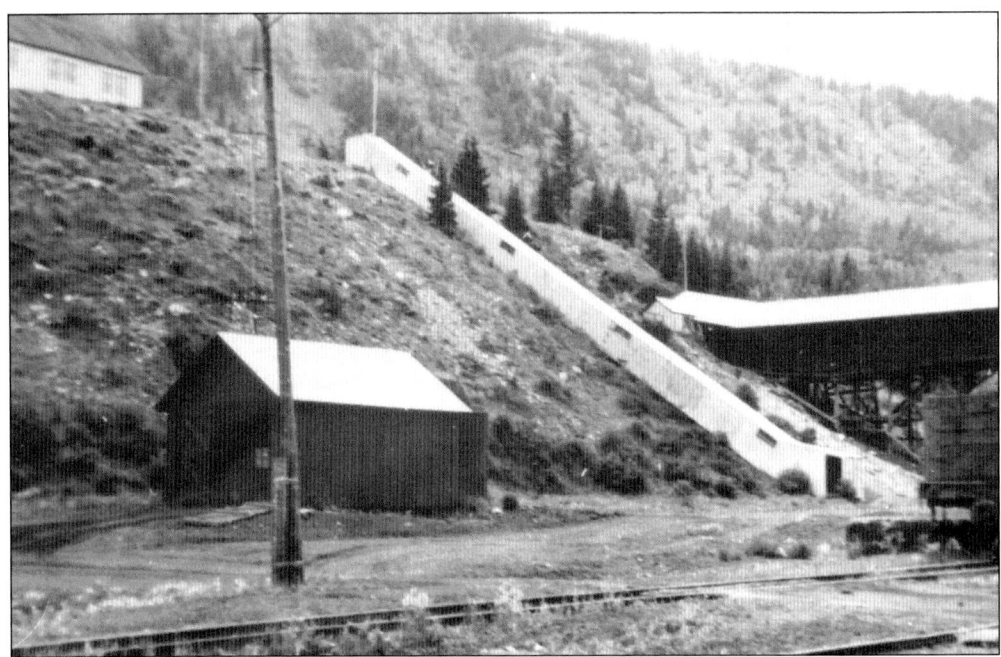

STEPS OF CRESTED BUTTE. The famous 127 steps of Crested Butte ran from the Bench where the Big Mine was located to the edge of town. The steps were covered to ward off winter snows and were used by miners to get to work and then back home after their shifts and by children going to and from school down below.

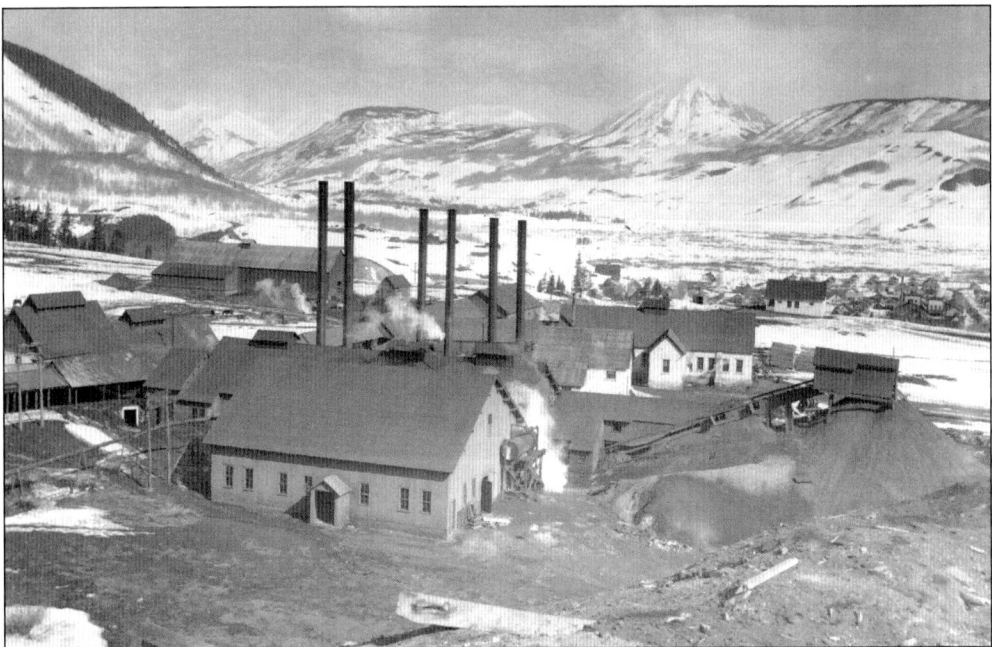

CF&I BIG MINE. The Colorado Fuel and Iron Company's Big Mine was the major employer in Crested Butte from 1894 to its closing in 1952. The mine was above Crested Butte on the Bench and included a power plant, mule barn, superintendent's house, and repair shops. A number of private homes were also on the Bench. (BHS.)

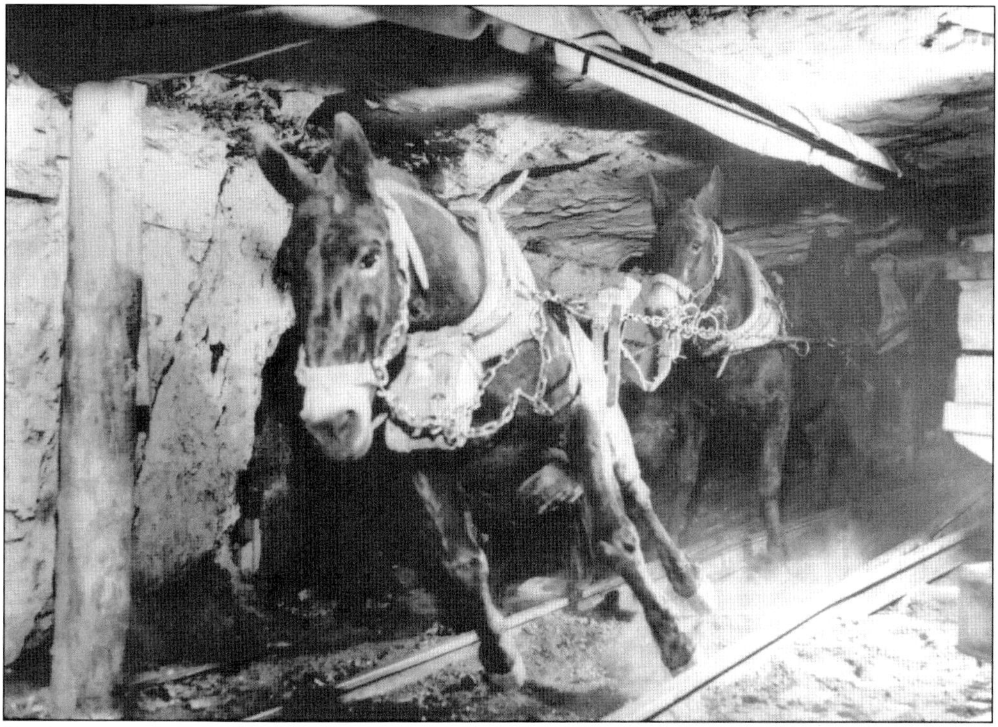

BIG MINE MULES. Mules did much of the work in Crested Butte's Big Mine and in most of the coal mines in Colorado and the West. They were responsible for pulling heavy cars laden with coal to the mine entrance where, in many mines, a tram carried the ore to a tipple below. Here, mules strain to pull their heavy load.

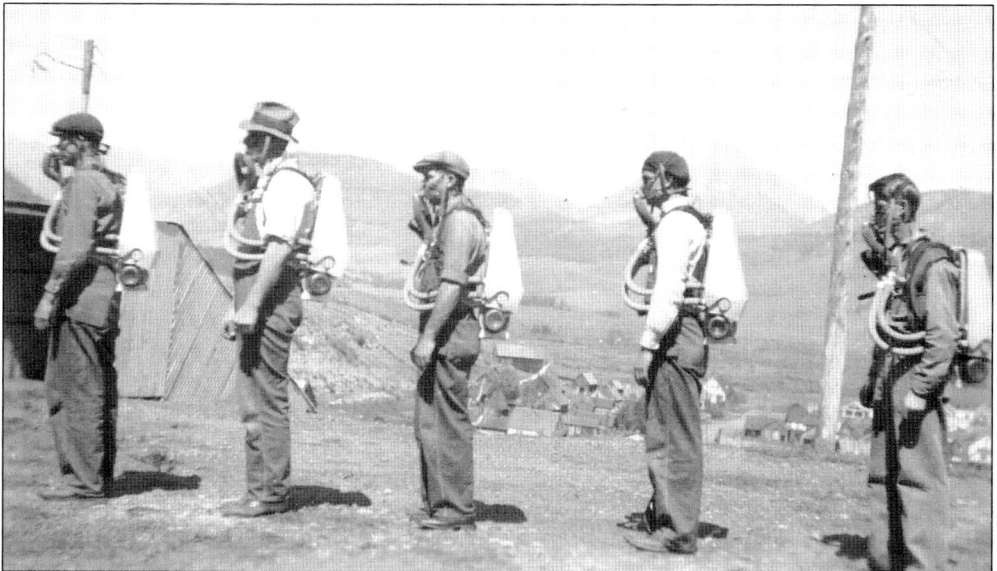

MINE RESCUE WORKERS. A mine rescue training exercise is underway at the Big Mine in Crested Butte in the 1920s. The men are, from left to right, Aust, Hultenan, Kerr, Miller, and Benton; they made up the Crested Butte rescue team. All of them are equipped with masks and oxygen tanks and are well trained in rescue procedures. (BHS.)

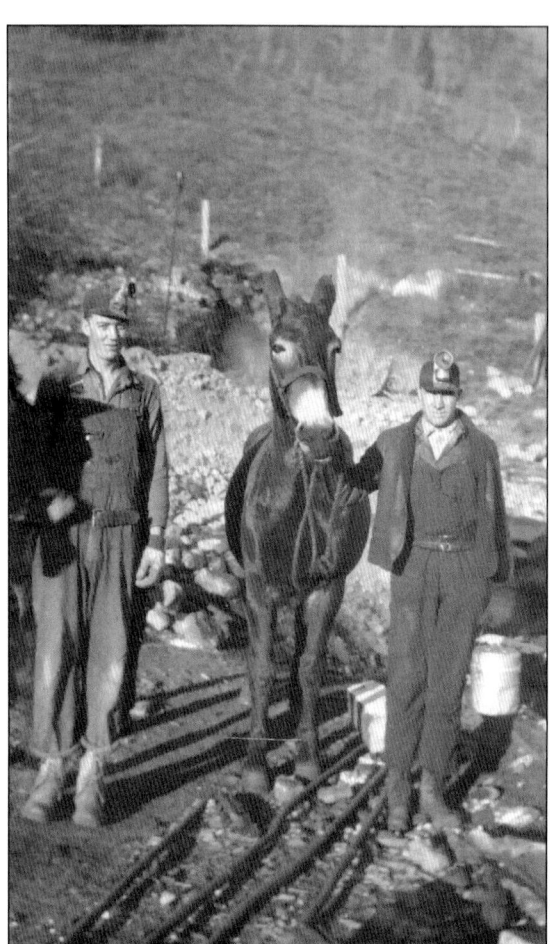

MULE SKINNERS. Two mule skinners stand next to one of their mules near the opening of the CF&I Big Mine in Crested Butte. The mule skinners were responsible for handling the mules inside of the mine, making sure they did their jobs. The men were also responsible for the mules' well-being outside of the mine.

PUEBLO MINE, CRESTED BUTTE. Located less than a mile south of Crested Butte, the Pueblo coal mine opened in 1904. The mine produced bituminous coal and was owned by Henry and Ira Littel. A tram carried coal from two openings on Robinson Hill 600 feet down the hill. A wooden shed six feet high protected the tram from the mine to the tipple, and 60 to 100 miners produced 150 to 200 tons of coal a day from the Pueblo Mine.

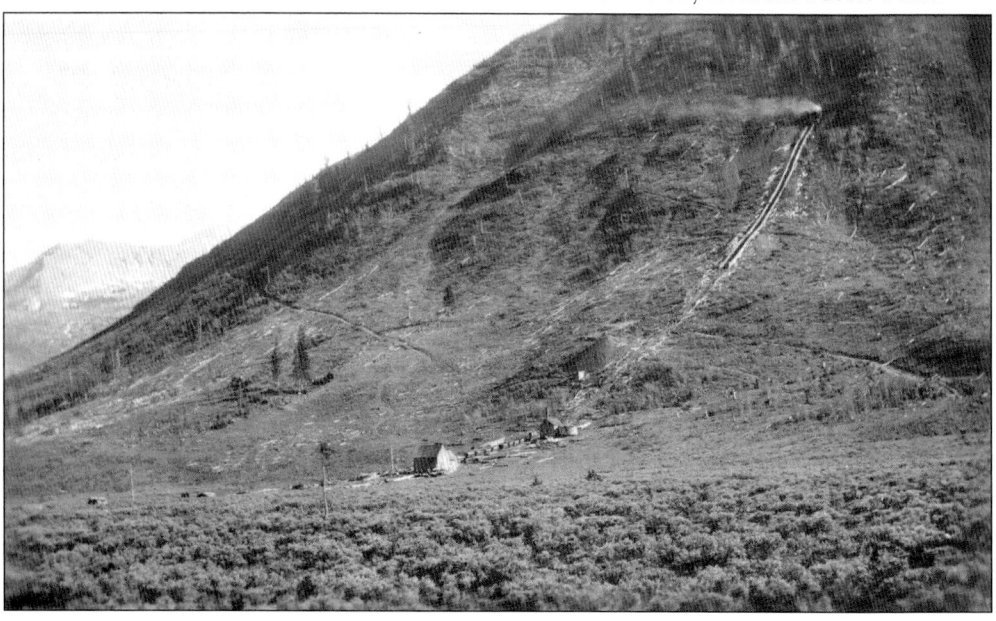

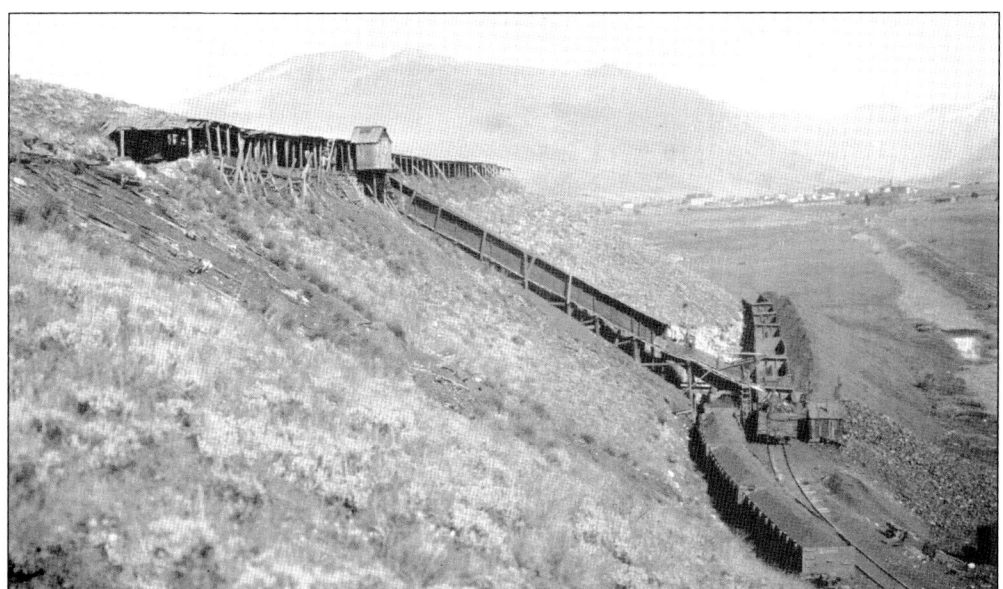

ROBINSON MINE. Crested Butte's Robinson bituminous coal mine, also called Horace, was only a couple of hundred yards away from the Pueblo Mine south of town. Named for Sant Robinson, one of the founders of Crested Butte, the mine began in 1905. The Robinson employed 40 men and from 1905 to 1912 produced 11,000 to 42,000 tons of coal a year. A tram brought coal from two mine openings to the tipple on the Denver and Rio Grande spur below.

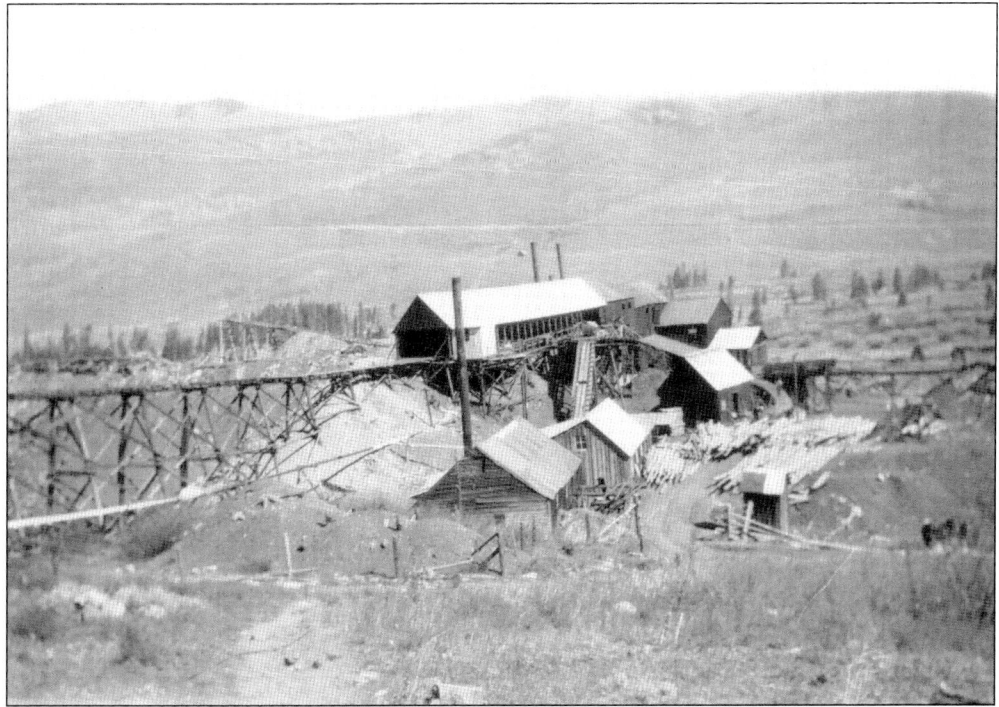

PEANUT MINE. The Peanut Mine was opened by Henry and Ira Littel in 1904 just north of Crested Butte and the Pershing Mine. The mine produced high quality coal and enjoyed the honor of being renowned as "Pennsylvania's only rival" in the field of anthracite coal.

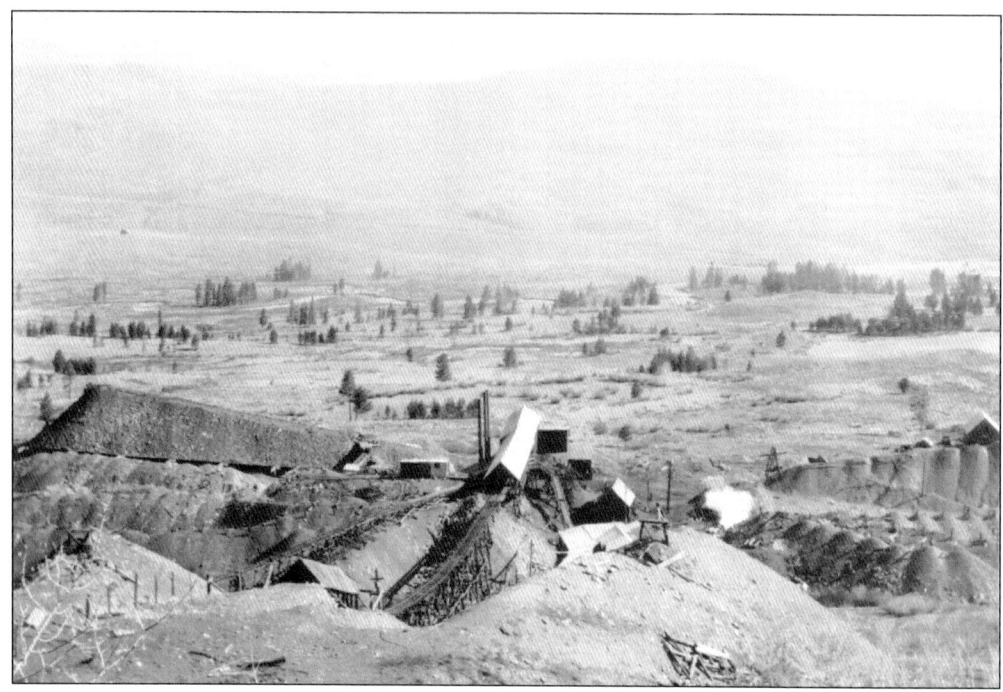

OVERLOOKING THE SLATE RIVER VALLEY. The Peanut Mine faces east and overlooks the beautiful Slate River Valley in the 1920s. The mine had a very low vein of coal, 18 inches to two feet high, making it very difficult for miners to get to. Often, a miner had to lie on his side or work on his knees using gunnysacks and old auto tires for pads.

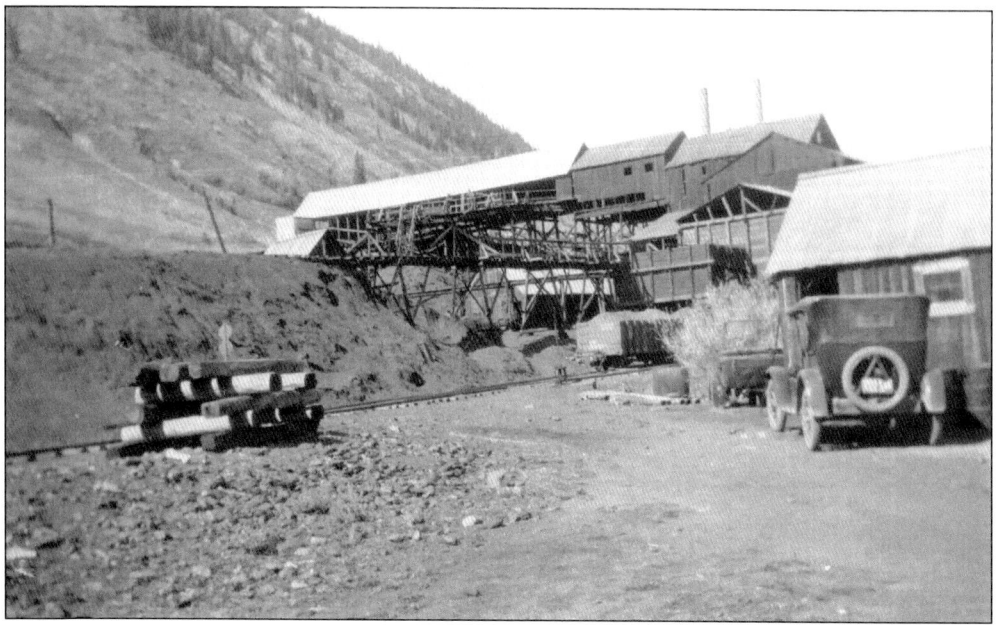

COAL IN THE 1920s. The Peanut Mine of Crested Butte is seen here in the 1920s. The anthracite mine employed 60 men and shipped out 30,000 tons of coal annually. The Peanut temporarily closed in 1931 because of the Depression and operated sporadically during the remainder of the 1930s and early 1940s.

ANTHRACITE TRAM. Crested Butte's second-largest coal mine was located four miles north of town, 1,600 feet above the Slate River on Smith Hill. A great coal breaker 80 feet high was built in 1883. Above the breaker in this photograph, a tramway ran for 1,628 feet from the anthracite mine to the breaker down a 33-degree incline. The town of Anthracite, which was on top of Smith Hill, had a population of 200.

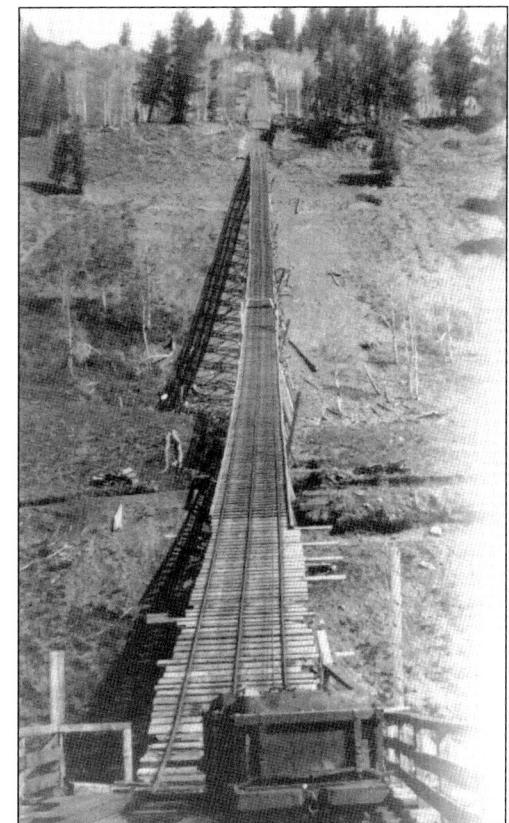

MULES AND MULE BARN. With Mount Emmons in the background, mules feed outside of the mule barn next to the CF&I Big Mine during early winter in 1917. The mine company used 70 mules in its operation, and each mule was valued at $200. Doing the heavy work of getting the coal to the tipple, mules were the unsung heroes of the coal mine.

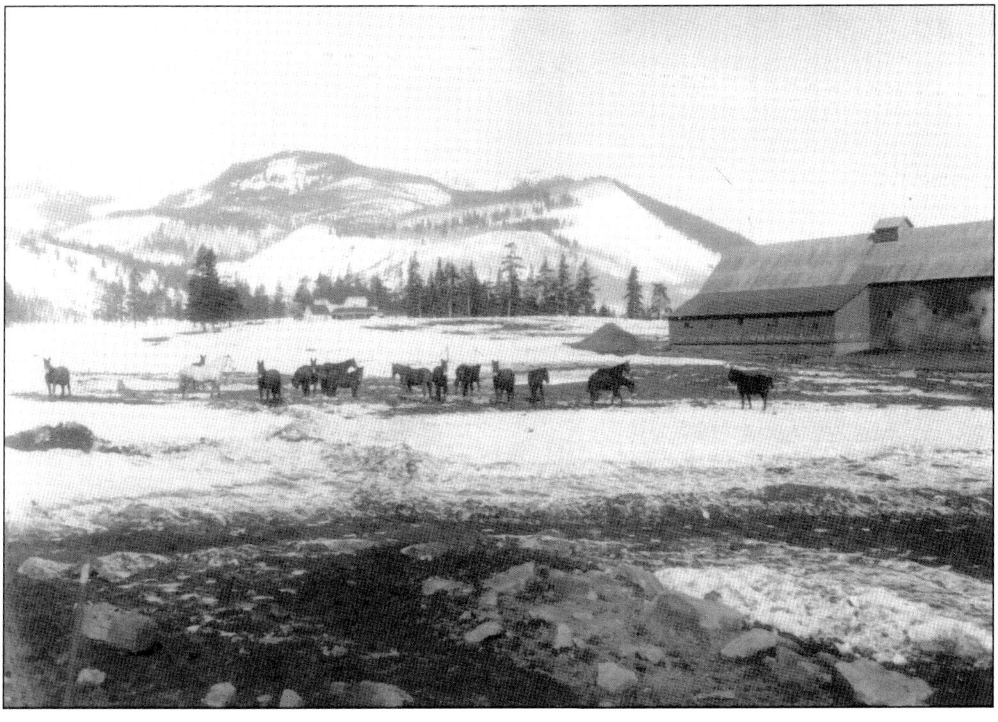

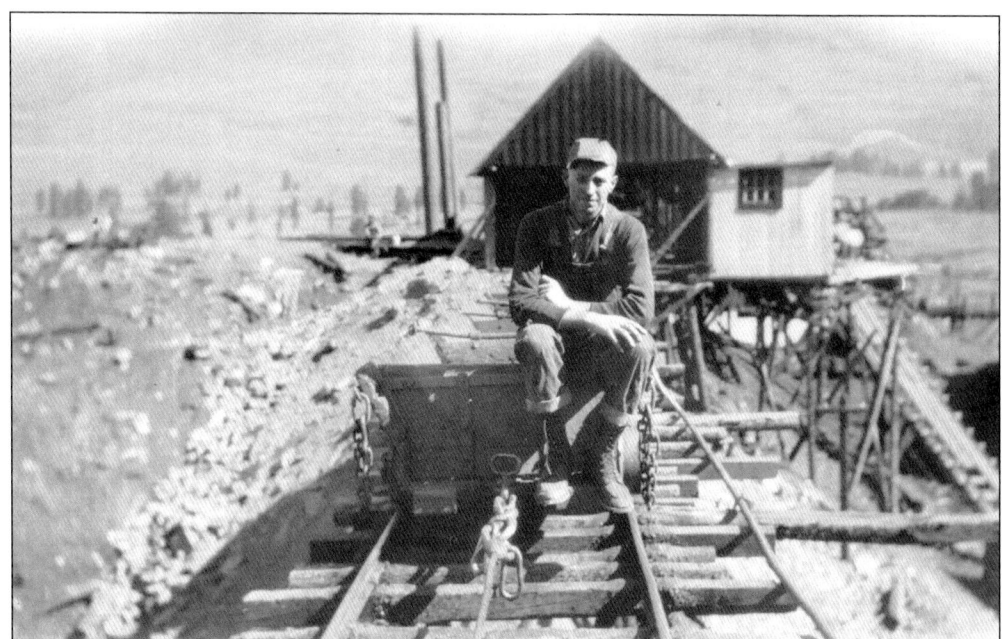

LONE EAGLE. A coal miner working at the Peanut Mine poses on a coal car in the 1920s. The Peanut was also known as the Littel Mine, after its first owners, and in 1919 became known as the Ross Coal Mine after Charlie Ross of the Crested Butte Bank, which had taken over the mine. The mine closed after the American Smelting and Refining Company purchased its 50,000-ton slack dump for $1.50 a ton.

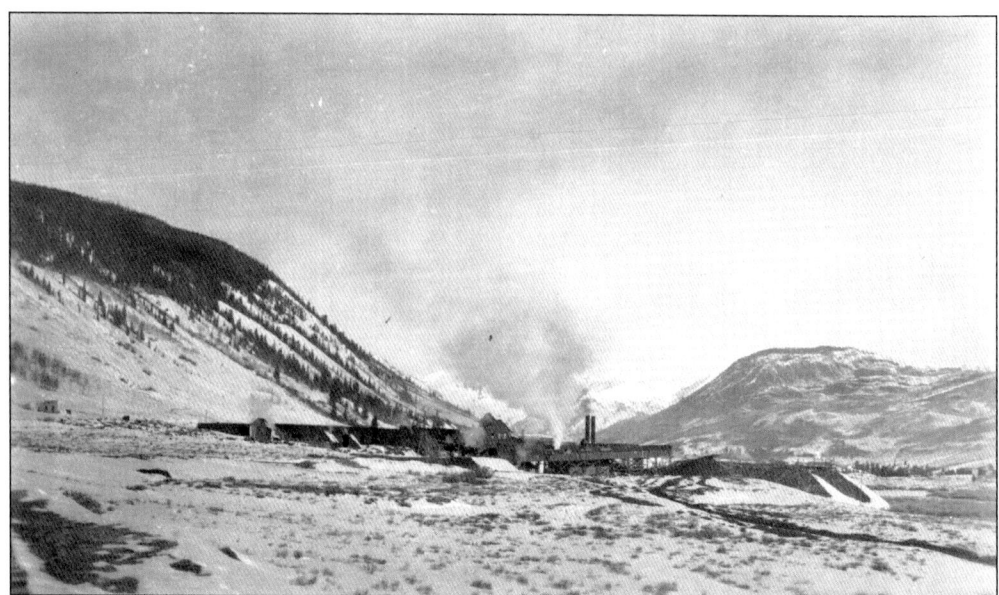

PERSHING MINE. Crested Butte's Pershing anthracite mine, located a mile north of the town near Peanut Lake, opened in 1919 and was owned by the Colorado Fuel and Iron Company. The mine was named for United States World War I general "Black Jack" Pershing. During its peak years in the 1920s, the Pershing shipped 40,000 tons of anthracite coal every year, while employing 60 men.

Six

PIONEER, ROZMAN, AND EARLY SKIING

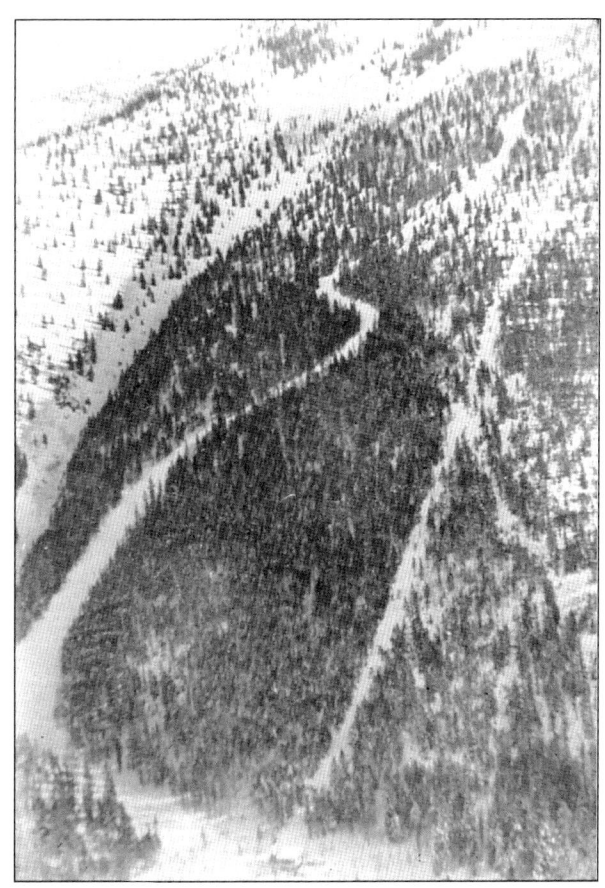

O' PIONEER. The Pioneer Ski Area was built during the winter of 1939–1940, three miles up Cement Creek and eight miles south of Crested Butte. Pioneer had the first chairlift in Colorado. This photograph shows the very steep cut for the chairlift and the equally steep Big Dipper run.

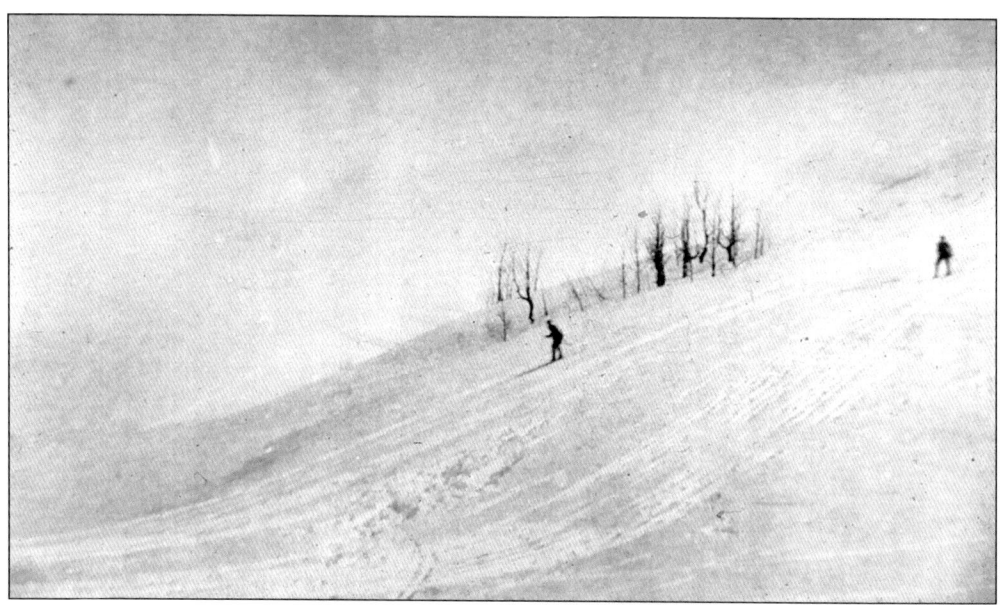

EARLY DAY SKIING, KEBLER PASS. Two Irwin miners with long skis and guide poles roar off a hill near Kebler Pass in 1883. Skiing was the only means of transportation during the winter in Gunnison Country mining camps. These two men are racing each other on Sunday, a day off from mining.

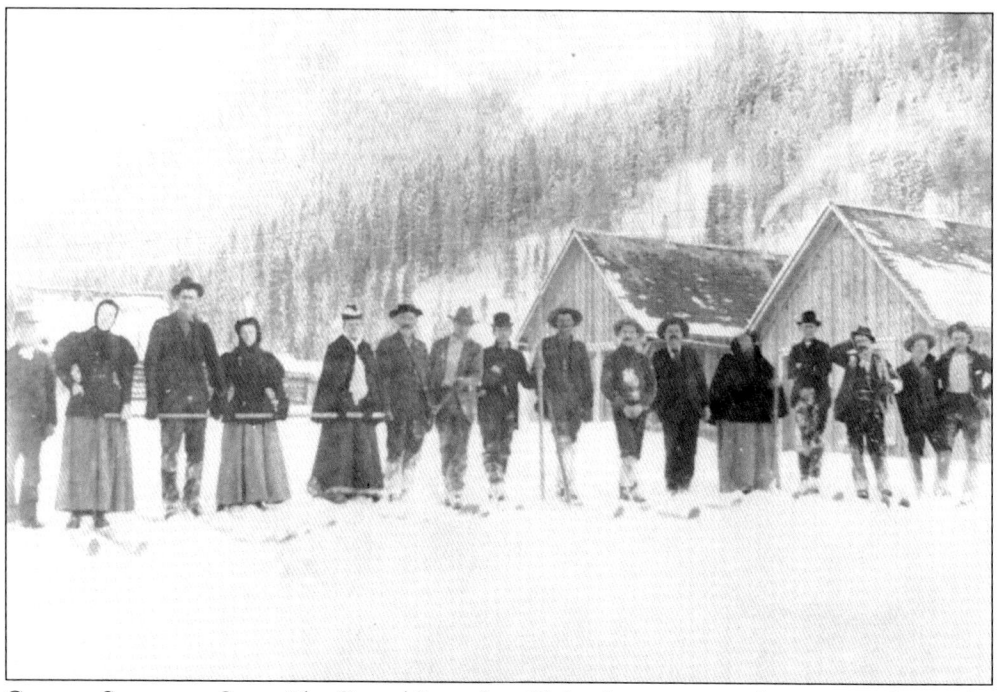

CRYSTAL SNOWSHOE CLUB. The Crystal Snowshoe Club takes a moment for a picture during the winter of 1898–1899. They are, from left to right, Ambrose Williams, Mrs. Horace Williams, Charles Melton, Mamie Wright, Mrs. O'Brien, Judge O'Brien, George Henniford, Ed Hurd, Bob Brown, Mr. Matthews, Mr. Trichberger, Mrs. Trichberger, Fred Holgaie, Frank Dempke, Rolle Hyers, and Frank Wright.

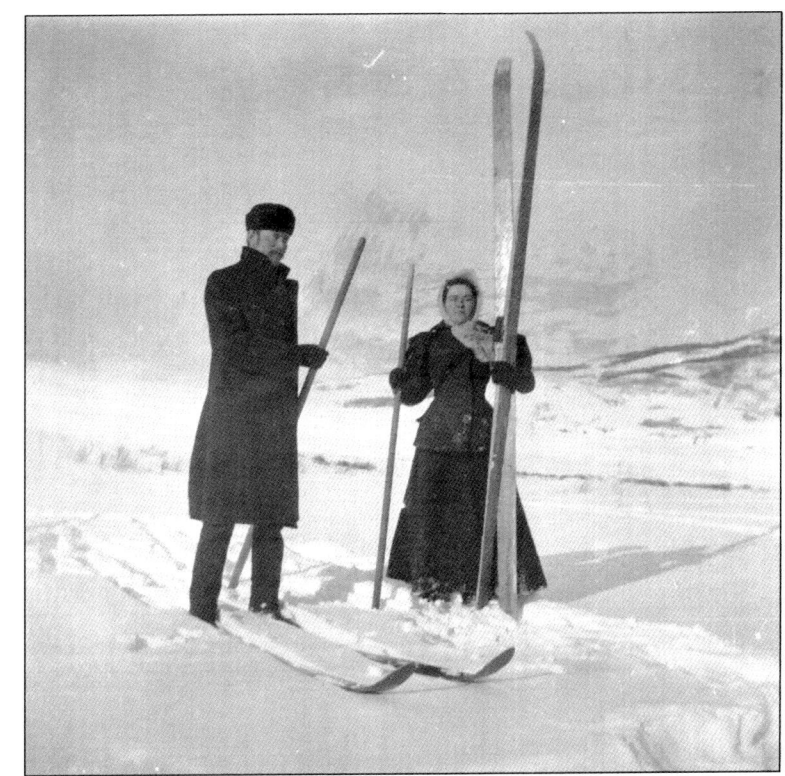

THE METZLERS FROM IRWIN. Vic Metzler and his wife, from Irwin, pose for a picture near Crested Butte in 1883. Metzler was a leading citizen of the Irwin camp and an outstanding skier. The skis that he and his wife are shown with were 11 feet long and weighed 8 pounds.

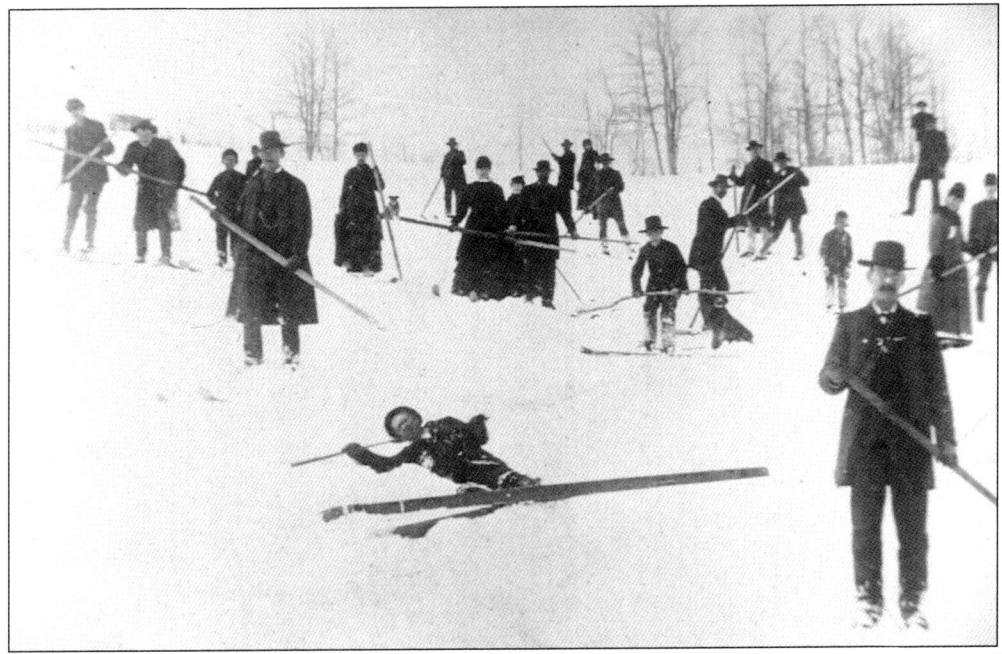

CRESTED BUTTE SNOWSHOERS, 1883. Men, women, and children ski on a hill just northwest of Crested Butte in 1883. Skiers were often called snowshoers then, and what people call snowshoes today were referred to as Canadian webs. All of the snowshoers (skiers) have long skis and guide poles and had to use the Telemark turn to be able to control their descents.

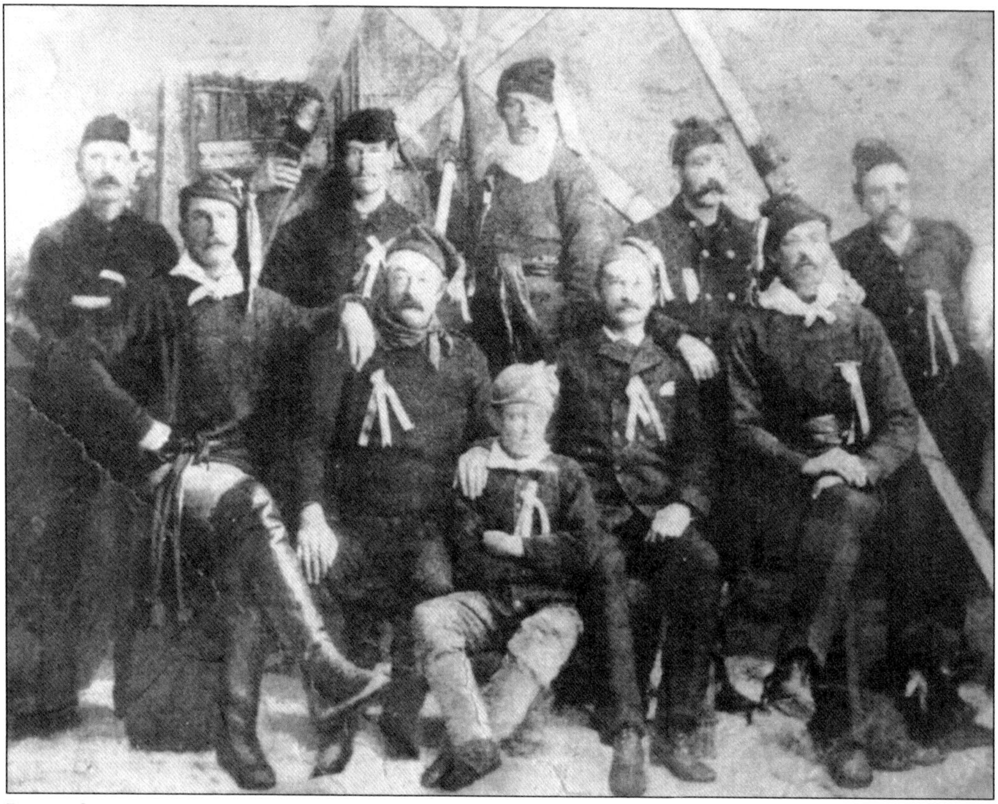

IRWIN SNOWSHOE CLUB, 1882. Irwin was still a booming mining camp in the early 1880s, and skiing was the number one form of recreation. Here, the Irwin Snowshoe Club poses for a picture. Included in the photograph but not specifically identified are Charles Ramsden, John E. Phillips, Vic Metzler, and P.F. Ropell. (CBMHM.)

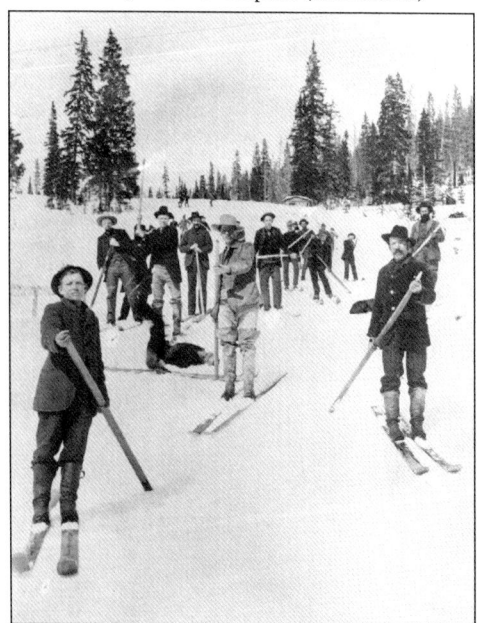

EARLY DAY SKIERS. A group of skiers from the mining camp of Irwin pleasure ski on a Sunday morning in 1883. Joining them (left front) is Charlie Baney of Crested Butte, one of the Gunnison Country's greatest skiers and the boy who defeated the legendary Al Johnson in a famous downhill race three years later.

"Hollins and Fred." Two men, identified only as Hollins and Fred, pose with their skis and guide poles in Crested Butte in 1881. Skis at that time ranged from 9 to 14 feet long and were heavy. Guide poles averaged 7 feet. Skiers had a leather tow attachment on the skis and a four-inch heel block preventing the foot from slipping backward on the ski. (CBMHM.)

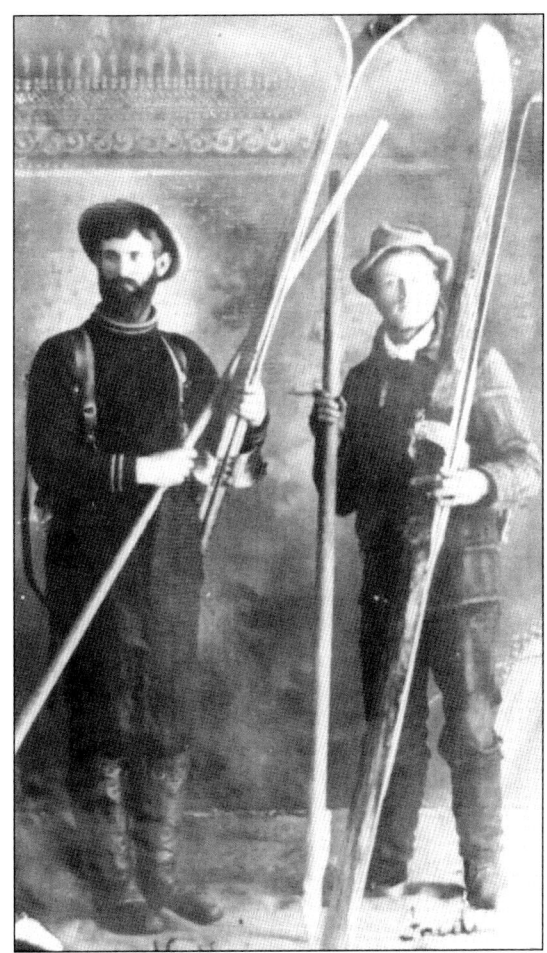

Splain's Gulch Skiing. Two Crested Butte women are seen in Splain's Gulch next to a mine building almost completely covered with snow in 1900. Splain's Gulch is located about six miles west of Crested Butte, and the head of the gulch opens into a spectacular park at nearly 10,000 feet.

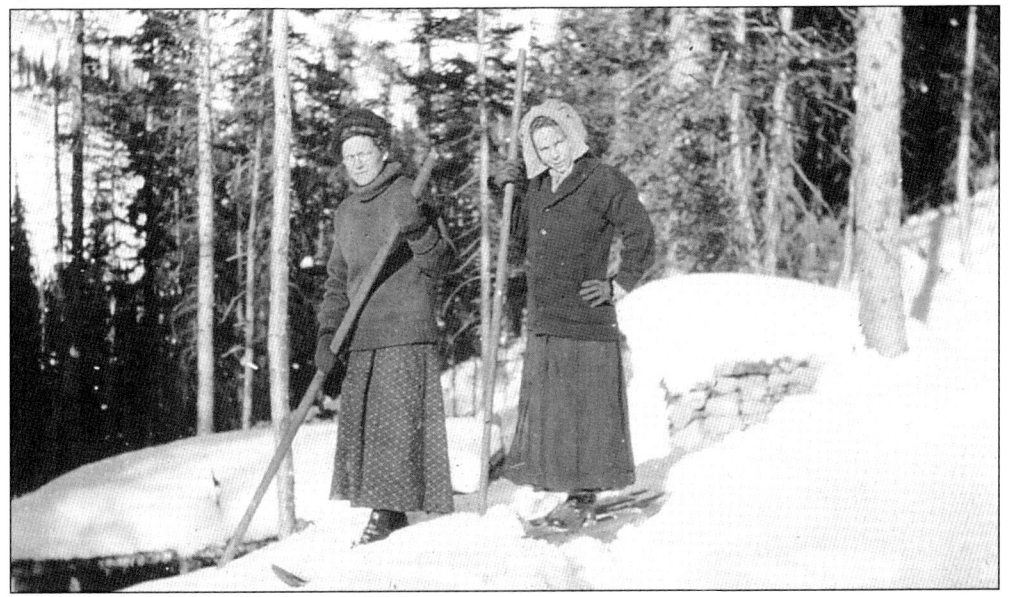

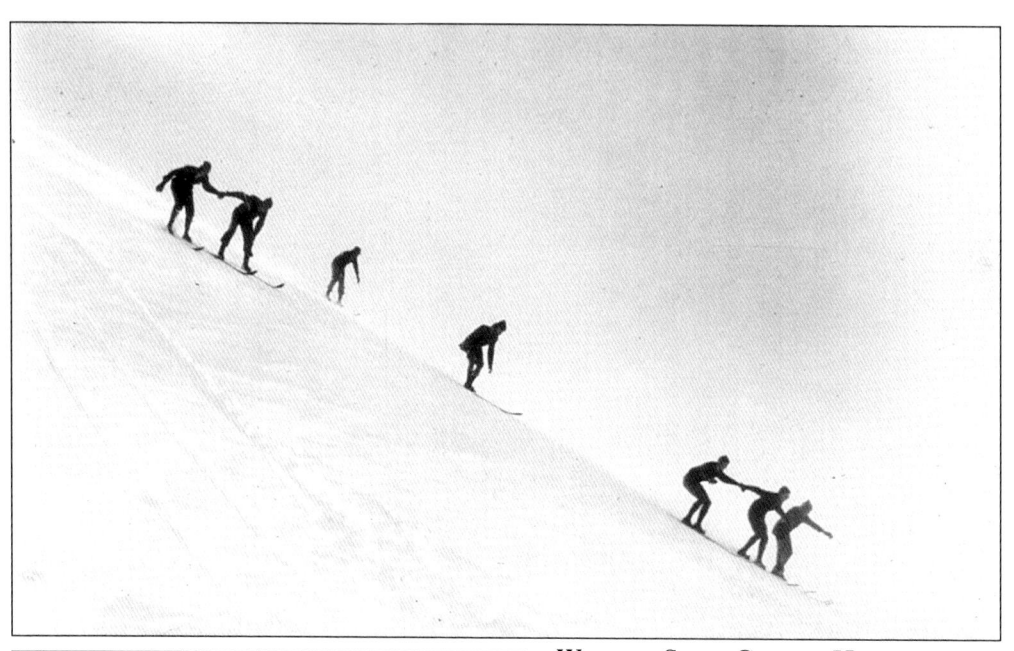

WESTERN STATE COLLEGE HIKING AND OUTING CLUB. The hiking and outing club of Western State College in Gunnison engaged in winter activities long before the existence of ski areas. The club packed out its own ski area as early as the 1920s on Quick's Hill, eight miles south of Crested Butte and near the mouth of Cement Creek. In this photograph, college men are playing "crack the whip" on Quick's Hill.

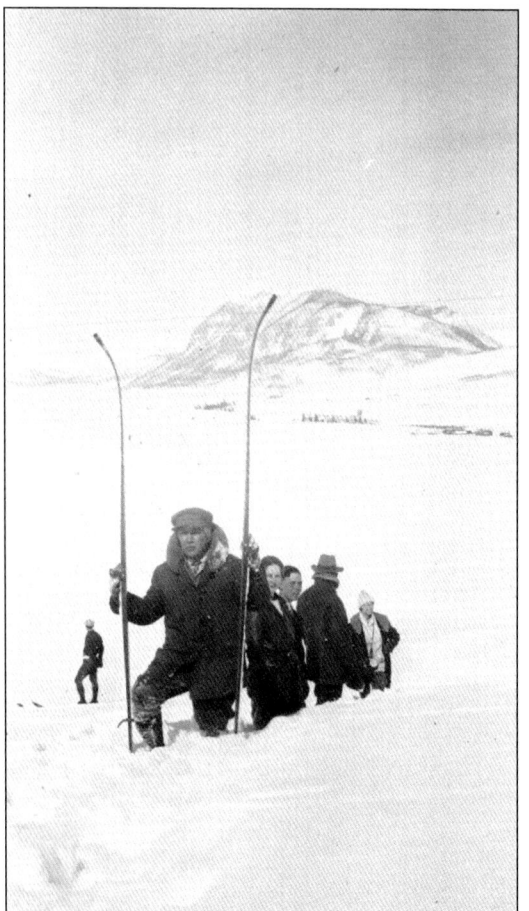

WORKING THE WAY UPHILL. With Mount Crested Butte providing a spectacular backdrop, a Western State College skier helps pack a trail up to the top of Quick's Hill in January 1931. The hill was 300 feet up from the valley floor below and provided a long ski run down. With only foot power to get to the top of the hill, seven runs a day was considered very good.

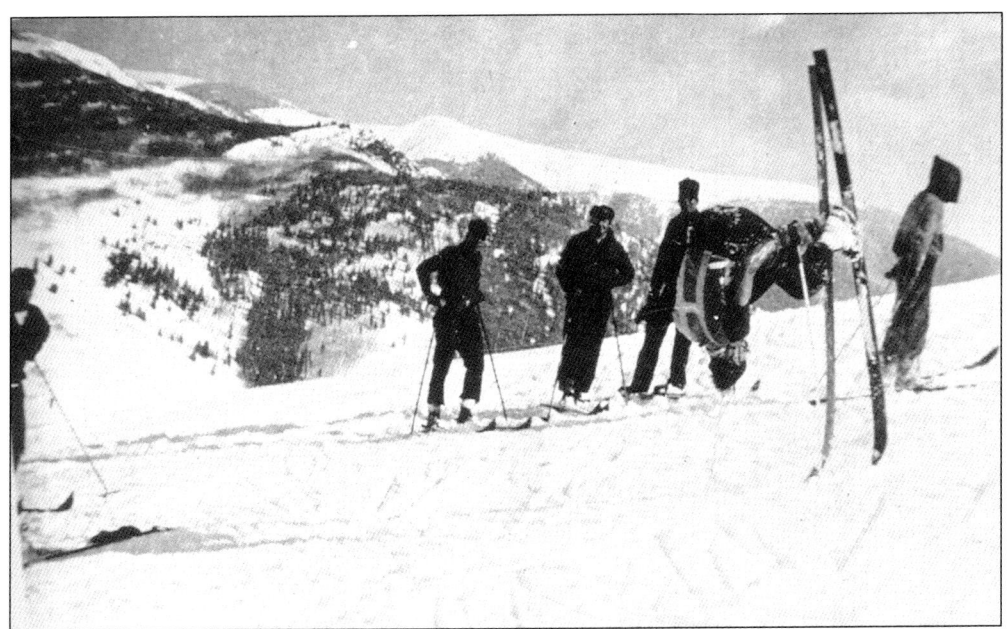

THE GREATEST OF THEM ALL. The greatest skier in the history of the Gunnison Country was Gunnison native Karl Easterly, a man ahead of his time. In this 1938 photograph on Quick's Hill, Easterly performs a backflip, long before anyone in the country even thought of it. In 1947, Easterly performed backflips on skis while being pulled by a helicopter in Sun Valley, Idaho. The footage was shown on early television.

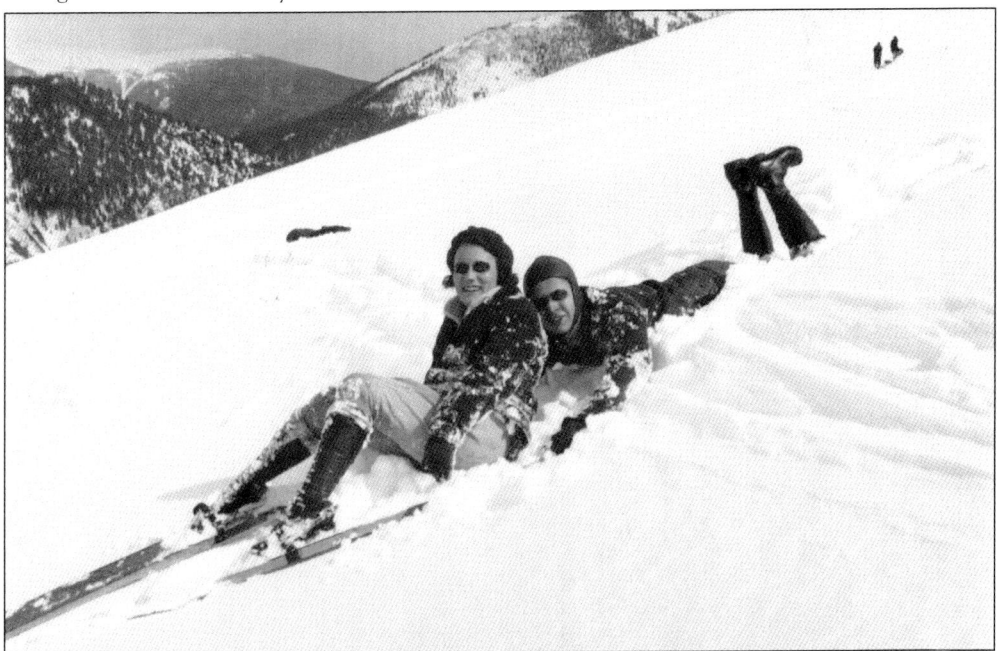

WESTERN STATE COLLEGE WOMEN. Two Western State College skiing coeds have crashed on Quick's Hill (named for the rancher who owned the land) in 1932. Helen McCormick is on the left. Many of the women skiers in the hiking and outing club at the college were as good as the top male skiers.

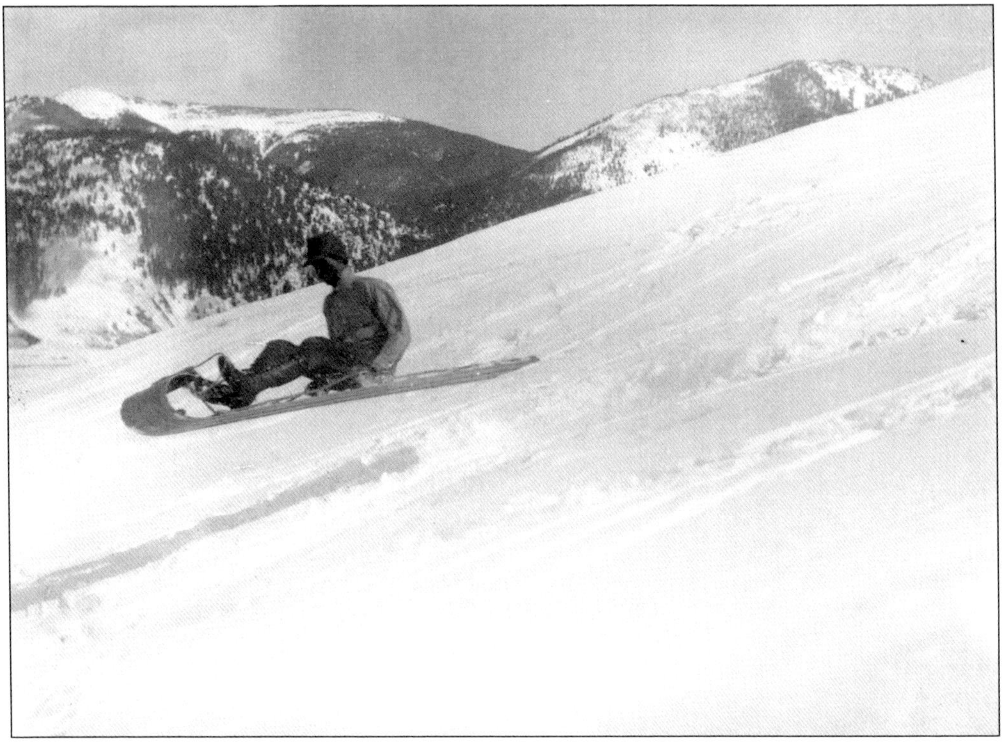

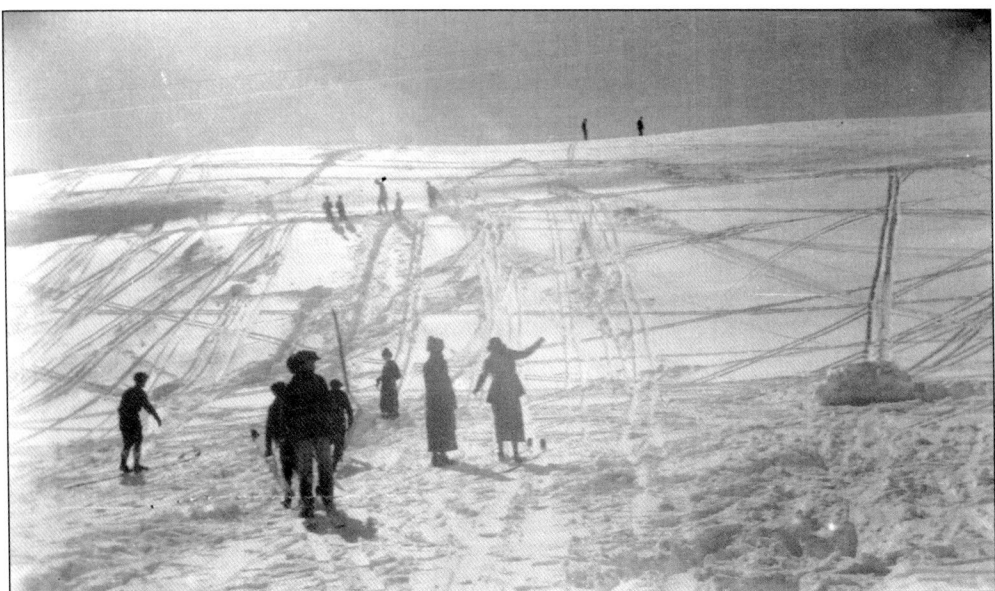

TOBOGGANING ON QUICK'S HILL. Fred Brand of the Western State Hiking and Outing club rides a toboggan off a jump on Quick's Hill in 1932. The speed of the toboggan was estimated at 35 miles per hour. The jump got the attention of all who went over it, and crashes were common.

CHICKEN RANCH. One mile north of Crested Butte along the Slate River, locals skied on a hill called Chicken Ranch, named for the sage hens that inhabited the area. In this 1935 photograph, locals have built jumps and are skiing powder snow during a weekend afternoon.

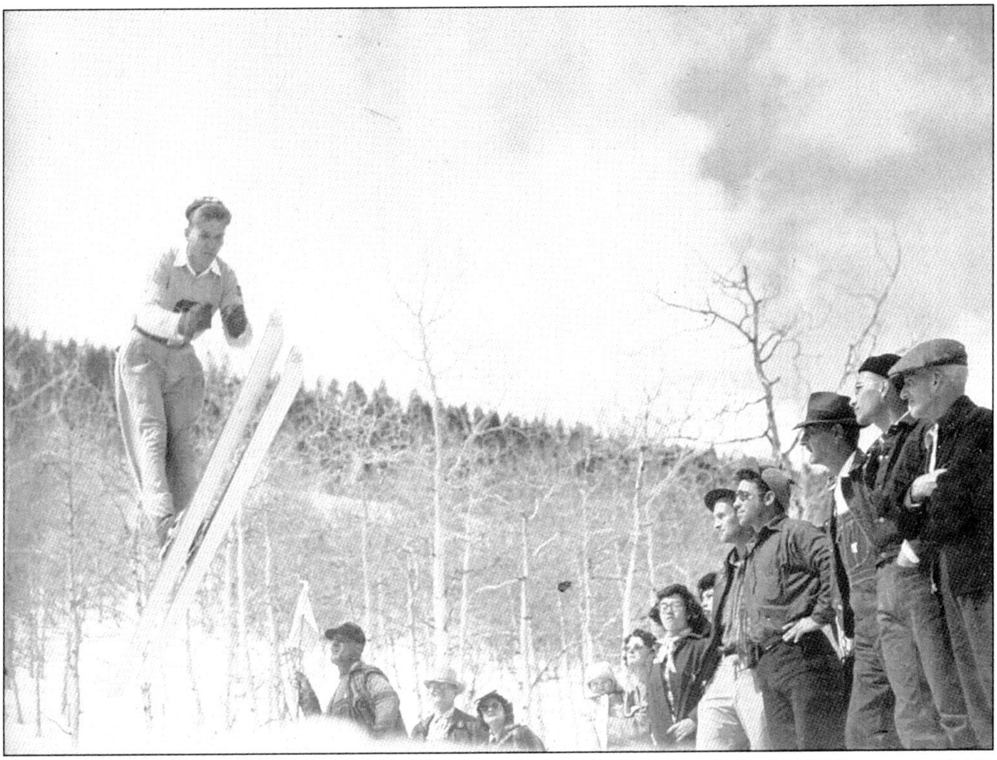

GOOD FORM OFF THE JUMP. John Gibson Jr. sails off the 20-meter Pershing Ski Hill jump in 1950. The starting point for skiers was 75 yards up the hill from the takeoff. The takeoff was made of log cribbing and snow. During the fall, rancher Joe Eacher used the land for grazing, so fences had to be taken down in the fall and put back up in the spring.

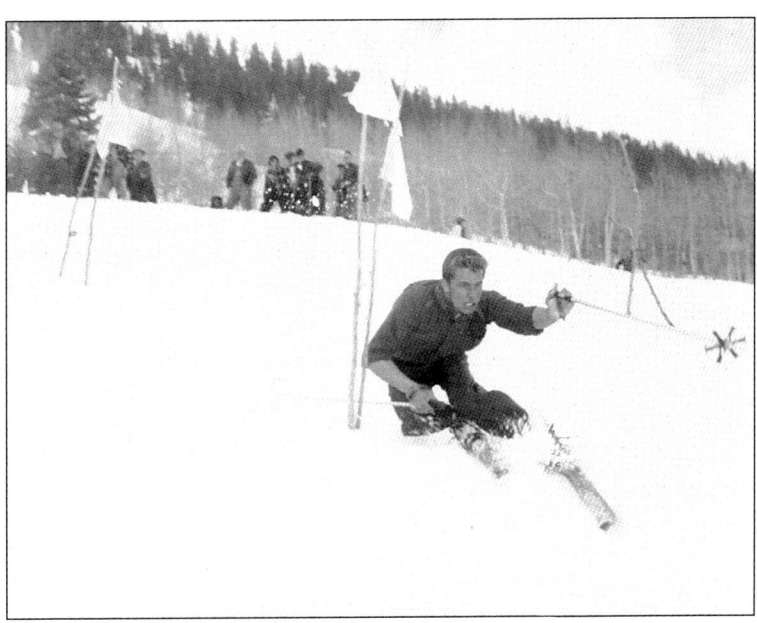

"KRIZ" IN ACTION. Steve "Beans" Krizmanich, a Crested Butte student, shows great form as he navigates a slalom course on Pershing Hill in 1951. The Pershing Ski Hill had a rope tow that could carry only two skiers at a time. A Model A engine, covered by an old coal shed, powered the tow. The warming house was a donated tin shed.

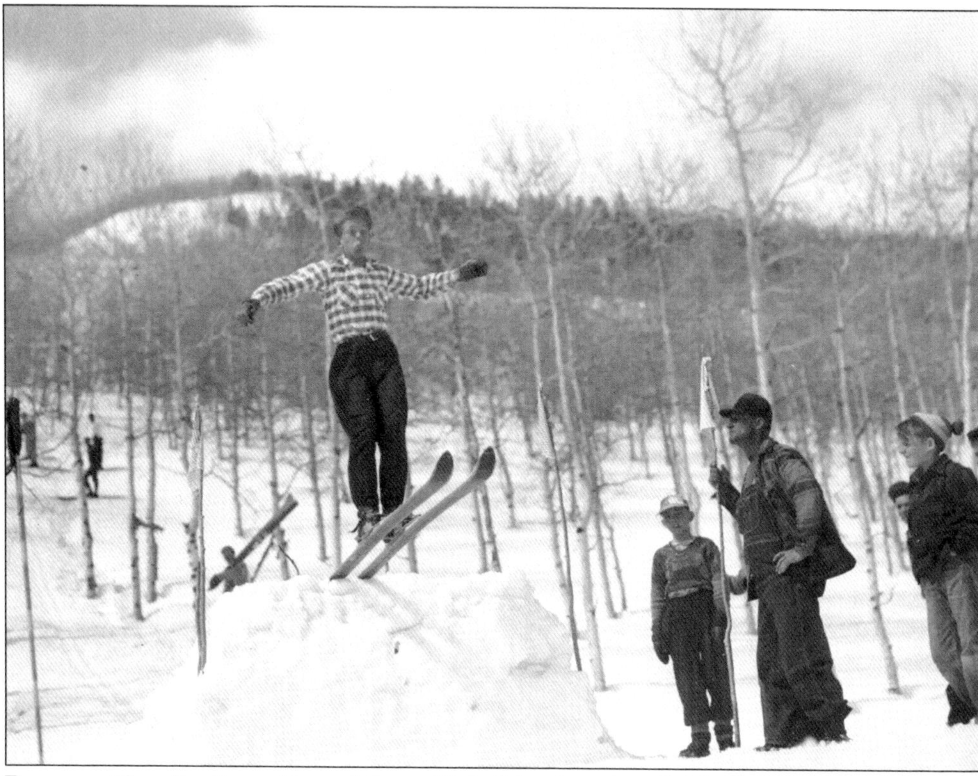

PERSHING HILL SKI JUMP. Crested Butte High School student Bobby Greenfield comes off the Pershing Hill ski jump during a competition in 1951. The Pershing Ski Hill was begun by local citizens in Crested Butte who received permission from the Colorado Fuel and Iron Company to use land near the Pershing Coal Mine. The hill was located a mile north of Crested Butte.

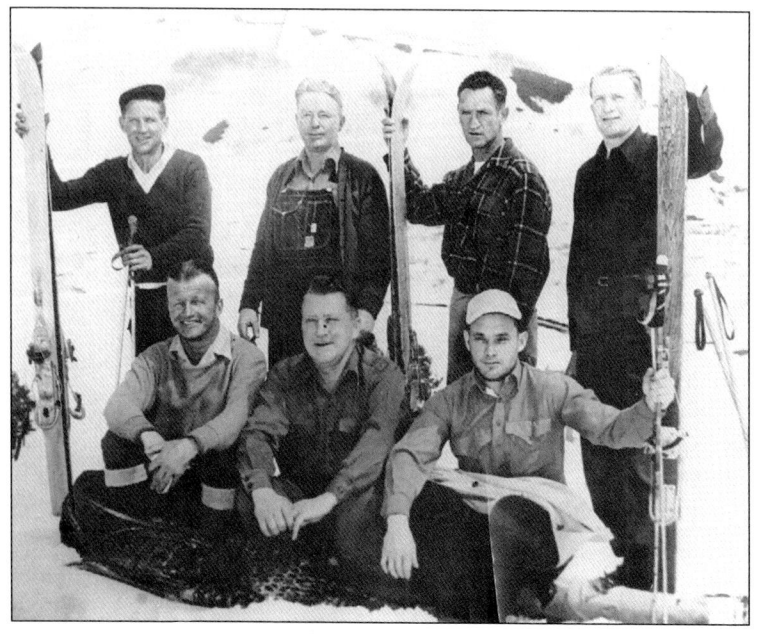

CRESTED BUTTE SKI CLUB DIRECTORS, 1950. Local citizens in Crested Butte provided the labor and funds to create the Pershing Hill Ski Area in 1950. Those on the board of directors included, from left to right, (first row) Joe Saya, Frank Starika, and Chick Mufich; (second row) Don Young (coach), Lyle McNeill, Chuck Songer, and Rudy Verzuh. (CBHM.)

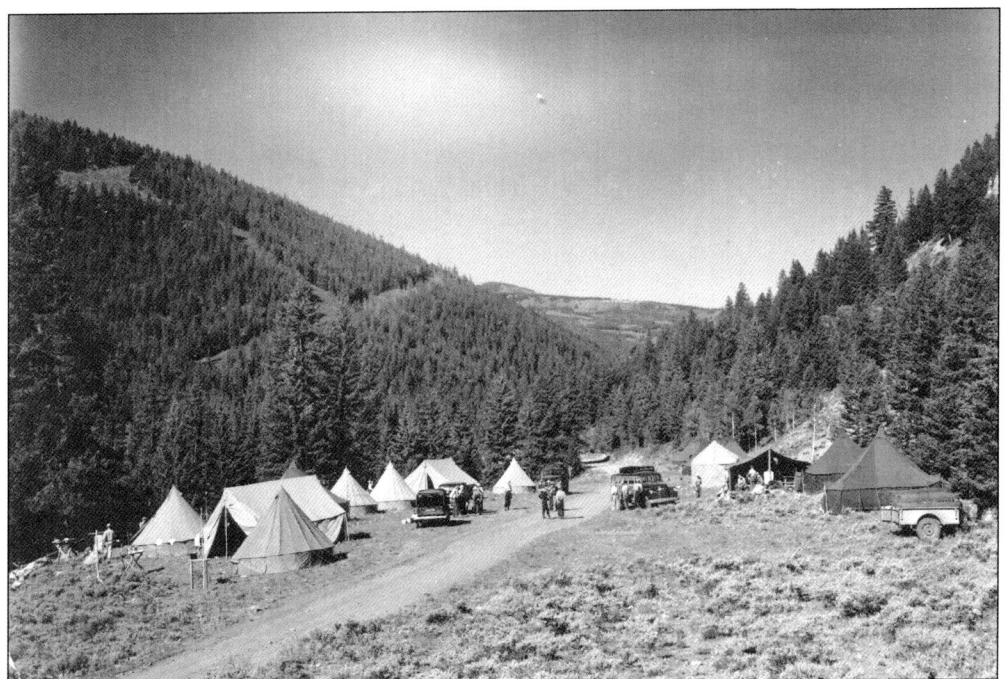

WPA IN ACTION. The Work Projects Administration, financed by Franklin Roosevelt's New Deal, worked on the Pioneer Ski Area during the fall of 1939. Up to 45 men camped out near Cement Creek and every day cut trees to clear runs on the hill above them.

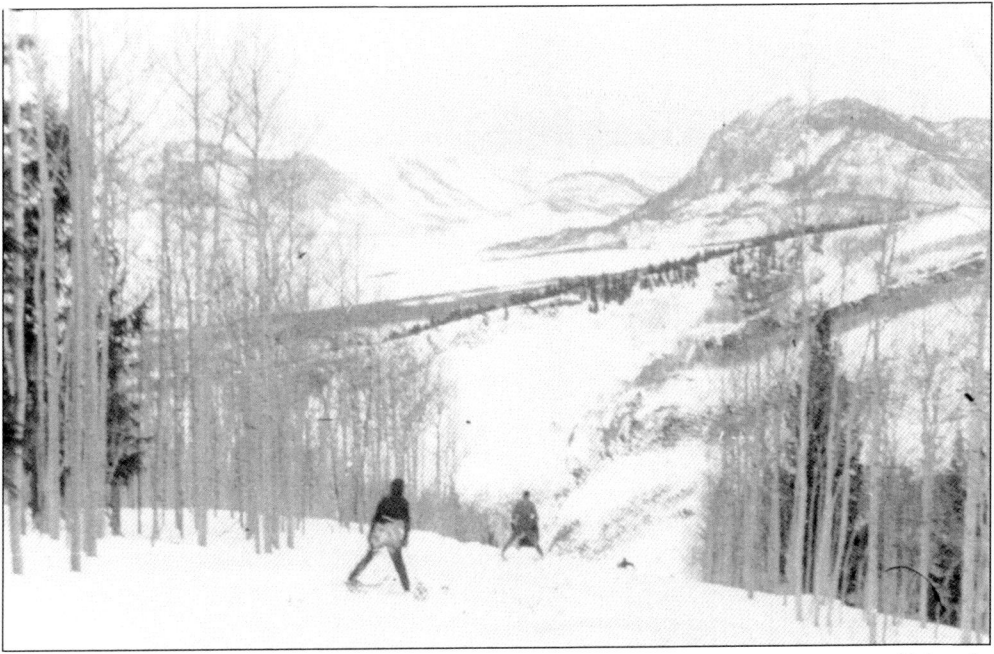

HEADING DOWNHILL ON THE BIG DIPPER. One of the steepest runs on any mountain in Colorado was the Pioneer Ski Area's Big Dipper. Not only was the long run steep but it also had many fall away turns that did not go straight down the mountain. The steepness of the run, coupled with primitive equipment, made skiing it very difficult.

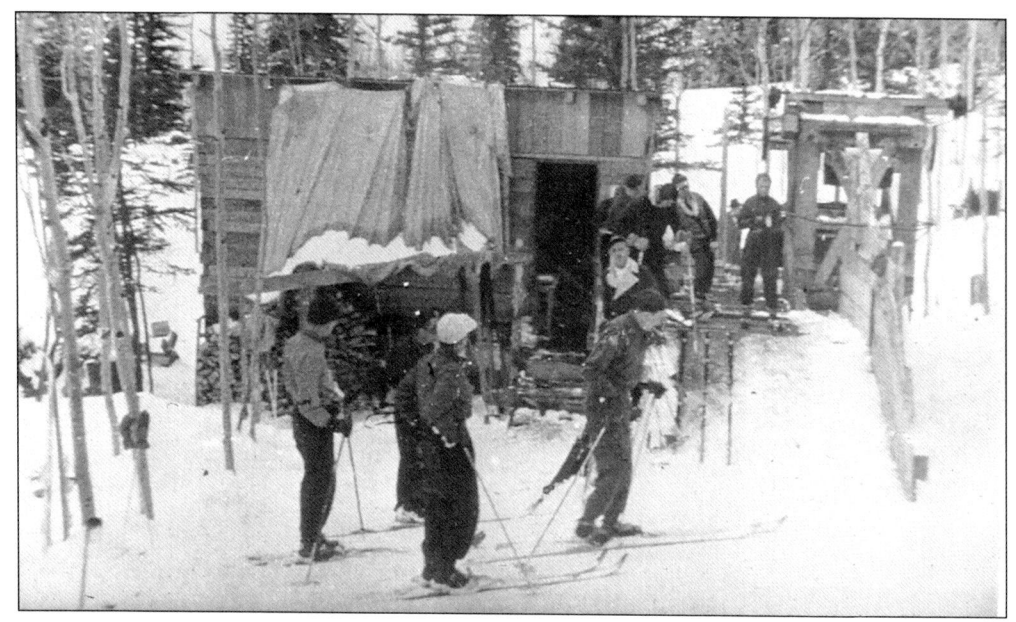

FIRST CHAIRLIFT IN COLORADO. A woman stands on the platform of the primitive Pioneer chairlift. The chairlift was called the Comet and took seven-and-a-half minutes to get skiers to the top of the ski area. Both the lift and steep runs at Pioneer proved hazardous, and the area closed following the winter of 1951–1952.

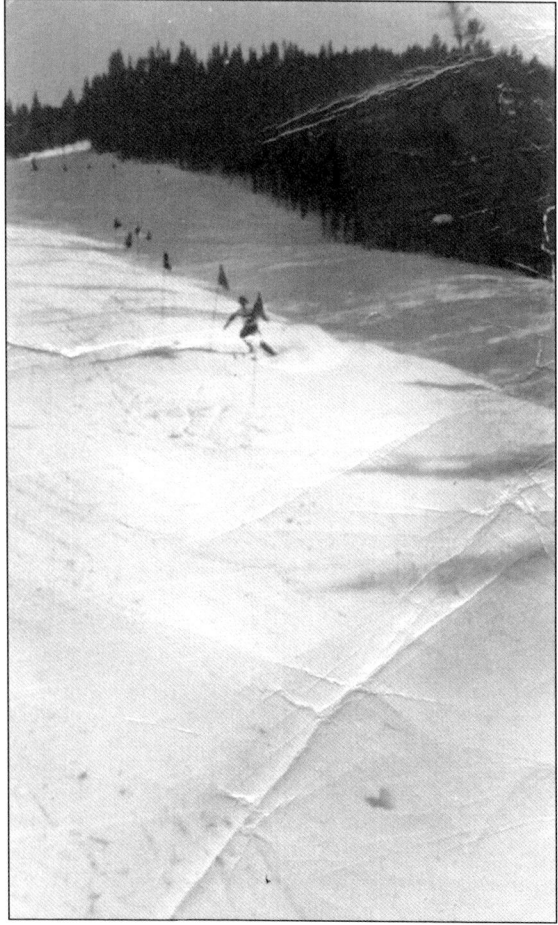

BIG DIPPER SLALOM. Shortly after the Pioneer Ski Area opened during the winter of 1939–1940, intercollegiate ski races were held there. Western State College, Denver University, Colorado, Utah, Wyoming, and Montana State were some of the schools that competed. In this photograph, an unidentified college skier is on the slalom course on the Big Dipper.

CEMENT CREEK CROSS COUNTRY. A Nordic skier from the University of Wyoming sets the pace in a 15 kilometer cross-country race in 1951 near the mouth of Cement Creek not far from the Pioneer Ski Area. Mount Emmons is in the background. The Cement Creek course was ideal for intercollegiate skiing because it was close to Highway 135 and only three miles from Pioneer.

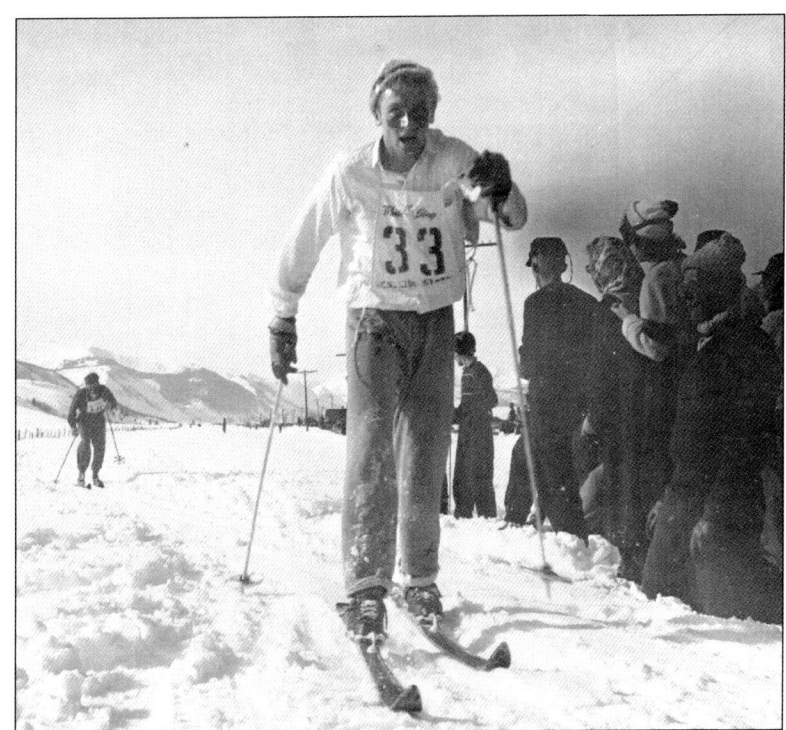

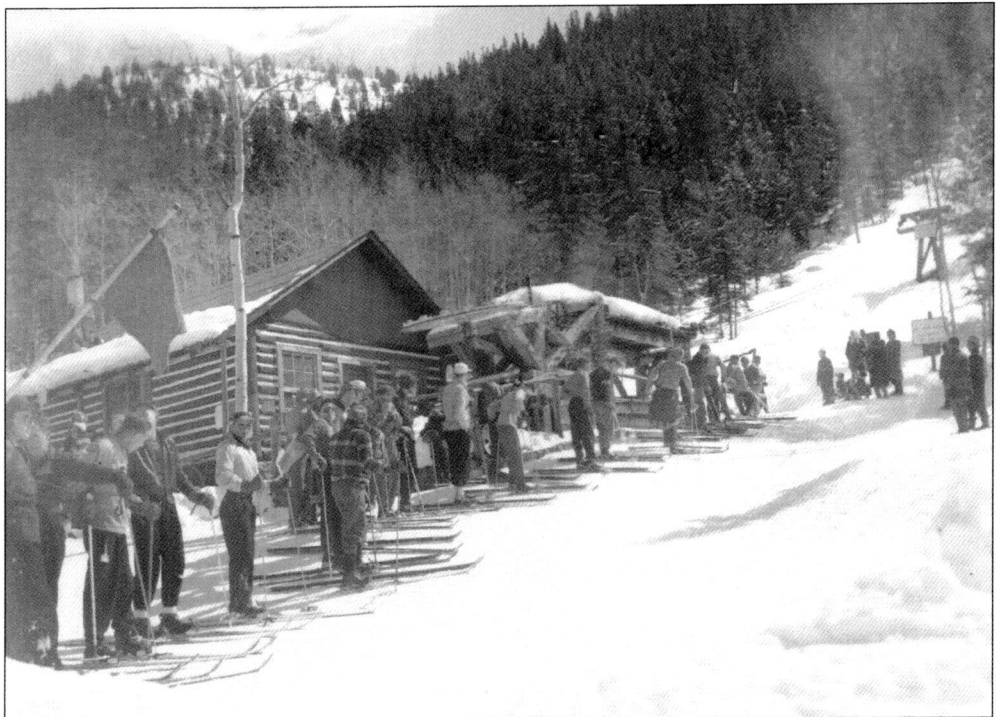

LIFT LINE. Skiers are lined up in February 1940 at the Pioneer Ski Area waiting to get on the primitive chairlift to carry them to the top of the runs. The towers, cables, and chairs came from the Blistered Horn Mine near Cumberland Pass, southeast of Crested Butte.

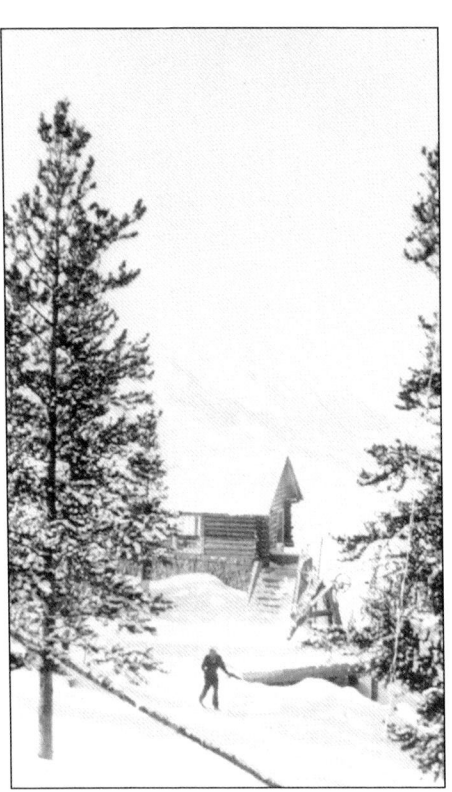

TOP OF THE LIFT. On a snowy and almost whiteout day in 1941, a lone skier heads downhill from the top of the Pioneer Ski Area. The cabin in the background was the warming house and was adjacent to the chairlift. Inside, a person could get coffee, hot chocolate, and sandwiches.

INTERCOLLEGIATE SKIING. Skiers from Colorado and Rocky Mountain Colleges line up near the bottom warming house of the Pioneer Ski Area in 1947. They are waiting to catch the Comet chairlift. Some of the greatest collegiate skiers in the country skied at Pioneer, including Barney McLean and Crosby Perry-Smith.

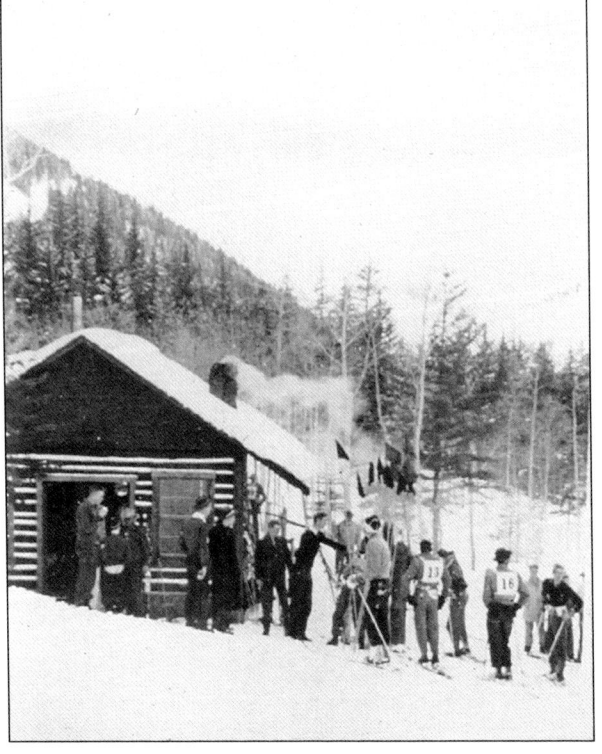

SKI JUMP. A ski jump was built at the Pioneer Ski Area in 1948. The jump was constructed for intercollegiate ski competition but was only used for one year. The landing area was not adequate and proved dangerous, so the jump was abandoned.

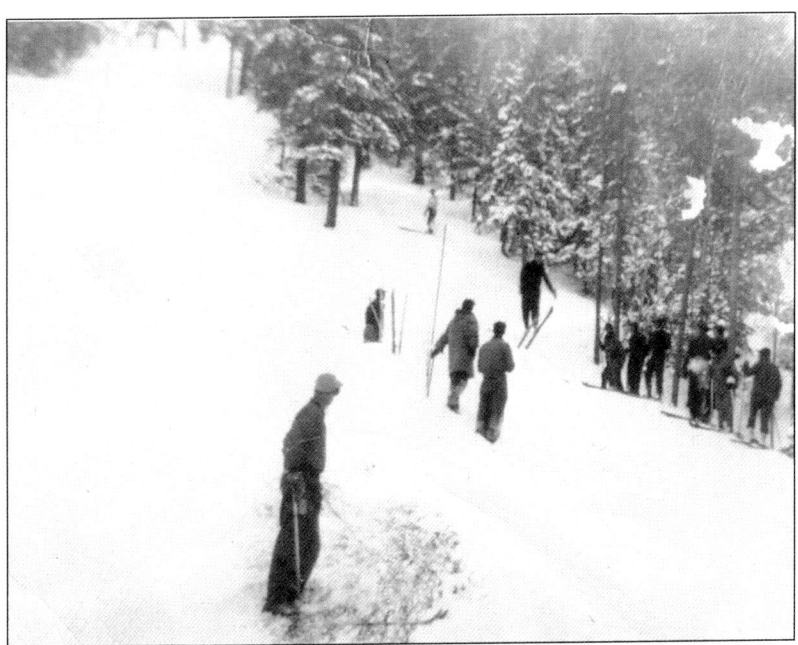

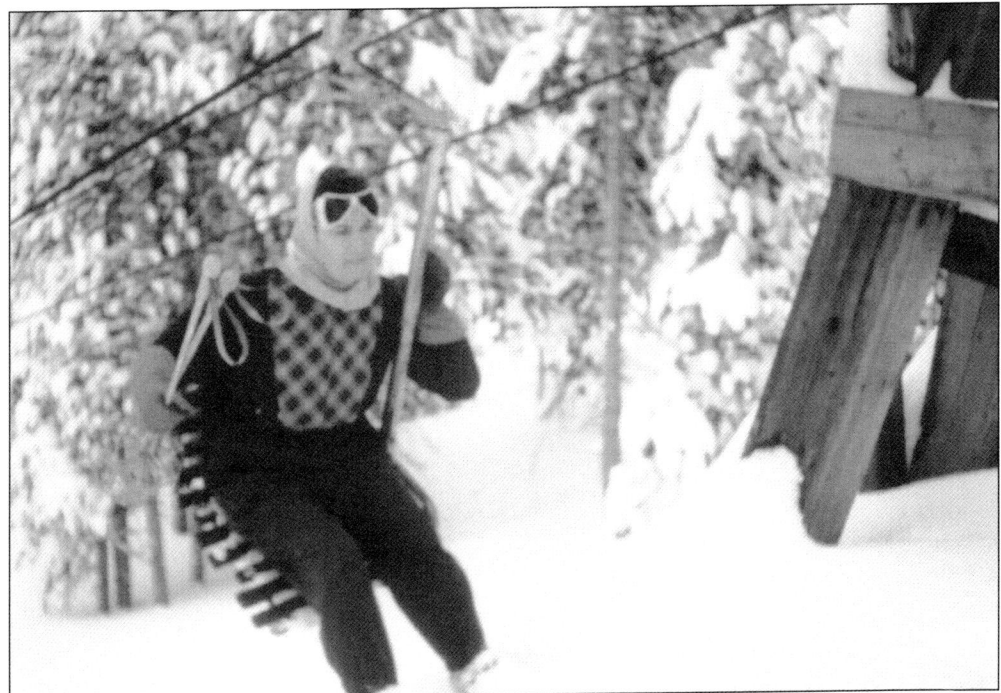

RIDING THE CHAIR. An unidentified woman rides a very primitive chair heading for the top of the Pioneer Ski Area in 1940. When the lift was put in during the fall, the US Forest Service made the builders lower the chairs because they were too high off the ground. When 20 feet of snow fell, skiers were flipped out of chairs because they were too close to the snow.

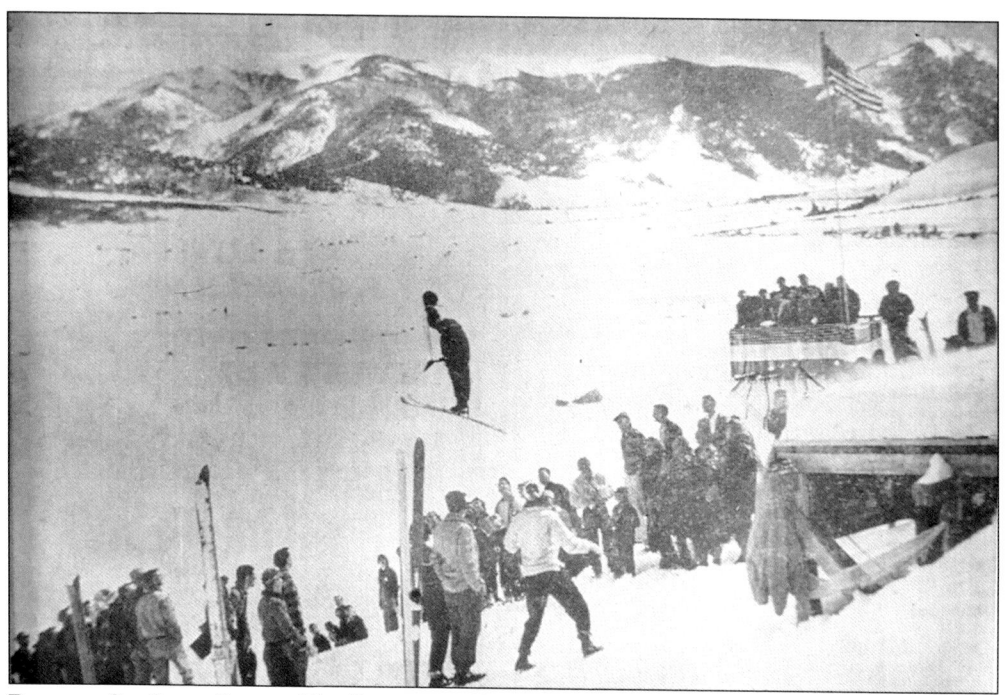

ROZMAN SKI JUMP OPENS. The Rozman Hill Ski Jump was located on John Rozman's ranch south of Crested Butte during the winter of 1949–1950. The first jump was made out of snow by the Western State College ski team. A better site was found on the hill next year, and a new jump was built. This photograph shows a jumper going off the jump on the first day it was used in intercollegiate competition.

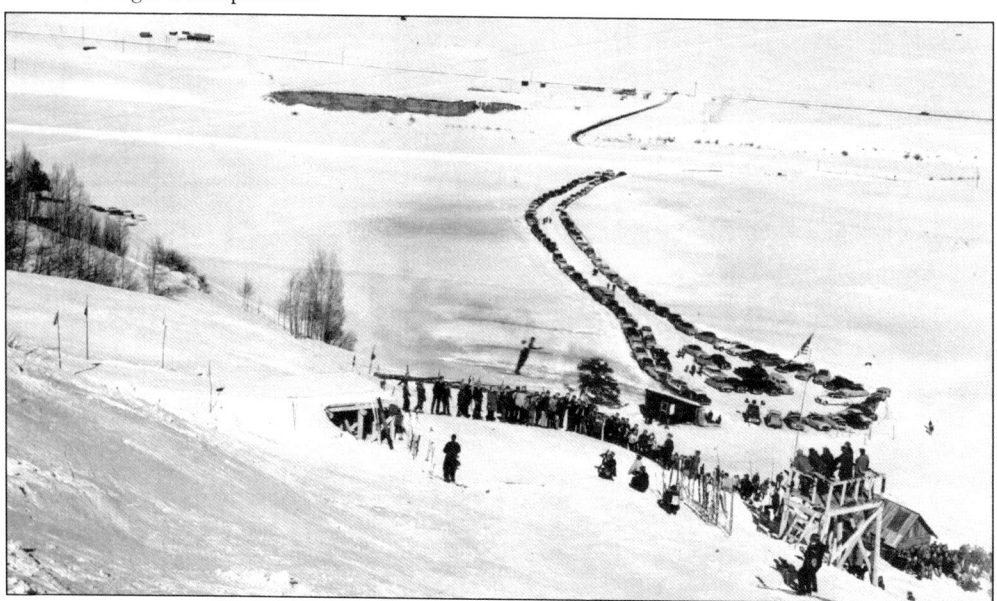

SKI JUMPING COMPETITION. A major intercollegiate ski meet is underway in this 1952 photograph. A big crowd has gathered to watch jumpers soar off the hill, and cars are parked almost to Highway 135 on John Rozman's ranch. Judges of the competition featuring Western State and the Universities of Denver, Colorado, Wyoming, and Utah are on the stand to the right.

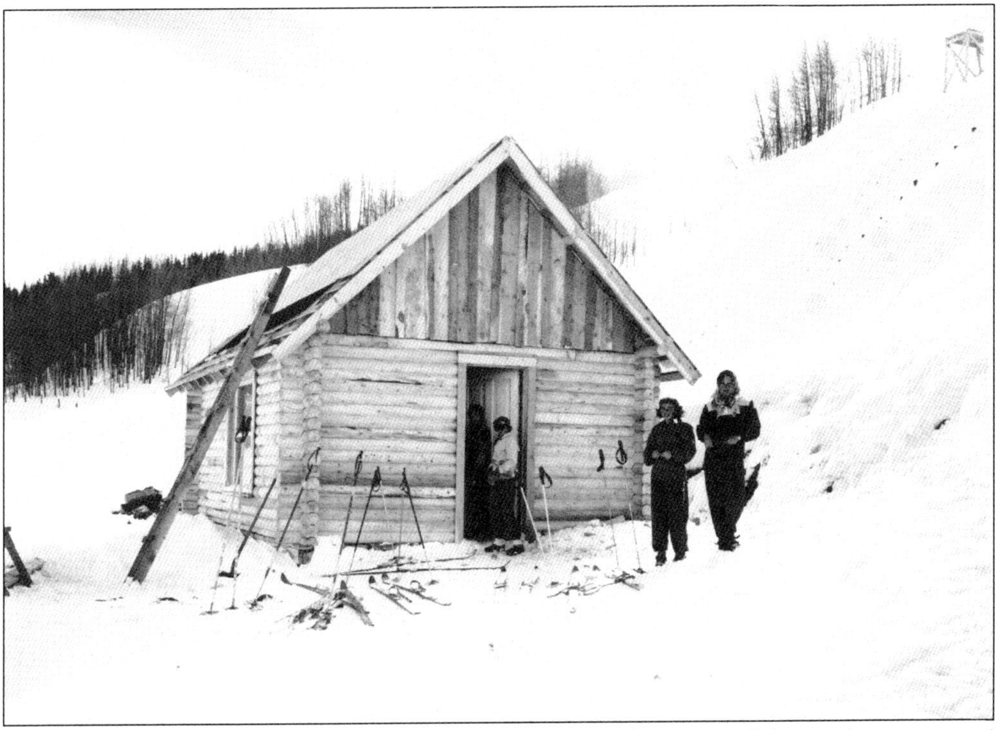

ROZMAN HILL WARMING HOUSE. Three female skiers stand in front of the newly constructed warming house at the Rozman Hill Ski Area in 1950. The judges' stand for ski jumping competitions is in the background. The warming house was spartan in its accommodations. Coffee and hot chocolate were served, and the building allowed people to warm up on bitterly cold days.

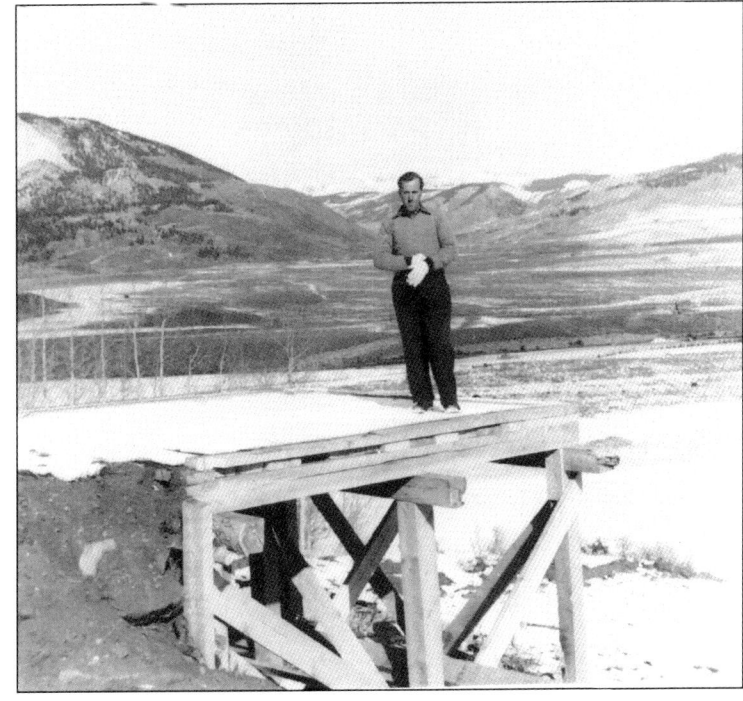

SVEN WIIK. Western State College ski coach Sven Wiik stands on the newly constructed ski jump at the Rozman Hill Ski Area during the fall of 1950. Wiik went on to become the US Olympic ski coach twice during his distinguished career.

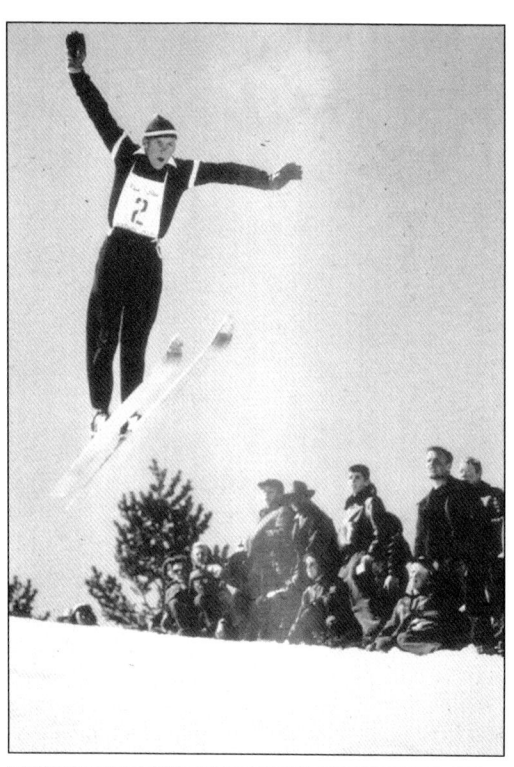

UPPER PENINSULA STAR. John Grodesky from Escanaba in Michigan's Upper Peninsula comes off the Rozman Hill takeoff in 1952. Grodesky was one of the top ski jumpers in the United States before coming to Western State College. He jumped off some of the most famous hills in the nation, including Suicide Hill in Ishpening, Michigan, and Howelson Hill in Steamboat Springs, Colorado.

THE JUMP. A giant W is on the front of the takeoff on the Rozman Hill ski jump as a Western State College skier begins to soar in January 1953. The judges on the viewing stand on the left are analyzing the jump for style points.

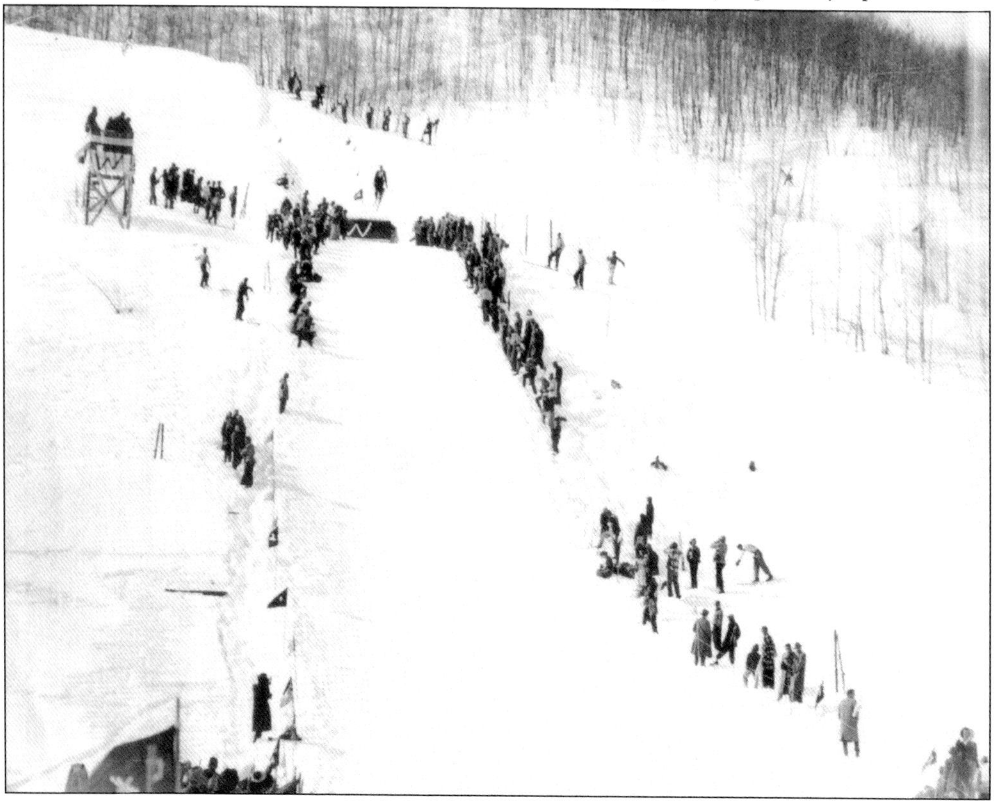

SKIING ROZMAN HILL. A skier makes his way down Rozman Hill on January 1, 1959. The ski area had three rope tows and was the creation of the Western State College ski team. Frank Le Fevre of the ski team signed up for four independent study classes from Western State College athletic director Paul Wright, worked on the ski lift during the fall of 1951, took one oral test, and received all As.

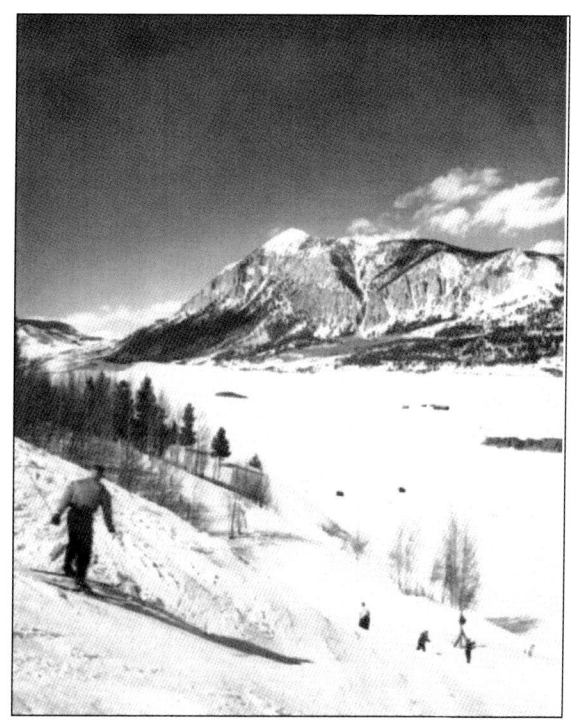

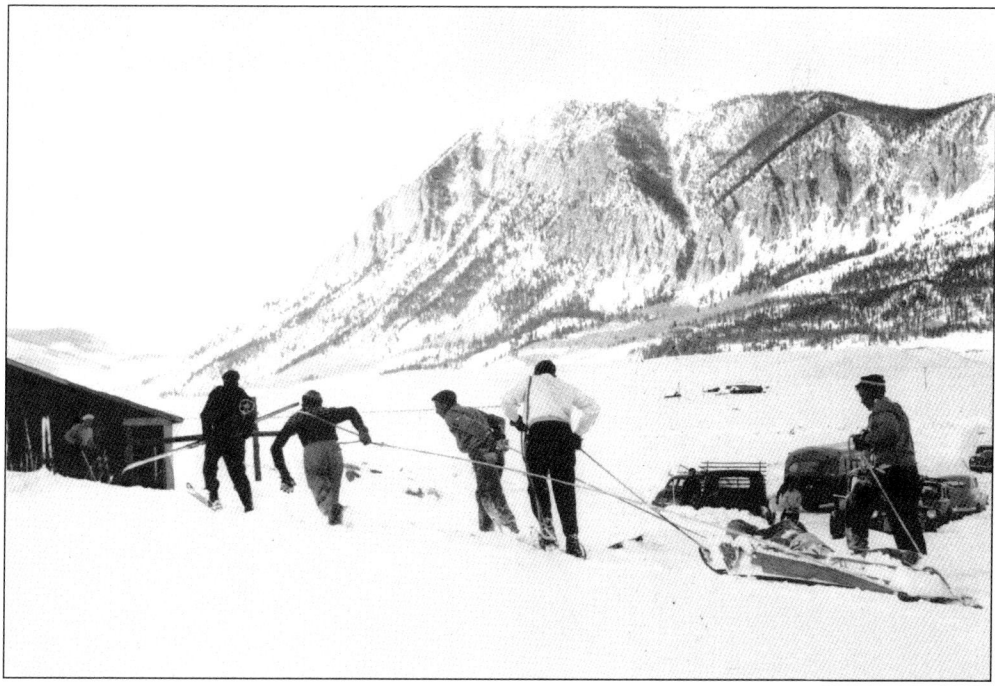

INJURED SKIER. The volunteer ski patrol pulls a toboggan carrying an injured skier at the Rozman Hill Ski Area in 1953. Rozman Hill had three rope tows servicing the area and they were referred to as "man killers." Many skiers did not have the strength to hold on for 1,000 feet and occasionally the tows snagged scarves, jackets, and loose articles of clothing. Going up the hill was just as hazardous as going down.

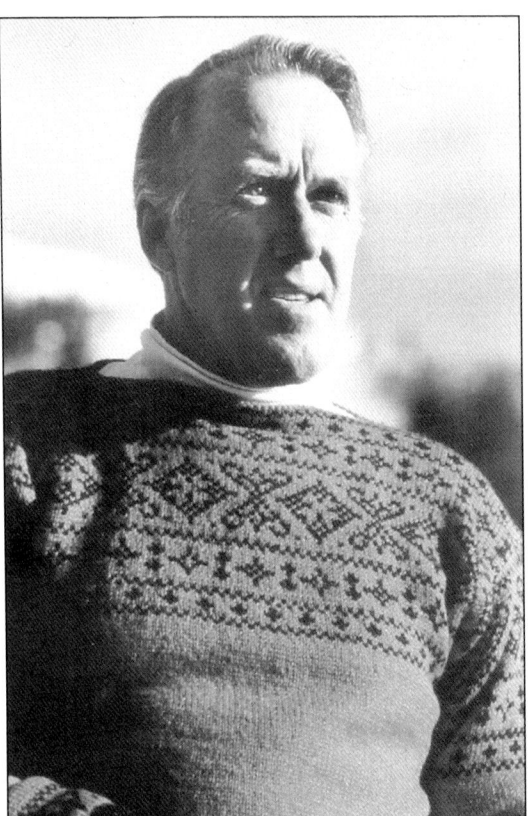

SVEN WIIK. One of the legendary ski coaches in United States history, Sven Wiik came to Western State College from Sweden in 1949, and he was still not very fluent in the English language. He served as a ski coach at the college until 1967 and twice coached the US Olympic team. Wiik is properly regarded as the father of Nordic skiing in the United States.

SOARING. A lone jumper soars off Rozman Hill in an intercollegiate ski meet in 1954. Distance marks will determine how far the jumper goes down the hill. The Rozman jump allowed skiers to attain distances of 120 feet or slightly more. The jump was good for collegiate skiers, but not for the nation's best.

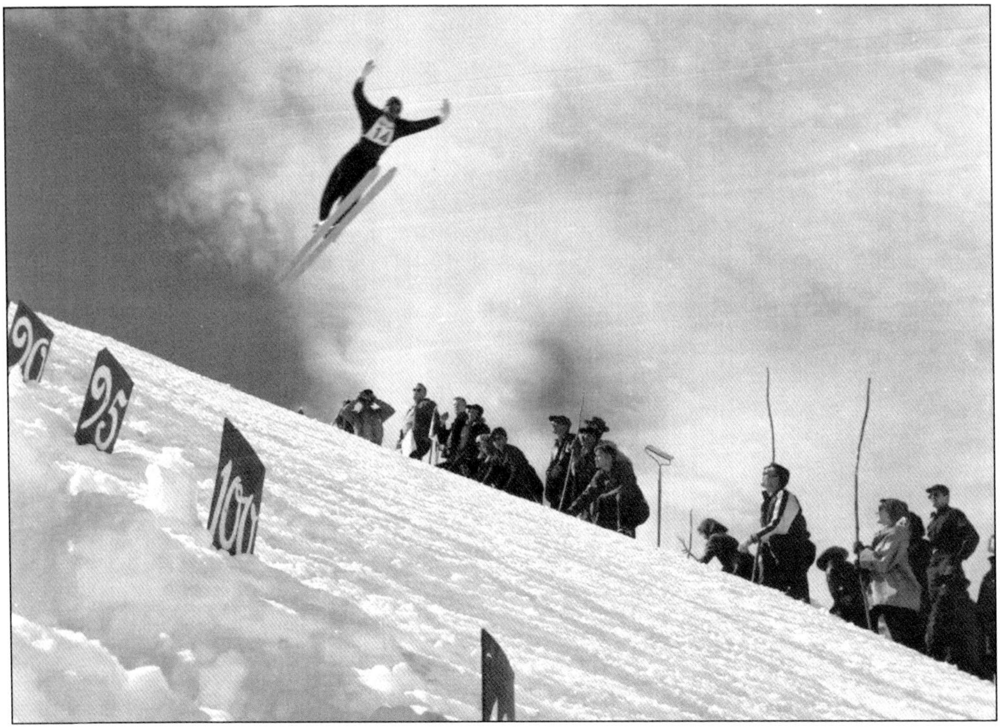

Seven
DENVER AND RIO GRANDE RAILROAD

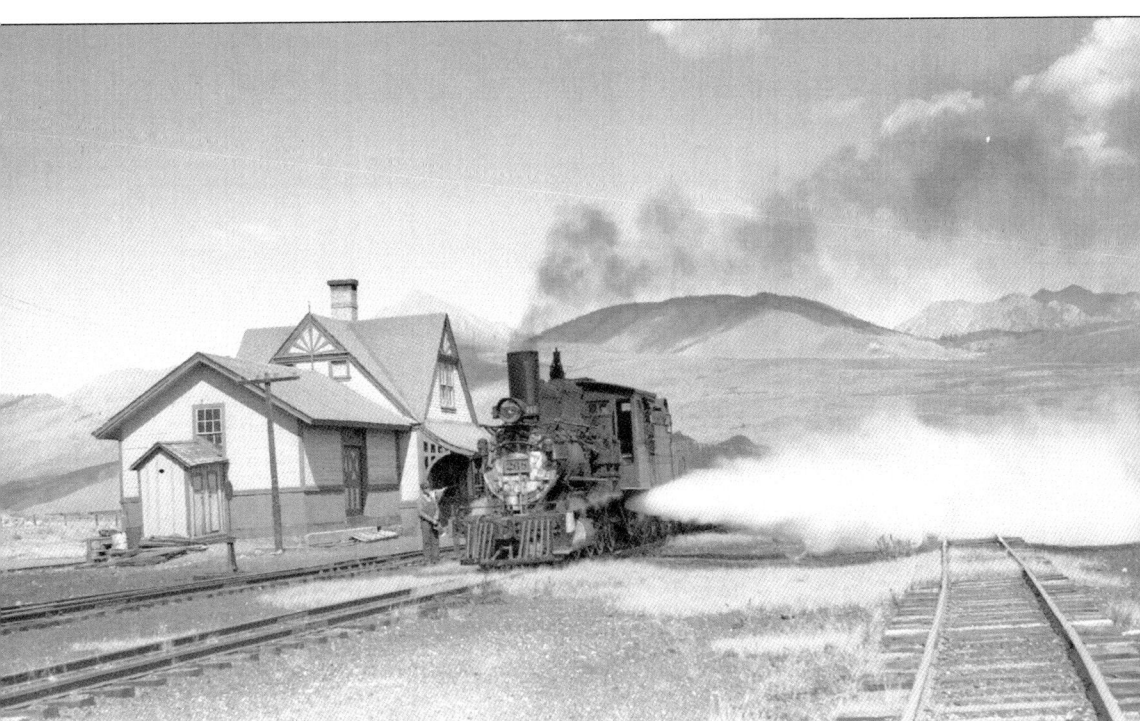

CRESTED BUTTE DEPOT. A Denver and Rio Grande engine blows off steam in front of the Crested Butte depot in the 1940s. The Rio Grande built from Gunnison into Crested Butte, 28 miles away, on November 21, 1881. The *Crested Butte Republican* newspaper exclaimed, "November 21 will ever be a red letter day in the history of Crested Butte."

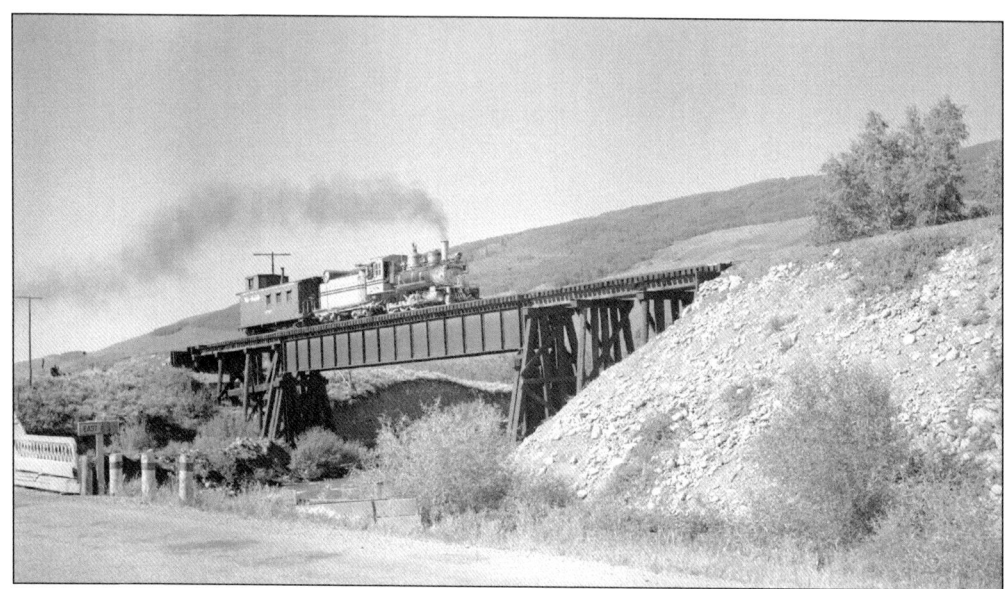

GLACIER. Denver and Rio Grande engine 268 and caboose cross a trestle over the East River in the 1940s. Glacier was eight miles south of Crested Butte and had a school that served ranch children from the area. Glacier was never much more than a D&RG railroad spur; it held four railroad cars and shipped out cattle, hay, and ore from nearby Taylor Park.

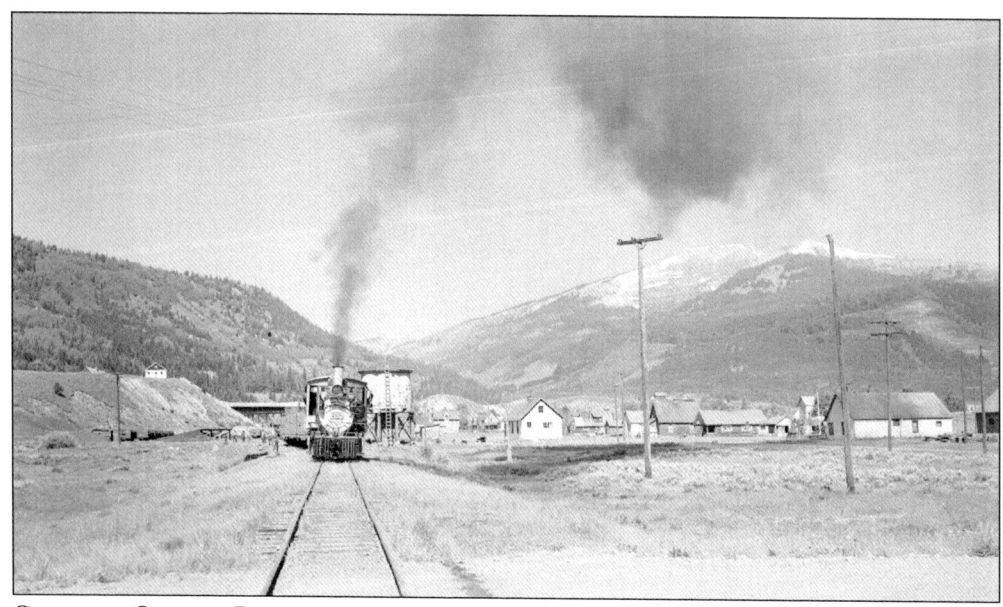

COAL AND CRESTED BUTTE. A Denver and Rio Grande coal train prepares to leave Crested Butte in the 1940s. Mount Emmons, site of one of the major molybdenum deposits in the world, forms a backdrop. The tipple of the Colorado Fuel and Iron Company's Big Mine can be seen behind the train.

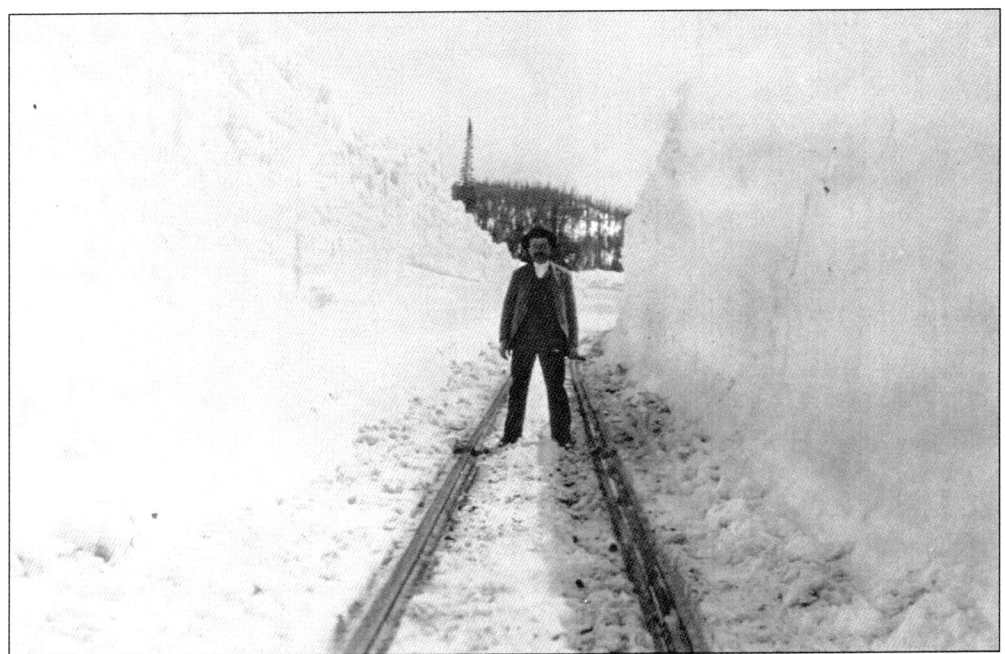

HEAVY SNOW IN THE HIGH COUNTRY. A railroad man stands on Denver and Rio Grande railroad tracks five miles west of Crested Butte in 1909. Plows have carved a route through snow 20 feet high. The tremendous snow that fell from Crested Butte to Floresta to the west shut down rail traffic for six months of the year.

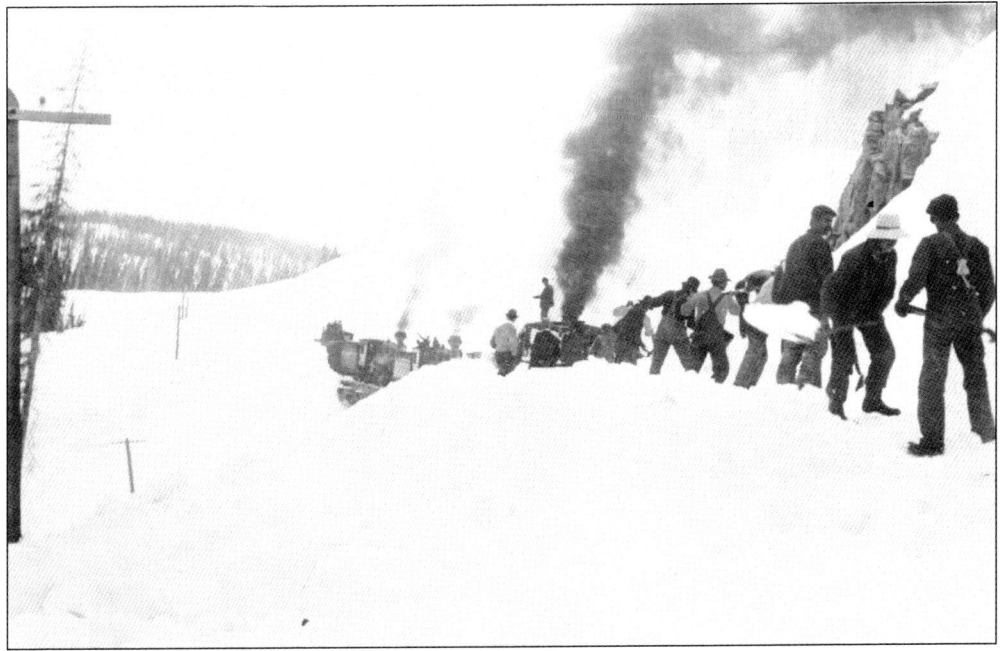

HARD LABOR. A tremendous avalanche of snow, along with trees and rocks, has buried Denver and Rio Grande railroad tracks near Floresta in 1902. A rotary engine could not be used to clear the tracks because of the trees and rocks, so manpower had to be utilized. Often, over 50 men would be hired to do the backbreaking work of clearing the tracks.

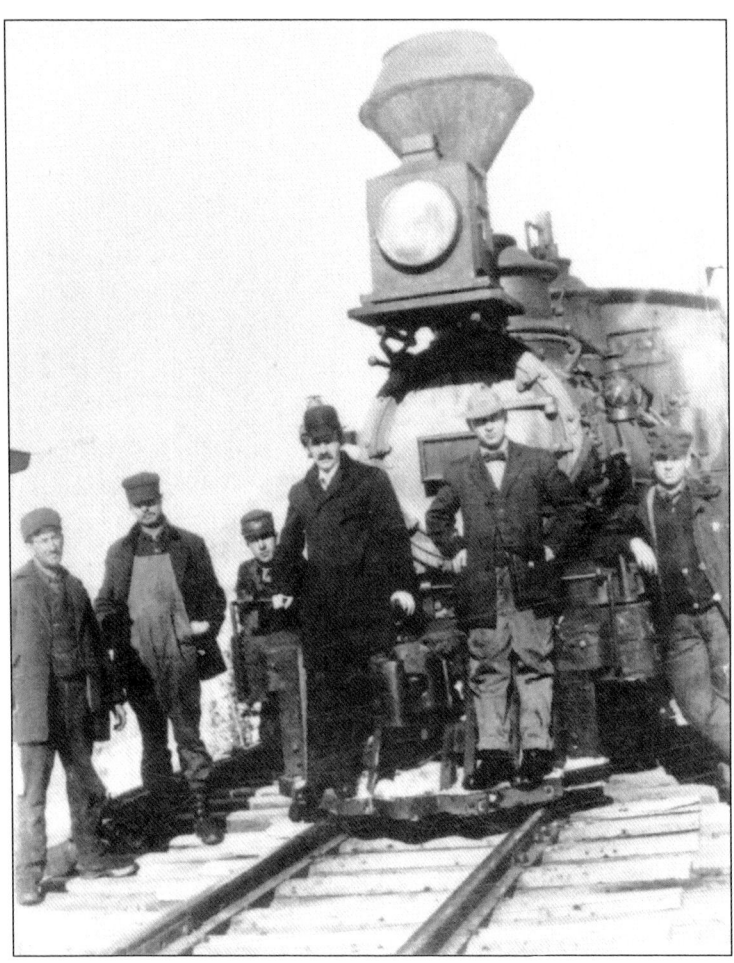

THE BRASS AND WORKMEN. Executives and workmen of the Denver and Rio Grande Railroad pose for a picture on a trestle between Gunnison and Crested Butte in the 1880s. The Gunnison, Taylor, East, and Slate Rivers between the two towns had to be crossed, forcing the building of many bridges.

COAL TRAIN. A long coal train prepares to leave Crested Butte heading for the Colorado Fuel and Iron Company steel mill in Pueblo. Engine 268 would take the train through Gunnison, over Marshall Pass, and then down the Arkansas River Valley to Pueblo.

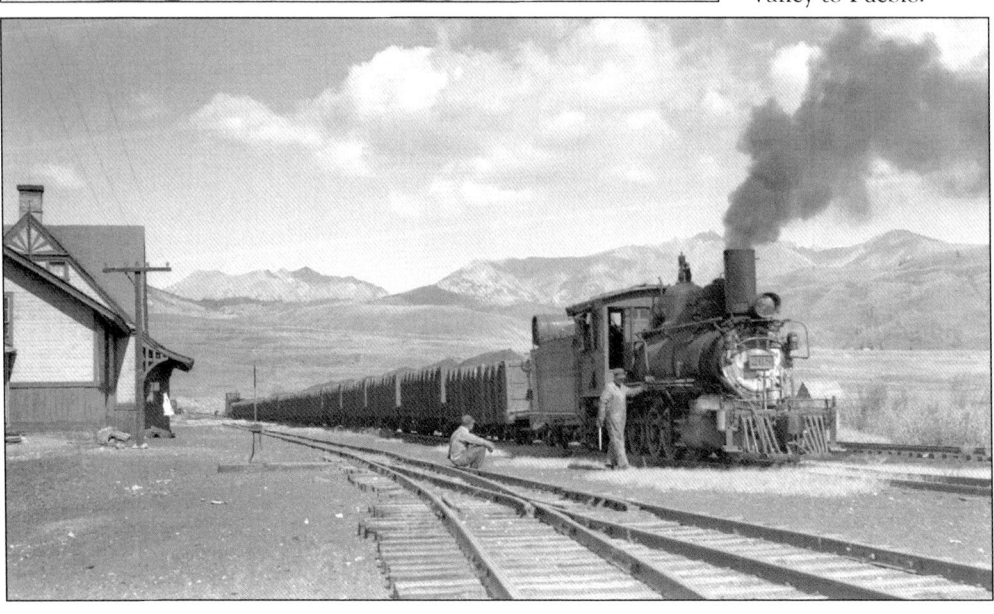

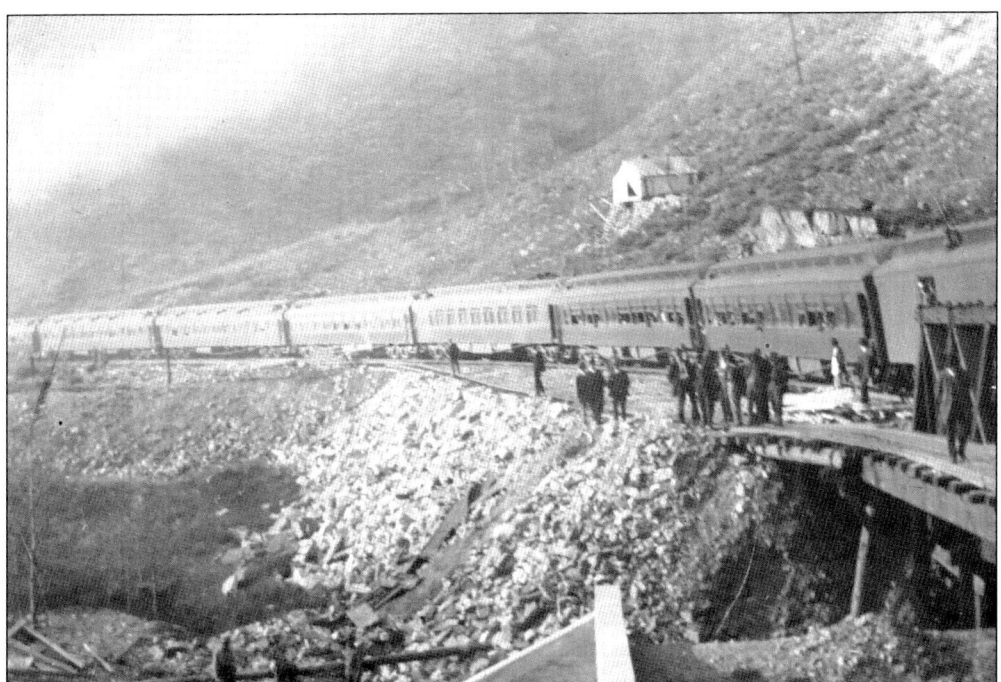

LABOR VIOLENCE. Crested Butte was a company town, run by the Colorado Fuel and Iron Company, the town's major employer. Strikes were common because of low wages, safety issues in the mines, and the paternalism of the company. A major strike came in 1927, during which a bridge south of Crested Butte was dynamited, with a passenger train derailed.

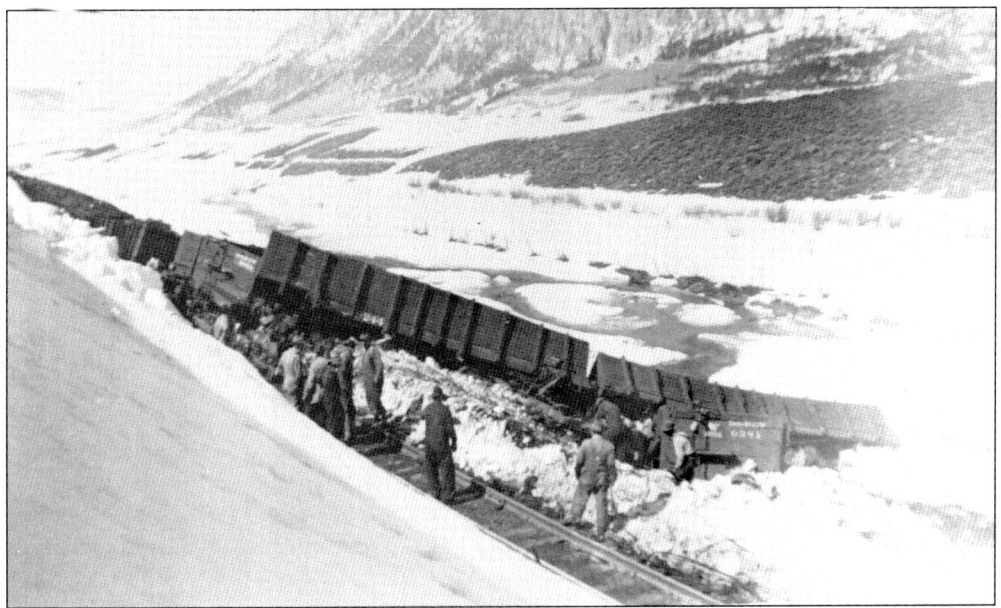

AVALANCHE. A Denver and Rio Grande train has been swept off the tracks south of Crested Butte in the 1940s. The area around the coal town vomited avalanches every winter, making railroading in the Upper East River Valley very dangerous.

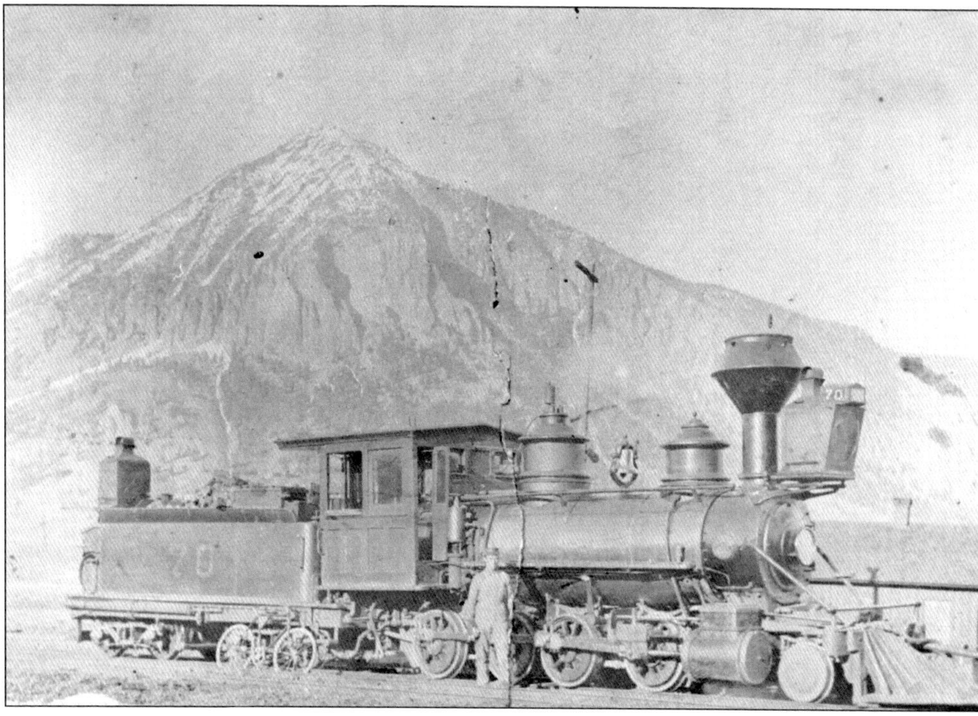

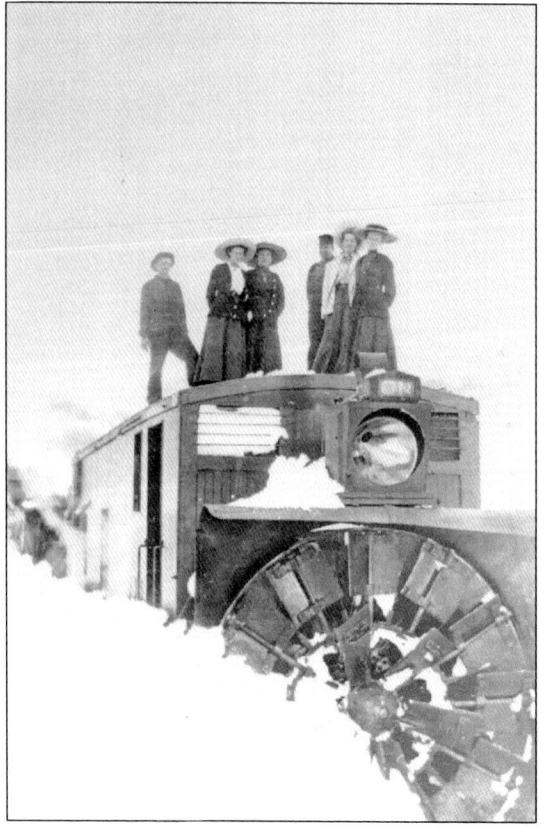

EARLY NARROW GAUGE. This Denver and Rio Grande narrow gauge engine was one of the first to enter Crested Butte in 1881. Gilbert Lathrop, in a classic book about narrow gauge railroads in the Gunnison Country, refers to them as "little engines run by big men." The little narrow gauge engines were indispensable in the opening of mountainous western Colorado.

D&RG ROTARY. Two trainmen and four women passengers pose on top of a Denver and Rio Grande rotary train as it carves its way through heavy snow just south of Crested Butte in the 1890s. Heavy snow and avalanches forced the Rio Grande to use the rotary often from December through April.

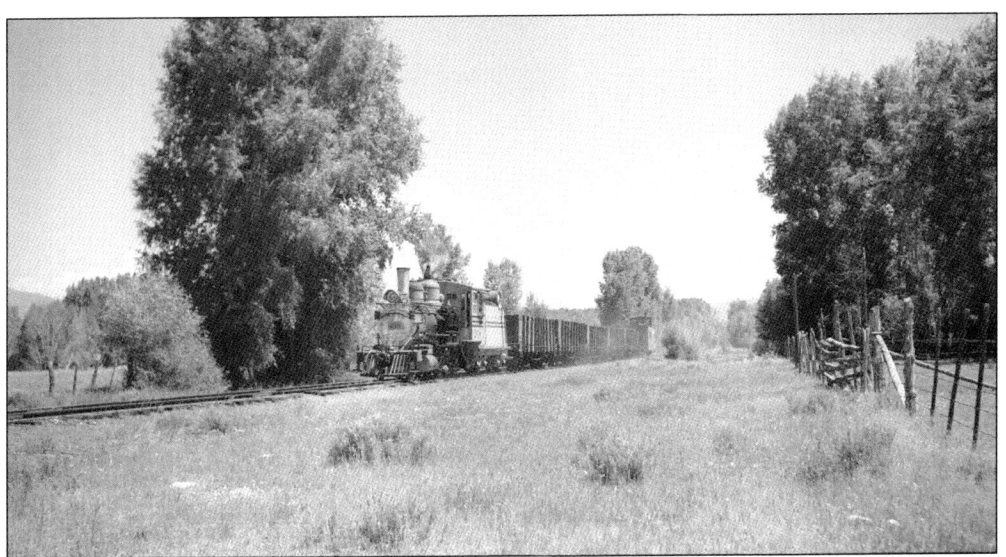

ALMONT. Engine 268 of the Denver and Rio Grande steams along the tracks near Almont with empty coal cars heading for Crested Butte. Almont, 10 miles north of Gunnison and 18 miles south of Crested Butte, began in 1879 and became a spur on the Denver and Rio Grande line as well as a hunting and fishing resort.

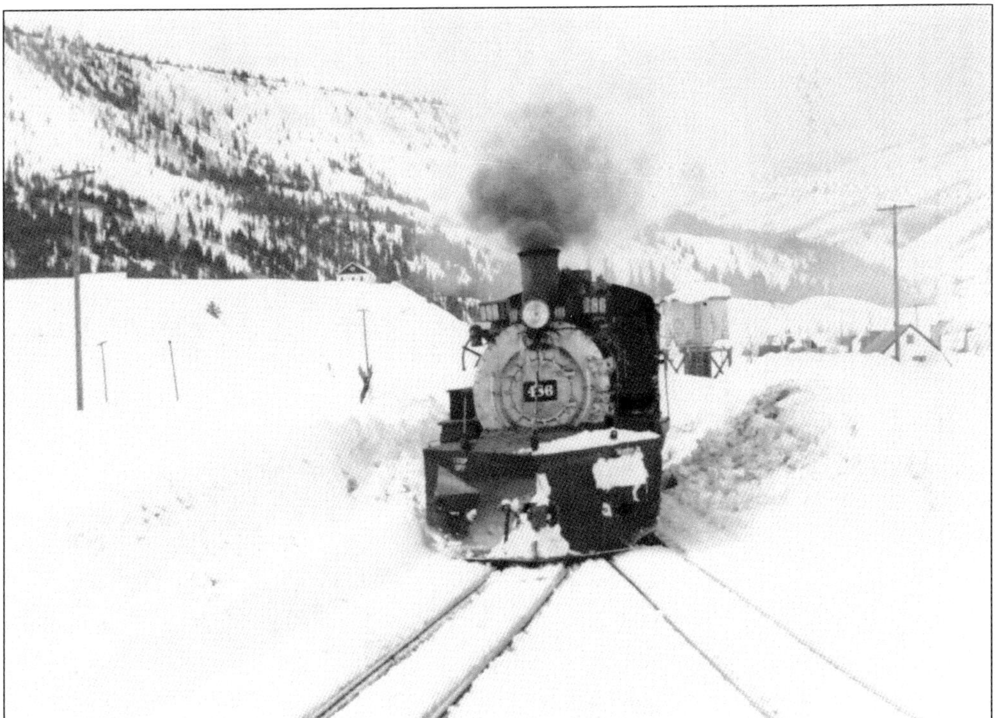

ENGINE 486. Denver and Rio Grande engine 486 prepares to depart Crested Butte during a stormy winter day in 1948. The water tank and Gibson Ridge are in the background. Below Gibson Ridge was Colorado's third-largest coal mine, the Big Mine of the Colorado Fuel and Iron Company.

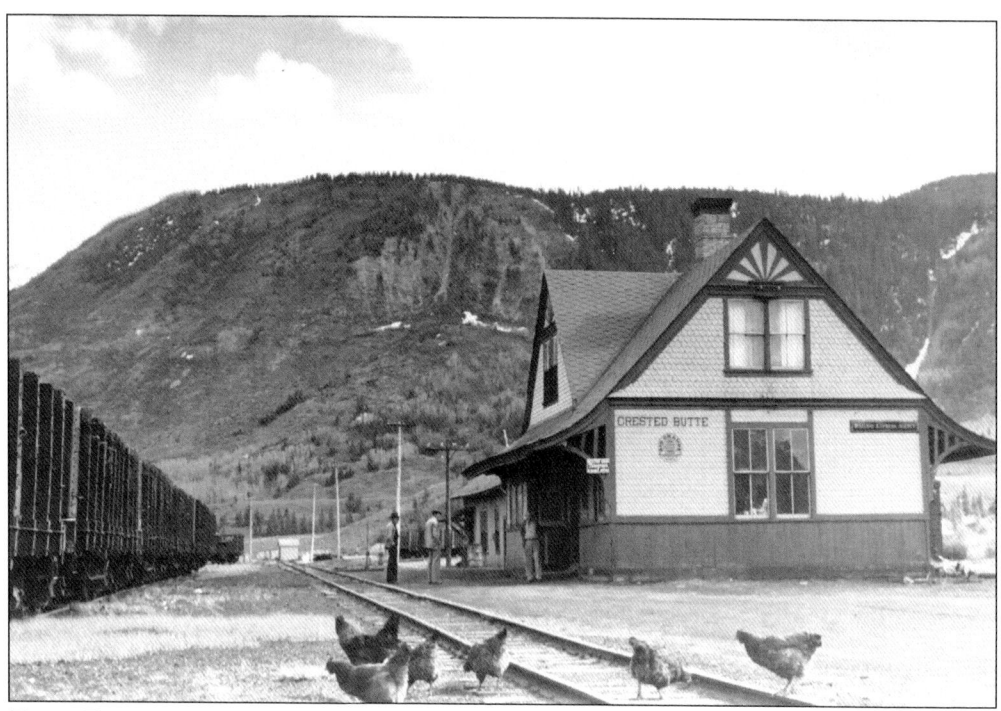

TRAIN TIME IN CRESTED BUTTE. While chickens feed along the railroad tracks, passengers await the arrival of the Denver and Rio Grande train in front of the Crested Butte depot in 1947. The depot operated until the Denver and Rio Grande ended passenger service and then was used as an arts center, library, and community center. The grand old building still stands today.

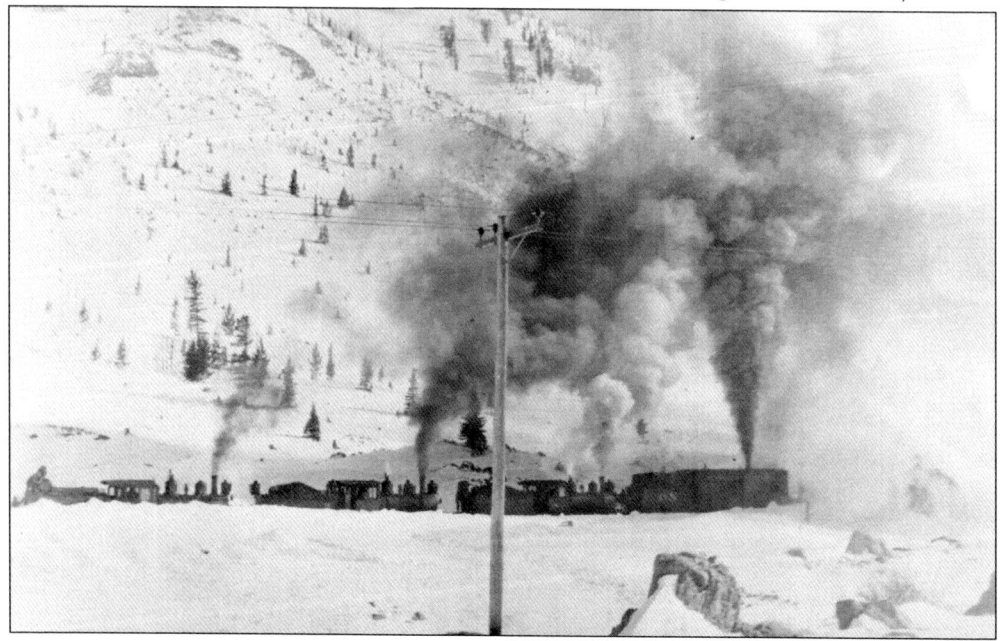

QUADRUPLE HEADER. On January 1, 1918, an avalanche has buried Denver and Rio Grande tracks just south of Crested Butte. The Rio Grande was forced to bring in four engines and a rotary to clear the tracks. Men worked around the clock to get the trains moving again.

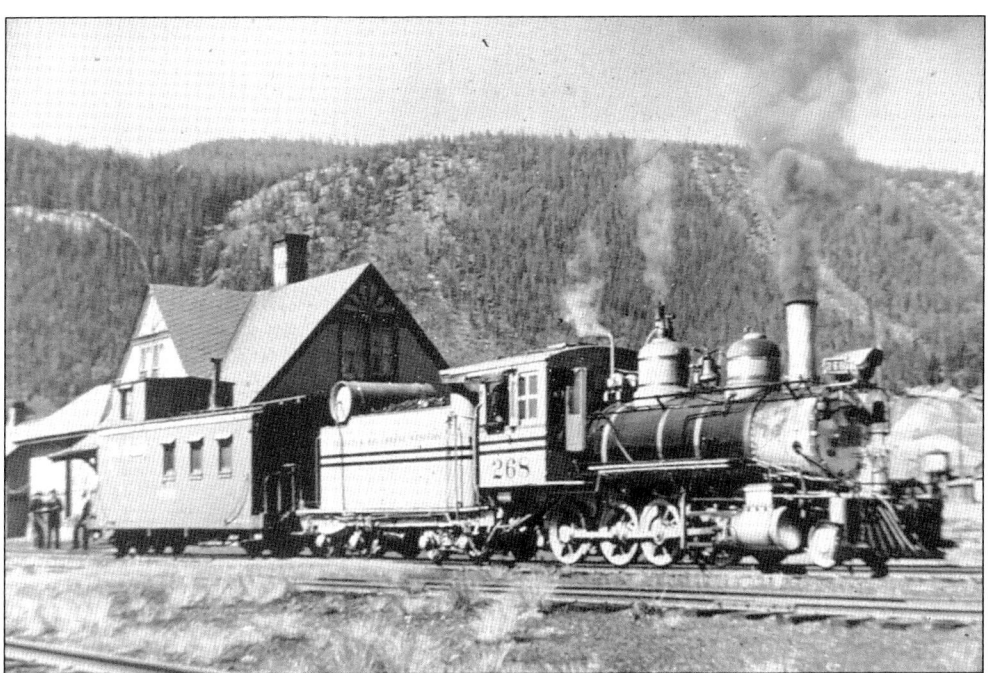

ENGINE 268. One of the Denver and Rio Grande workhorses in the Gunnison Country was engine 268. In this photograph the engine sits outside of the Crested Butte depot with Gibson Ridge and the CF&I Big Mine in the background.

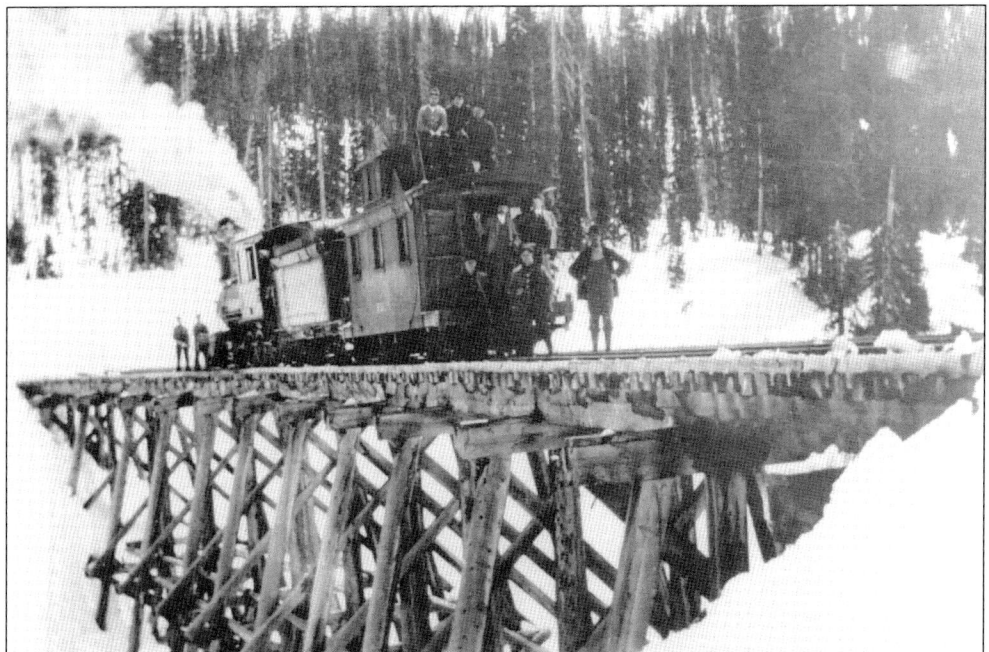

FLORESTA TRESTLE. A Denver and Rio Grande work train is stopped on a trestle near Floresta during January 1911. The great Floresta Mine turned out 800,000 tons of anthracite coal from 1898 to 1918, when operations ceased. The Denver and Rio Grande struggled mightily to keep the tracks clear of the tremendous amount of snow that fell every winter.

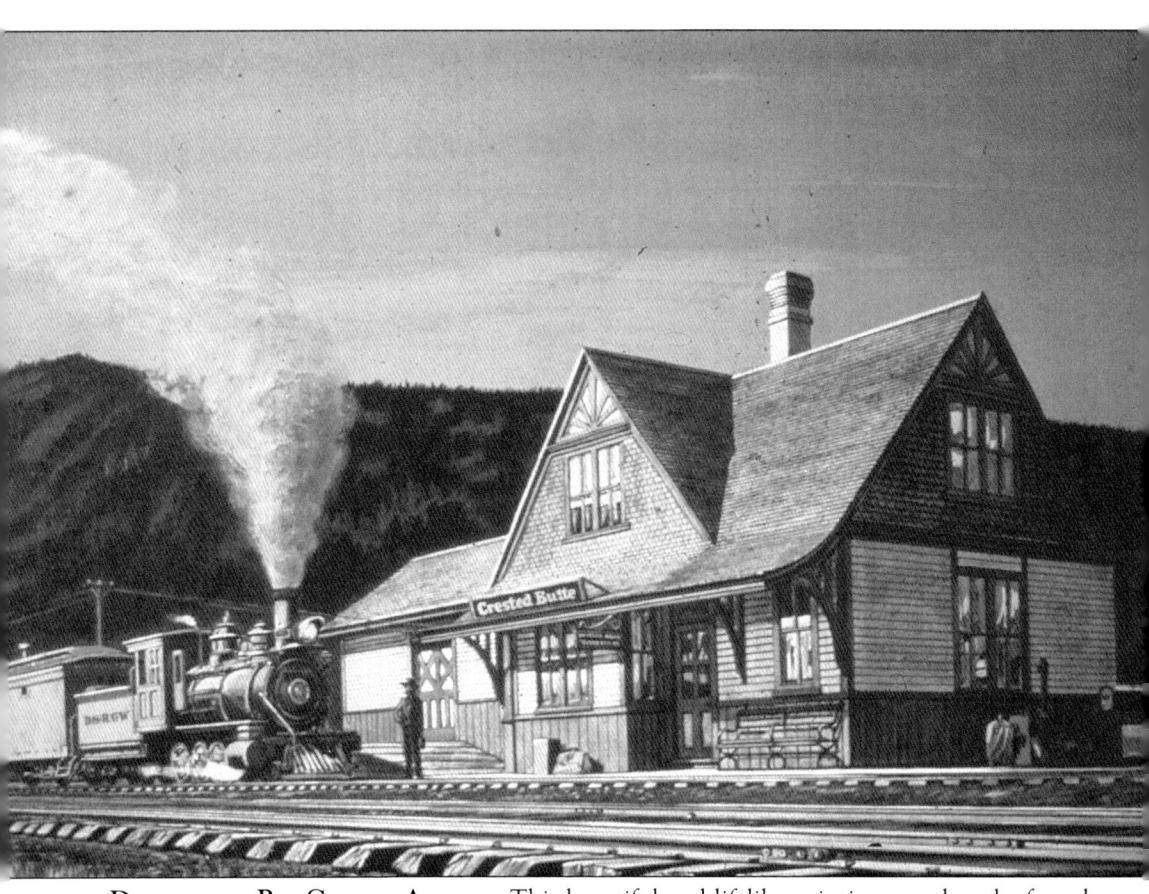

DENVER AND RIO GRANDE ARRIVAL. This beautiful and lifelike painting was done by famed artist Bill Duehren of Milwaukee, Wisconsin. It shows a Denver and Rio Grande train coming into the Crested Butte depot in the 1880s.

Eight
AGE OF SNOW
THE CRESTED BUTTE SKI AREA

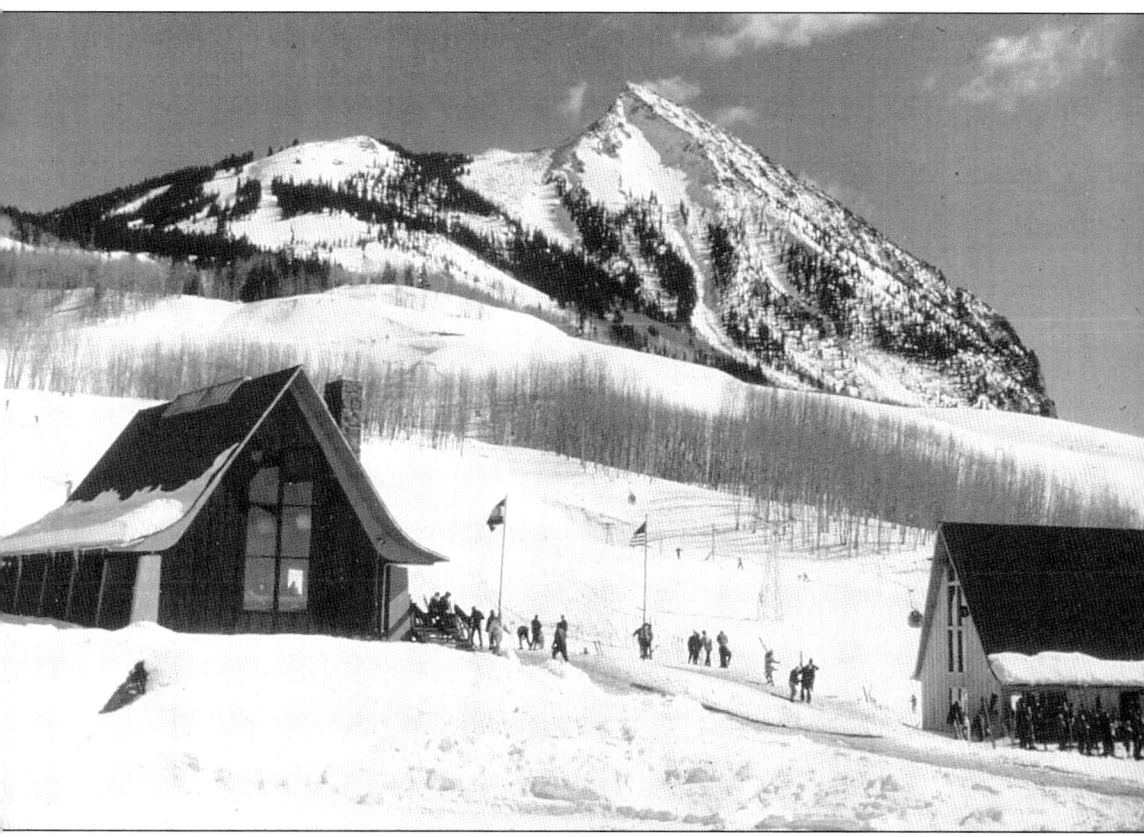

A NEW SKI AREA. The Crested Butte Ski Area was only a couple of years old when this photograph was taken. The warming house on the left and the gondola building on the right were the major buildings. The gondola, which carried skiers to the top of the mountain, opened in January 1963.

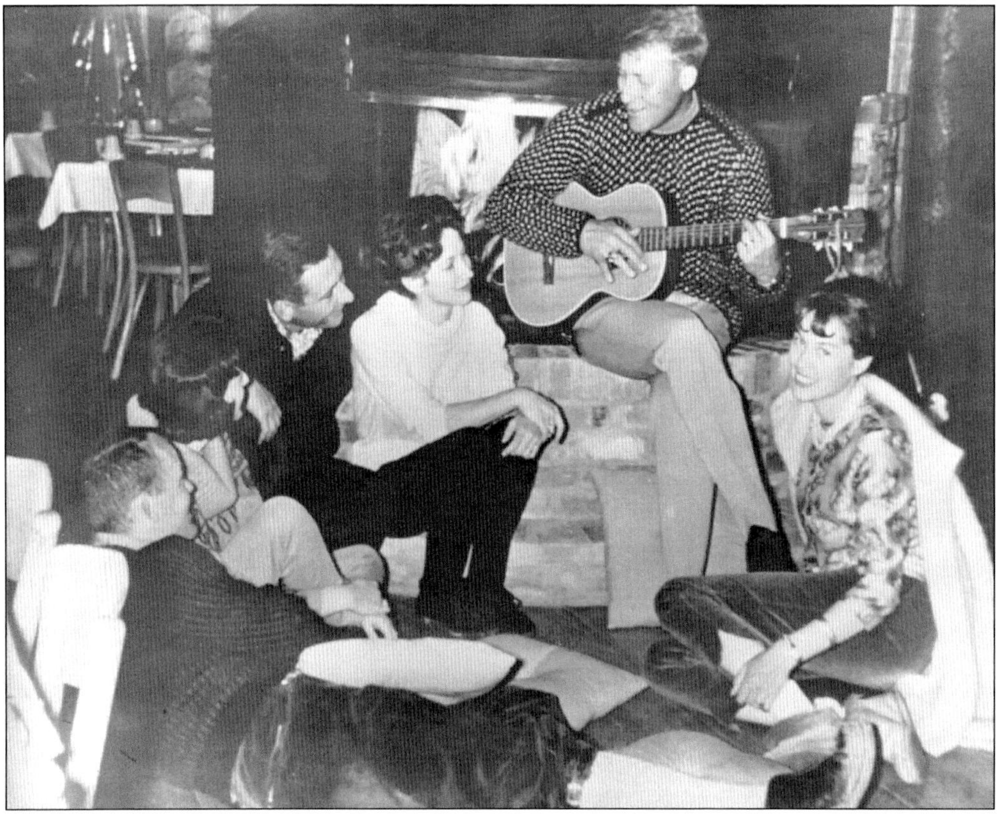

DICK EFLIN. In 1960, Dick Eflin (playing the guitar) and Fred Rice of Kansas purchased the Malensek Ranch three miles northeast of Crested Butte and announced they would build a major winter recreation area. By the winter of 1961–1962, the ski area had become a reality. Here, Eflin is entertaining early skiers at a steakhouse a mile north of Crested Butte, while his wife, Liz, is looking at the camera.

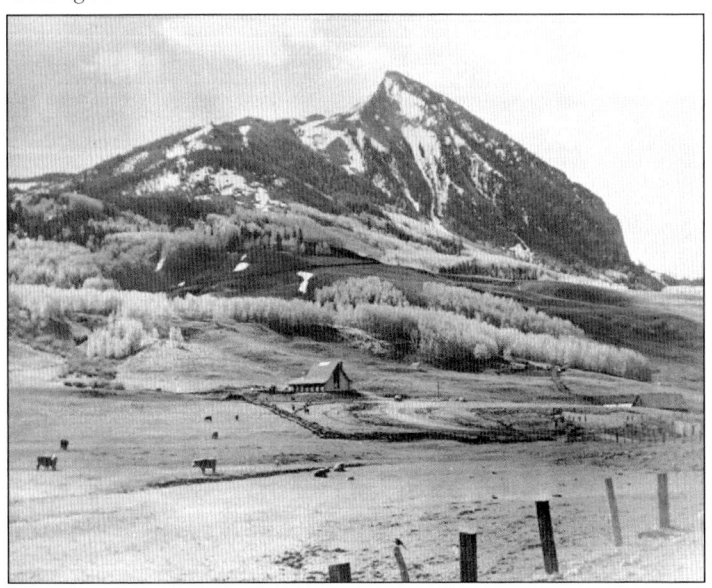

MALENSEK RANCH. Cows are still grazing on the Malensek Ranch in 1961 while buildings and lifts are being constructed at the new Crested Butte Ski Area. The warming house can be seen, and majestic Mount Crested Butte towers in the distance.

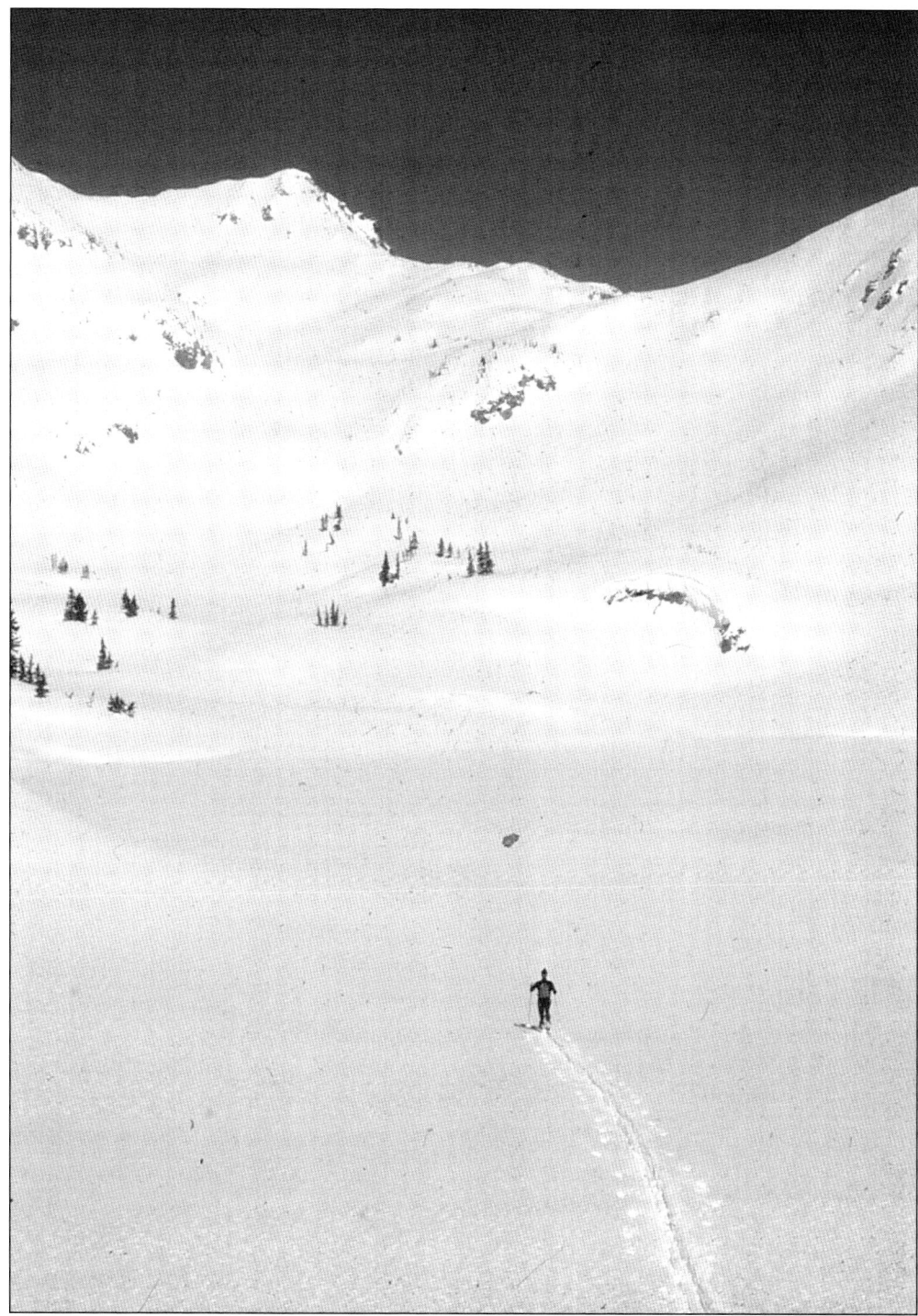

EAST MAROON PASS, 1969. A lone skier breaks trail up Copper Creek six miles from Gothic, heading for Aspen. East Maroon Pass, at 11,800 feet in elevation, is dead ahead; and from the top, it is all downhill skiing for nine miles to the Maroon Creek Road above the great silver camp of Aspen.

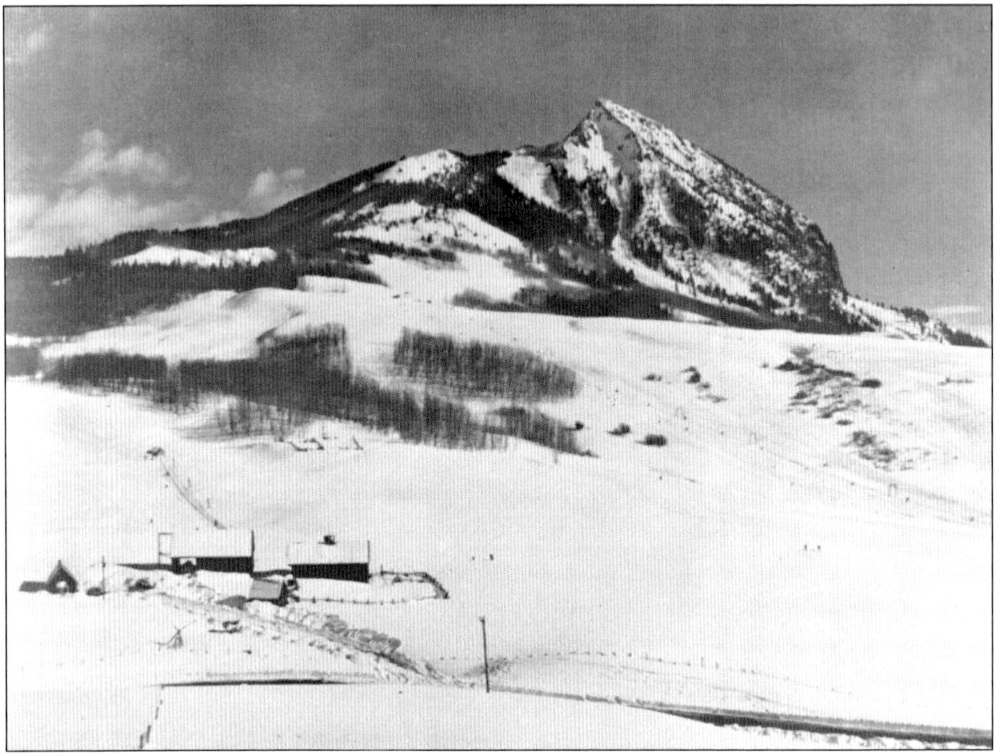

CRESTED BUTTE SKI AREA, 1961. The Crested Butte Ski Area had just gotten underway during the winter of 1961–1962. The Malensek barns and stables are just below the rope tow for beginners, while the T-bar for more advanced skiers can be seen on the right. (CBMHM.)

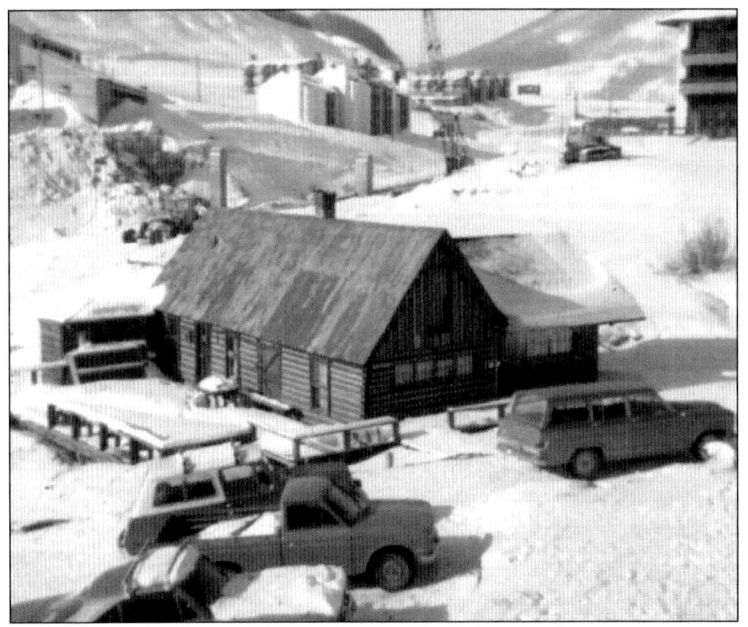

BEGINNING OF THE SKI AREA. While construction goes on during the early years of the Crested Butte Ski Area, one of the Malensek barns, now converted into the Bier Stube, is the center of action. The Bier Stube was where early skiers danced, drank beer, and had impromptu parties both inside and outside.

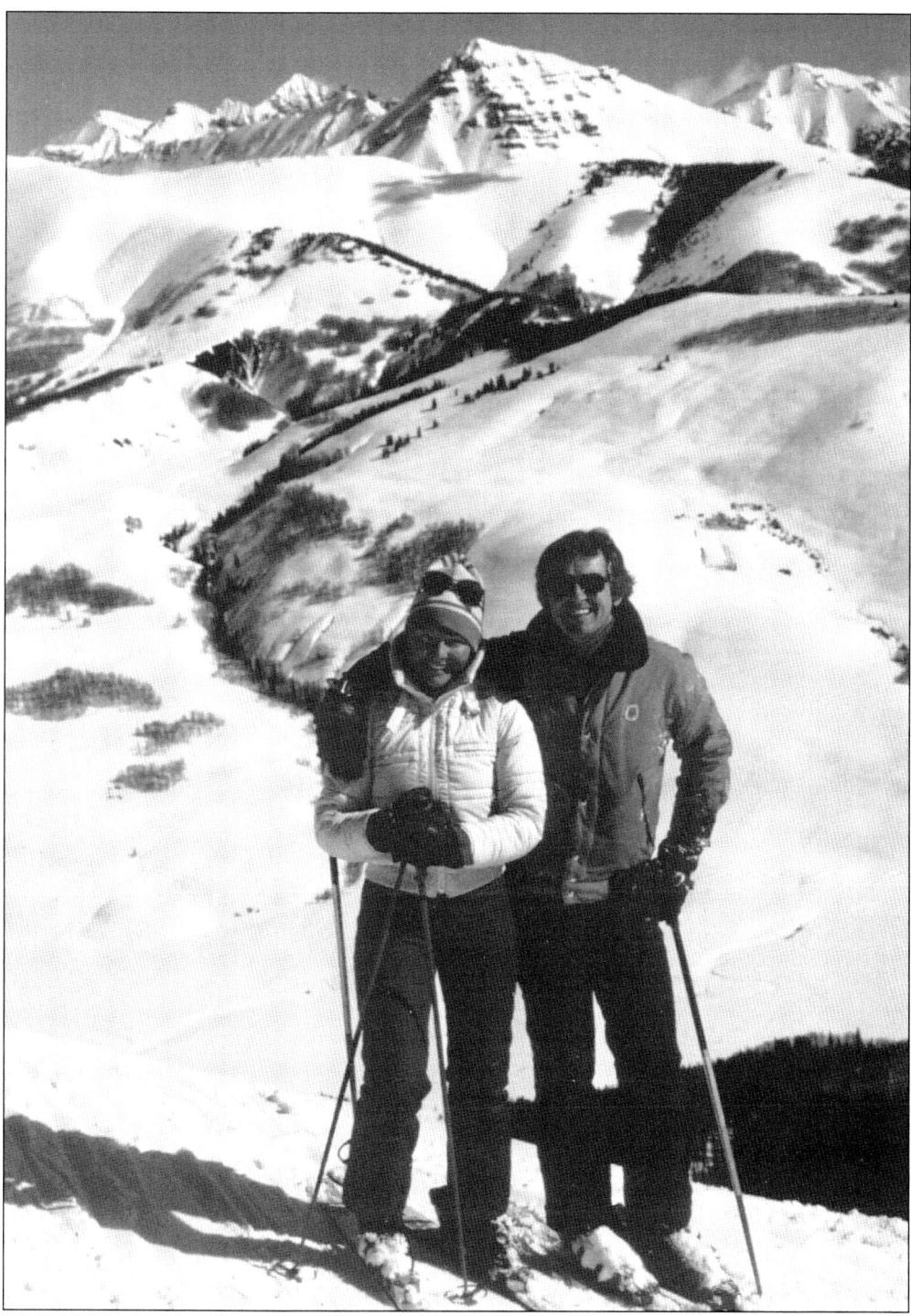

Sara and Jerry Davis, 1972. Two ex-Western State College ski team members, Sara and Jerry Davis, pose for a photograph near the top of the Hawksnest at the Crested Butte Ski Area. Mount Teocali highlights a spectacular panorama in the distance. The Hawksnest was one entrance to the Northface, a challenging extreme run of the ski area.

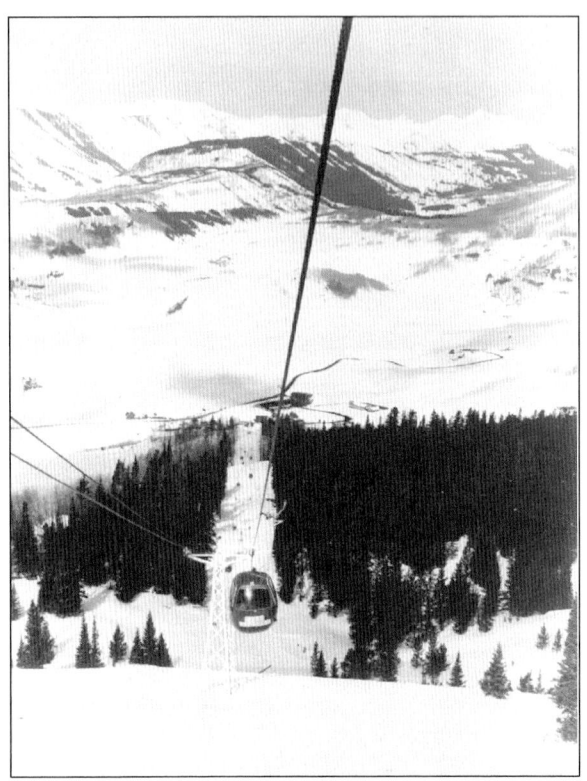

RIDING HIGH. The gondola is running at the Crested Butte Ski Area in March 1968. It carried three skiers and took 10 minutes to go from the gondola terminal at the bottom to the top of the area, a 2,000-foot elevation gain. By 2011 standards, the gondola was very slow and transported only a limited number of skiers to the top.

INSIDE THE BIER STUBE. A group of admirers listens as Buck Kelley plays the guitar inside the Bier Stube at the Crested Butte Ski Area in early 1963. Kelly was also a great banjo player and, after leaving Western State College where he was a student, played all over the world before his death in the 1990s. He was the chief entertainer at the Bier Stube.

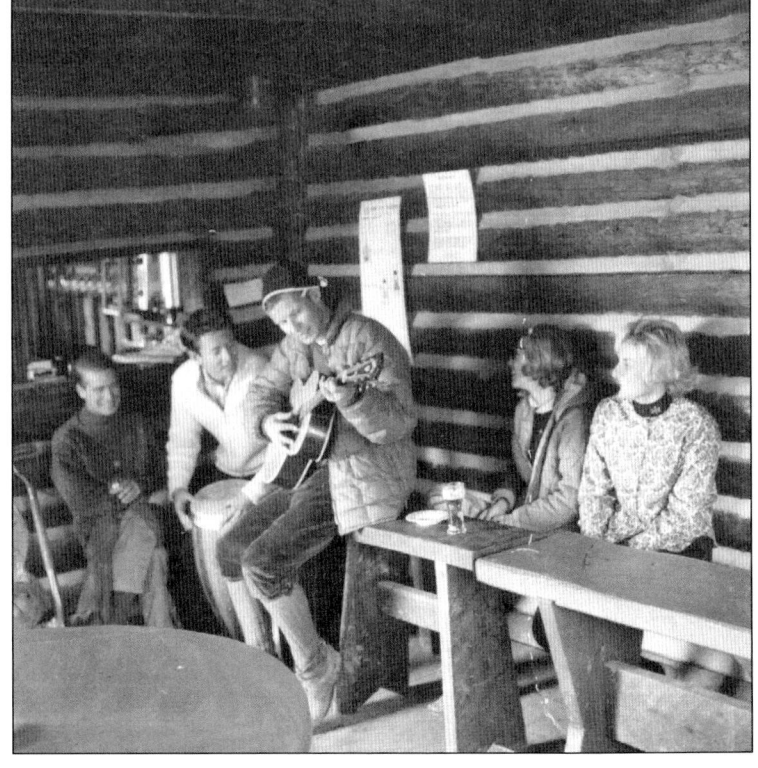

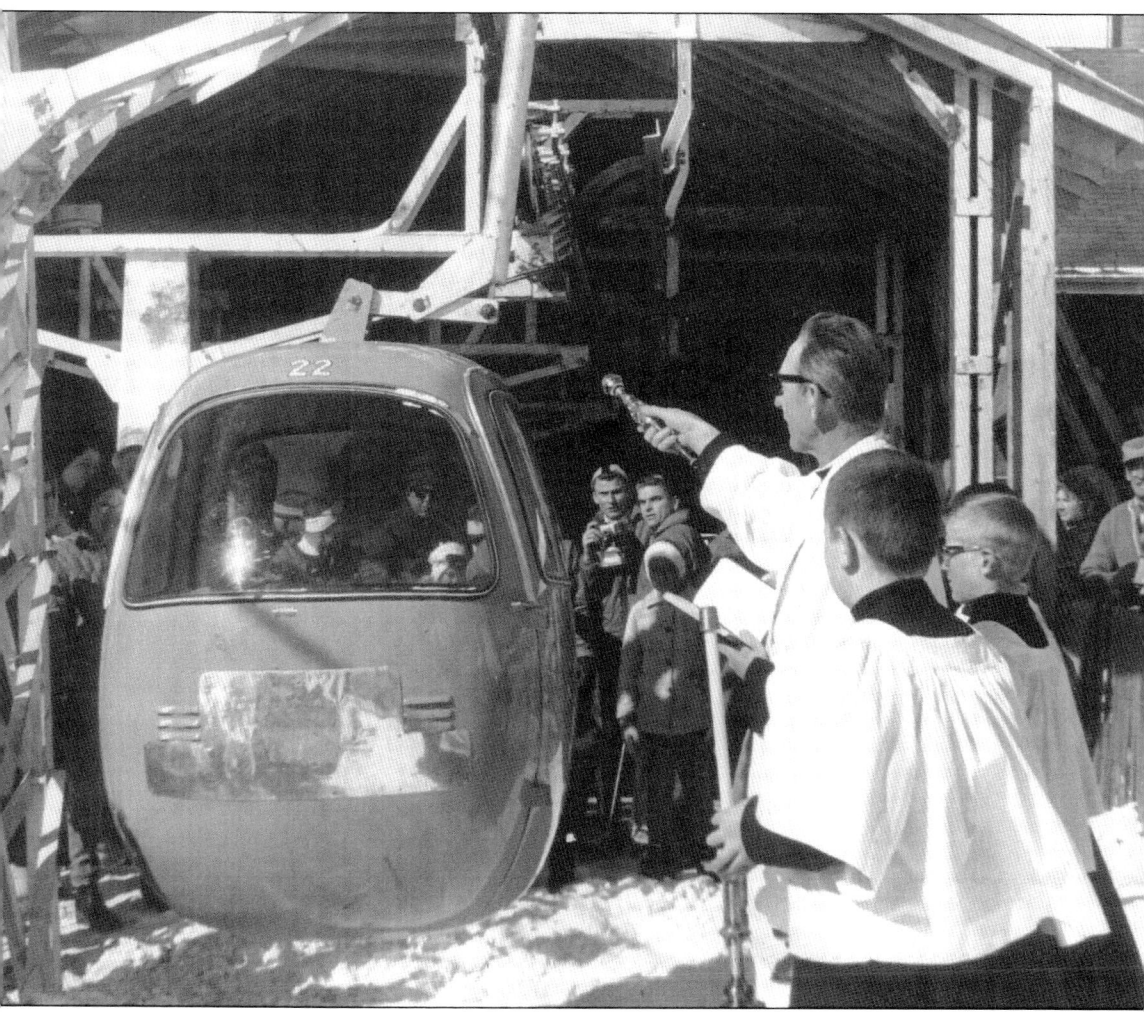

BLESSING THE GONDOLA. Following European tradition, Catholic priest Father Leo MacKenna of Gunnison blesses the new Italian gondola at the Crested Butte Ski Area in January 1963. Shortly after the gondola was blessed, it broke down for the rest of the day. To make matters worse, Father MacKenna slipped and fell in the parking lot while leaving, fracturing his kneecap.

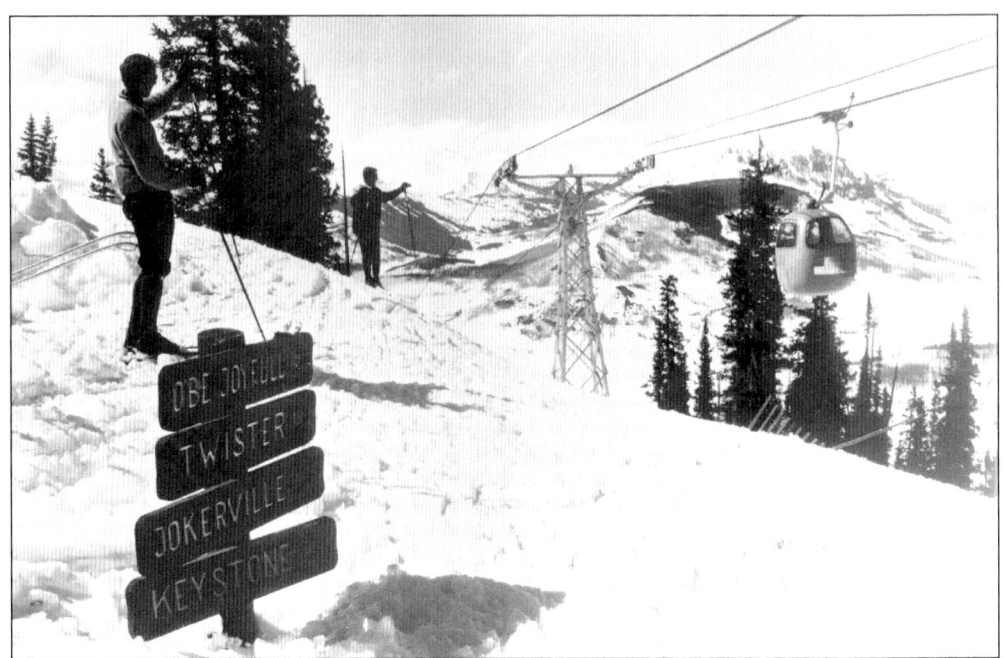

NEAR THE TOP. Two early skiers in 1964 watch a gondola car near the terminal at the top of the lift. The sign on the left lists four major runs at that time: O'Be Joyful, Twister, Jokerville, and Keystone. All of the runs at that time were relatively ungroomed and heavily moguled.

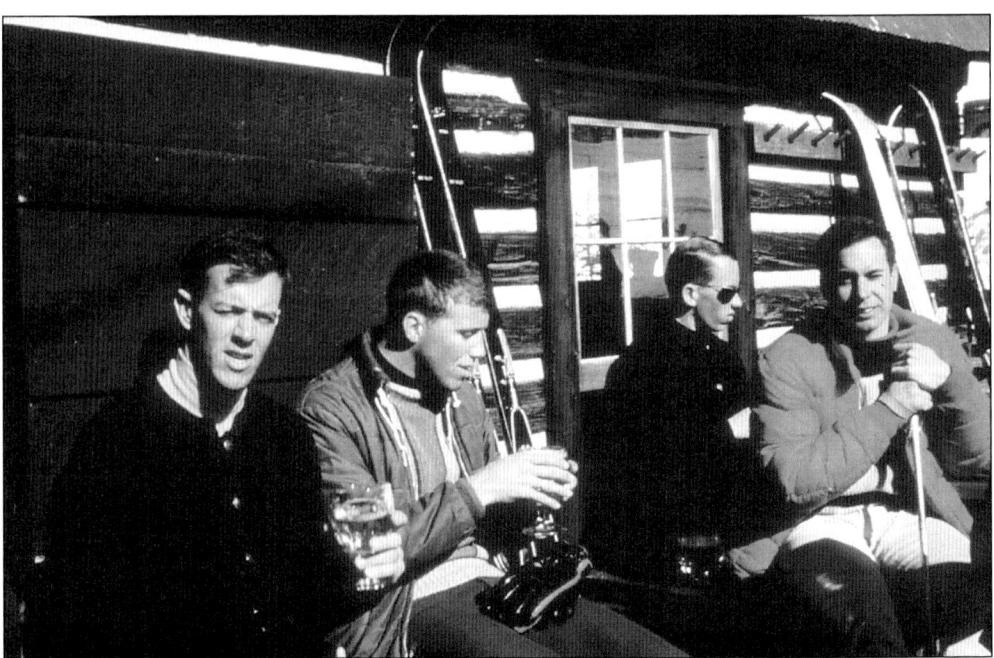

BIER STUBE, 1963. The Bier Stub at the newly opened Crested Butte Ski Area had been one of the buildings on Matt Malensek's ranch. When the ski area bought the property, the barn was converted into a beer garden. Here, enjoying a beer during lunch are, from left to right, Norm Simmons, Don Spicklemeyer, Bob Knowles, and Dick Erickson.

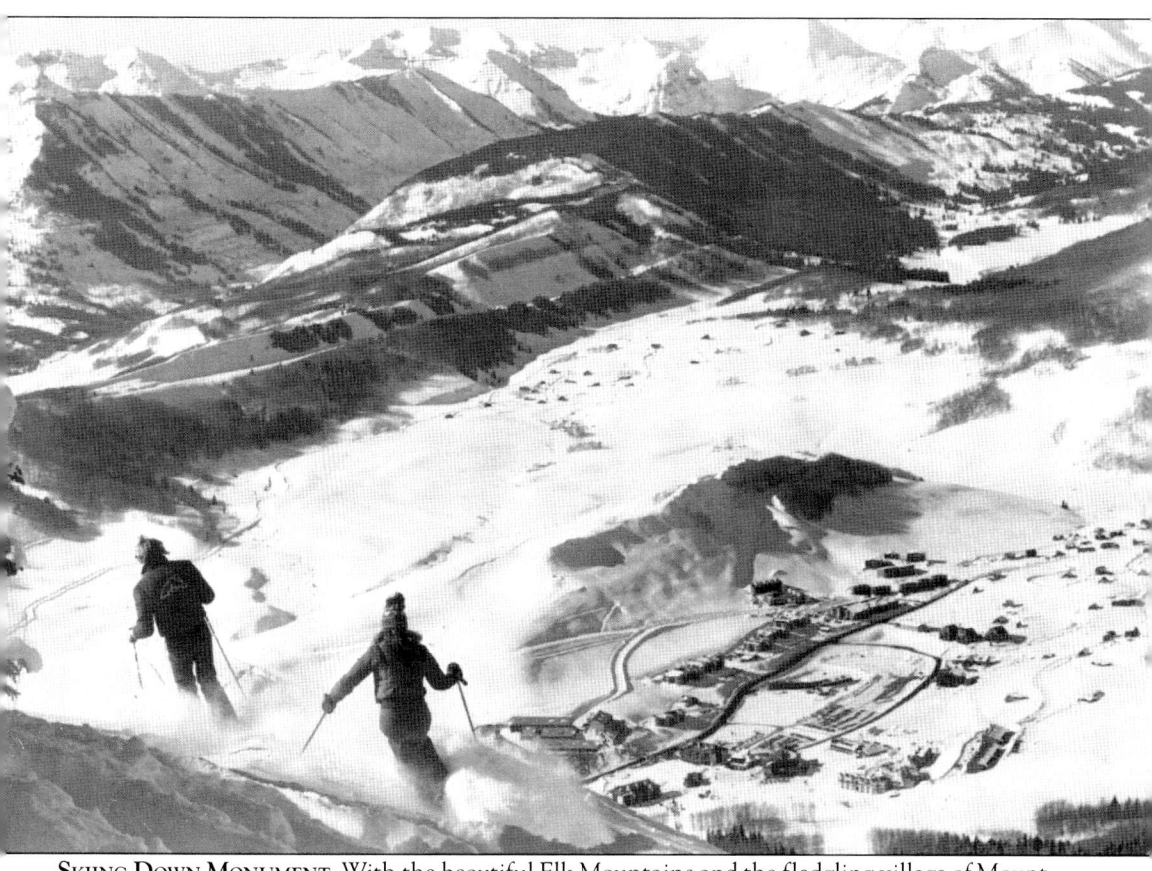

Skiing Down Monument. With the beautiful Elk Mountains and the fledgling village of Mount Crested Butte providing the background, two skiers ski the powder off of Monument Hill. From the top of this steep run to the bottom of the mountain is a 2,000-foot drop. (CBMHM.)

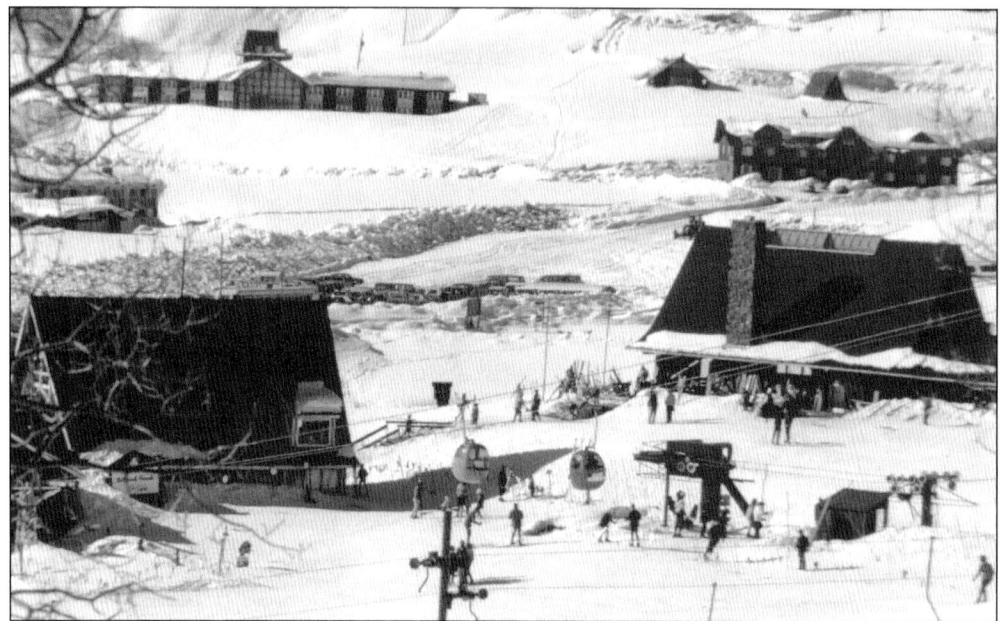

CRESTED BUTTE SKI AREA, 1960S. The Crested Butte Ski Area began to grow by the late 1960s. Lodges and chalets were built, and in 1974 the settlement around the ski area incorporated into a town called Mount Crested Butte. In this photograph, the gondola terminal is on the left and the warming house on the right; a small and slightly filled parking lot lies in the background. Mount Crested Butte has 765 residents in 2011.

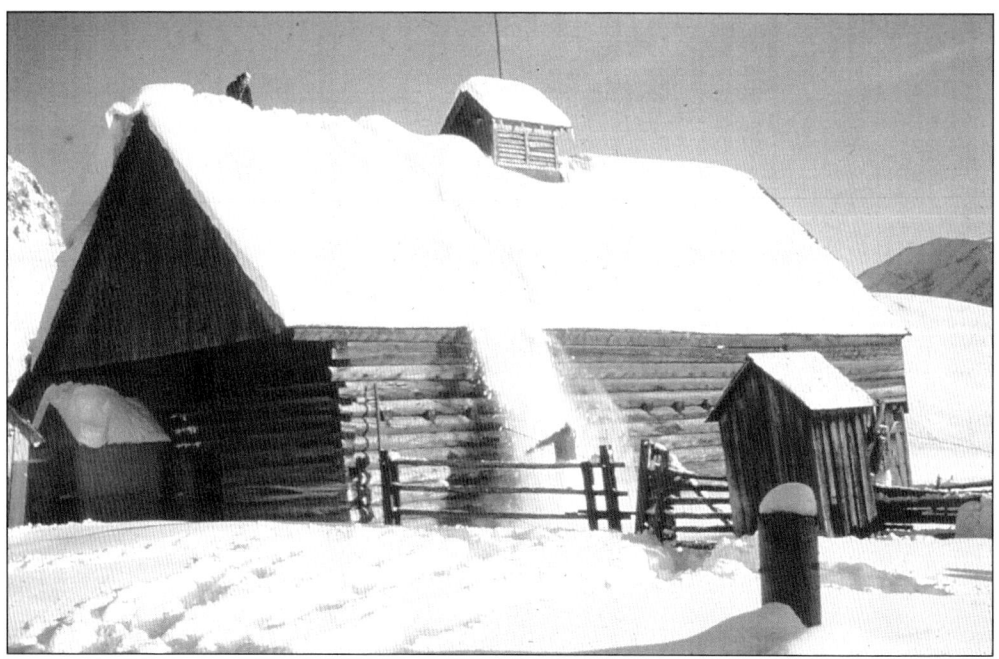

BARN JUMPING. Jay Miller, a Western State College skier, attempts a new sport—barn jumping—in January 1962. With fellow skier Bob Sweitzer on the top of the barn and ready to slide down, Miller lands in four feet of snow. The barn was on the Malensek Ranch, which had now become the Crested Butte Ski Area.

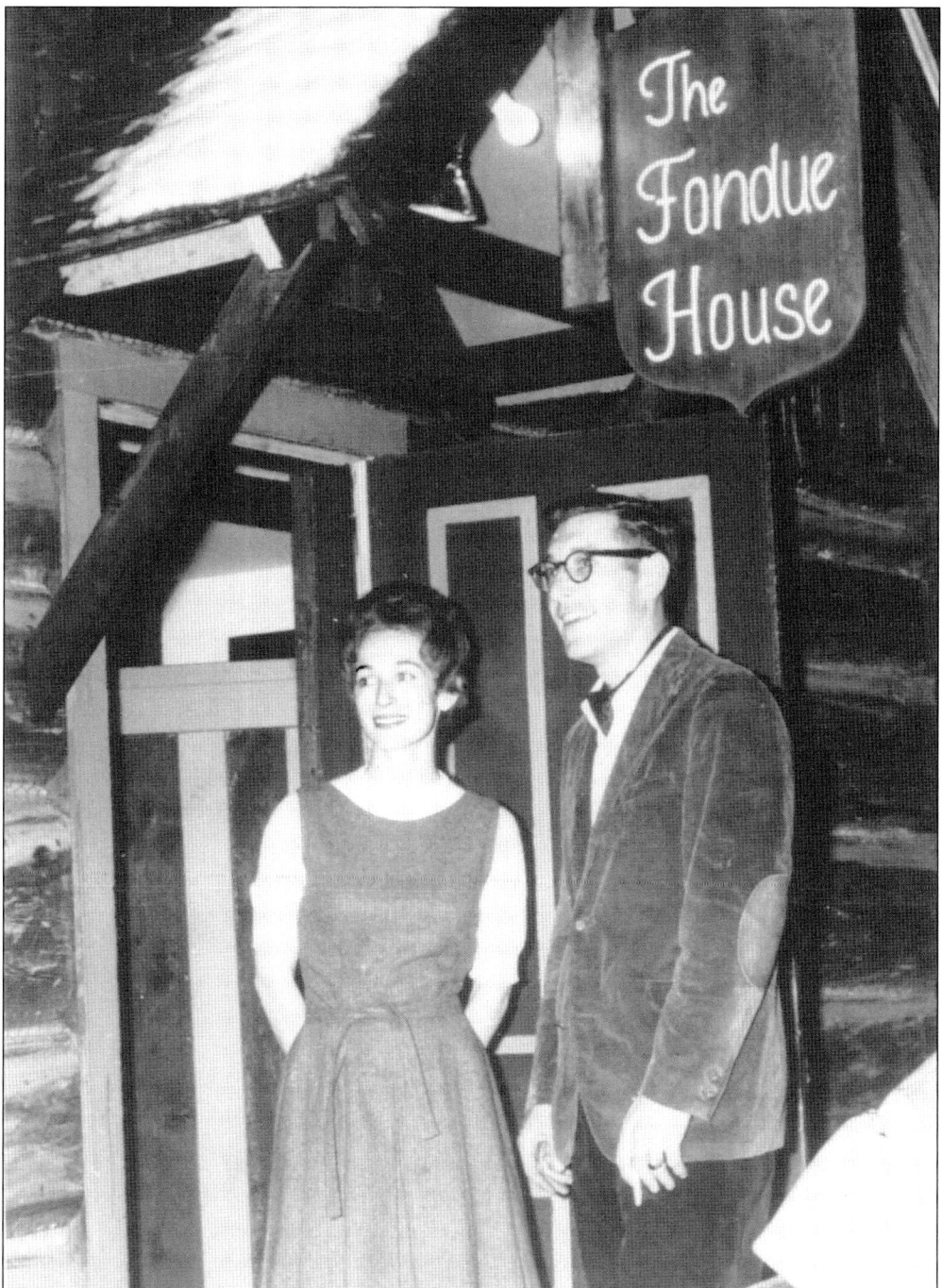

FONDUE HOUSE. Located in an alley between Elk and Maroon Avenues in Crested Butte, the Fondue House became a popular, if small, eatery in town. Started in the early 1960s by Colby and Lynn Schrichte (seen here), the small cabin was a favorite gathering place for early skiers. The Schrichtes were also the first to run the Warming House and Beir Stube at the Crested Butte Ski Area. One of Crested Butte's most popular eating places in 2011, Soupcon is located in the same building where the Fondue House was. (CBMHM.)

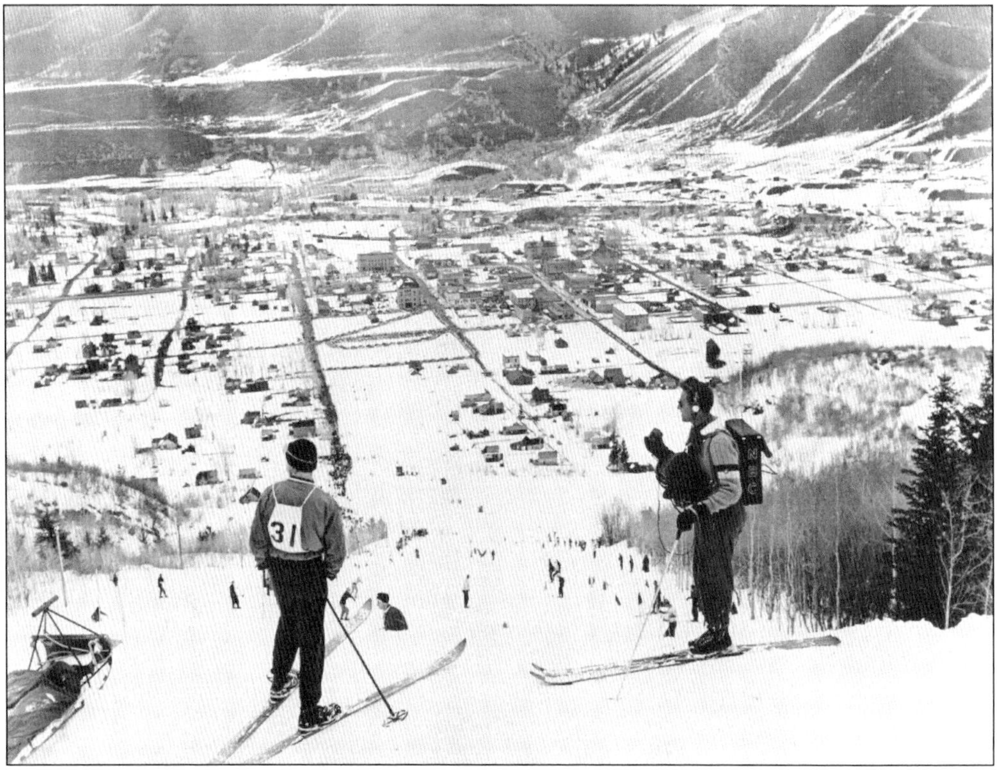

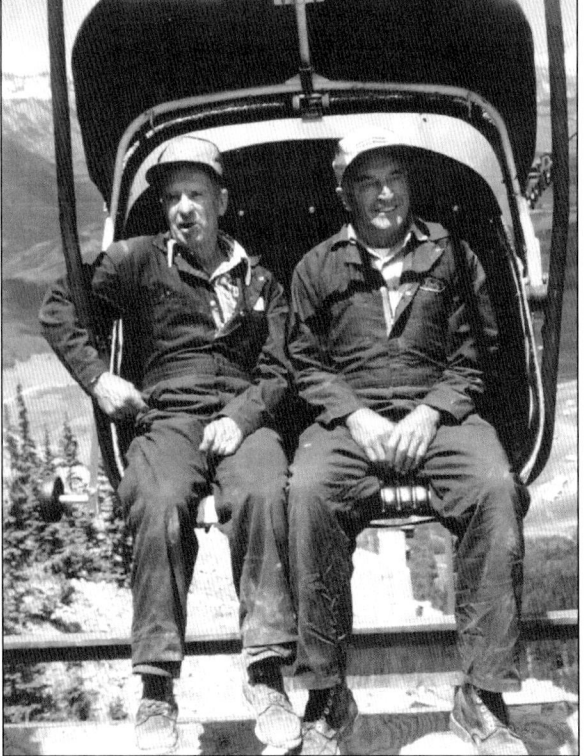

ASPEN: THE EARLY YEARS. Two skiers on Little Nell on Aspen Mountain look out at the historic silver town in the late 1940s. Once one of the greatest silver towns in the world, Aspen became a great ski town with the arrival of Walter Papaecke after World War II. The old silver town just north of Crested Butte soon became one of the world's premier ski resorts.

TWO OLD-TIMERS. John Krizmanich and Rudy Sedmak sit on the upper chairlift at the Crested Butte Ski Area while taking a break from work during the summer of 1978. The two ex-miners both came from southeast European immigrant families, like many other residents of Crested Butte.

Nine
Potpourri

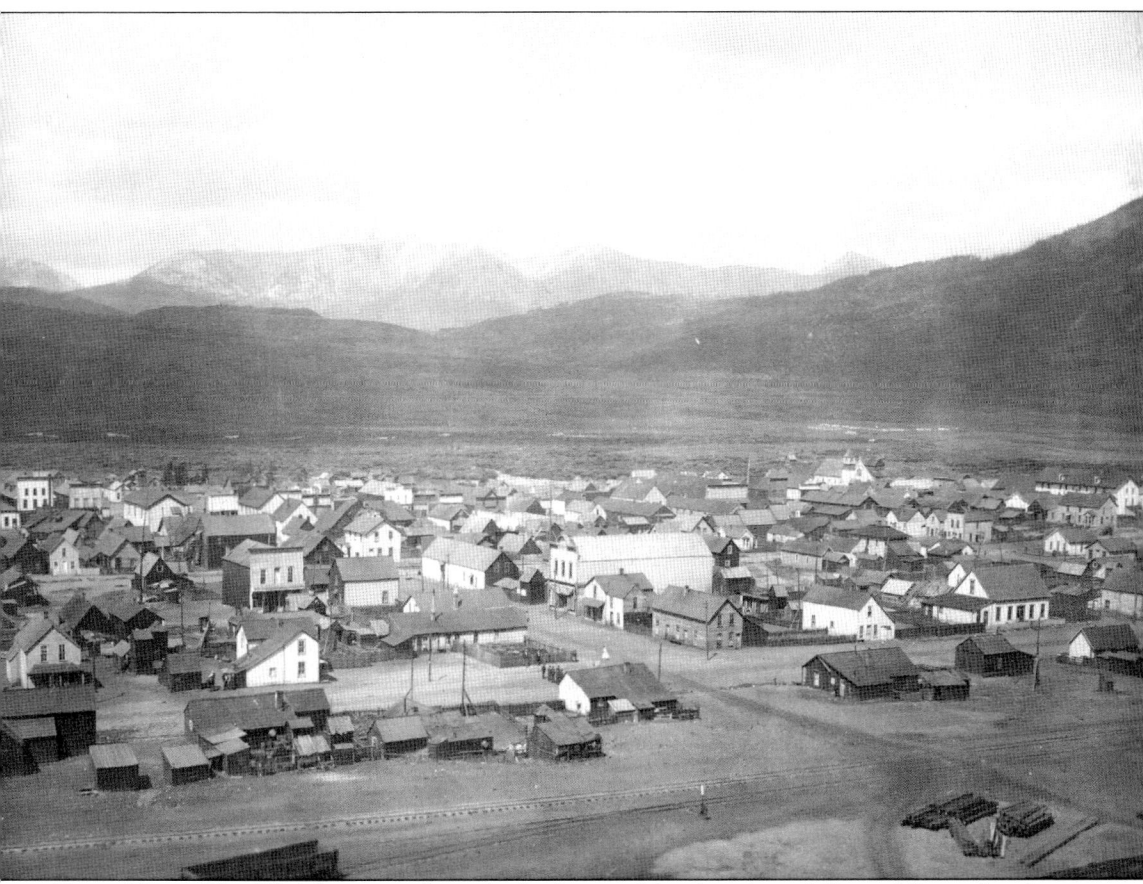

TOWN VISTA. The Elk Mountains form the background for this vista of Crested Butte shortly after 1900. The coal town was at the peak of its prosperity, with coal mines producing bituminous and anthracite coal and the Denver and Rio Grande Railroad taking long trains of coal to the CF&I steel mills in Pueblo. (BHS.)

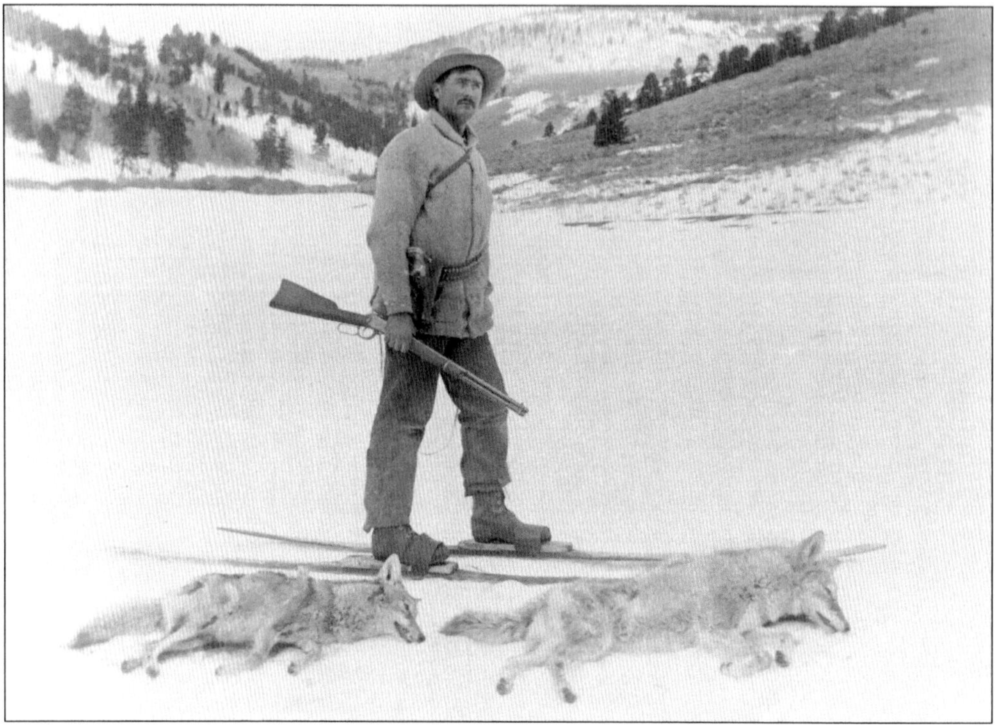

PREDATORS. A hunter on skis stands beside two wolves he has just killed in the Elk Mountains in 1913. Wolves, like coyotes, preyed on cattle and were considered fair game for hunters hired by ranchers or for ranchers themselves.

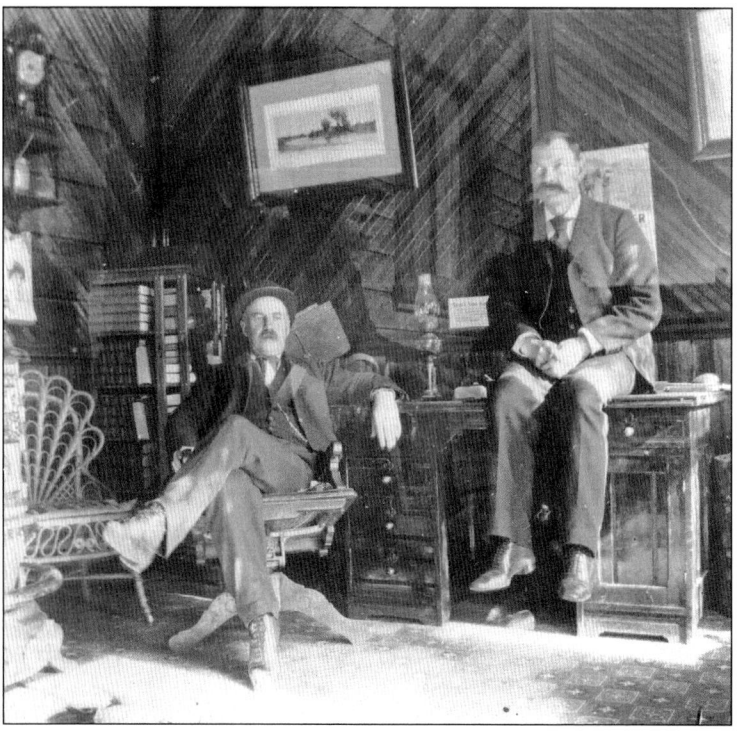

CRESTED BUTTE DOCTORS. Doctors J.W. Rockefeller and J.D. Walker have a quiet moment in Rockefeller's office in Crested Butte in the 1880s. Both doctors were employed by the Colorado Fuel and Iron Company and were kept busy by the many injuries and deaths caused by hazardous duty in the mines. (DPL.)

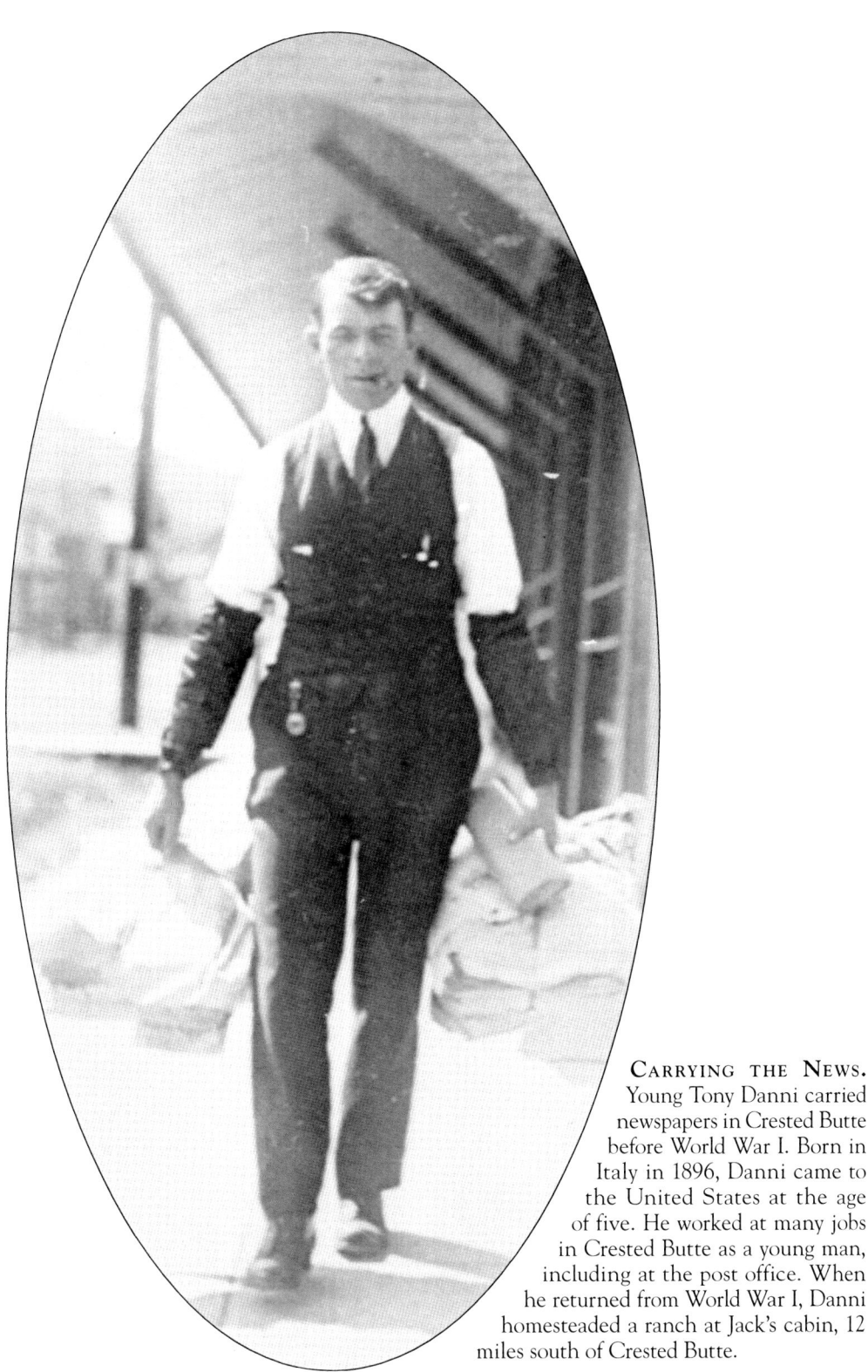

CARRYING THE NEWS. Young Tony Danni carried newspapers in Crested Butte before World War I. Born in Italy in 1896, Danni came to the United States at the age of five. He worked at many jobs in Crested Butte as a young man, including at the post office. When he returned from World War I, Danni homesteaded a ranch at Jack's cabin, 12 miles south of Crested Butte.

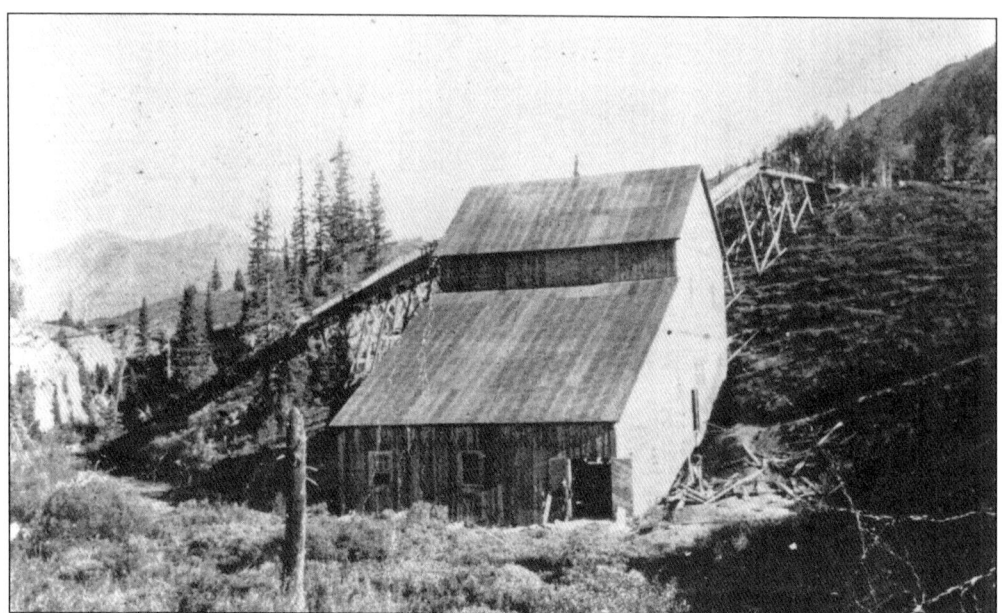

BLAINE MILL. The Blaine Mill in Gothic reduced silver ore from the Jim Blaine Mine. The 10-stamp mill was built in 1880 but was never very effective in smelting the ore. It closed after only two years of operation.

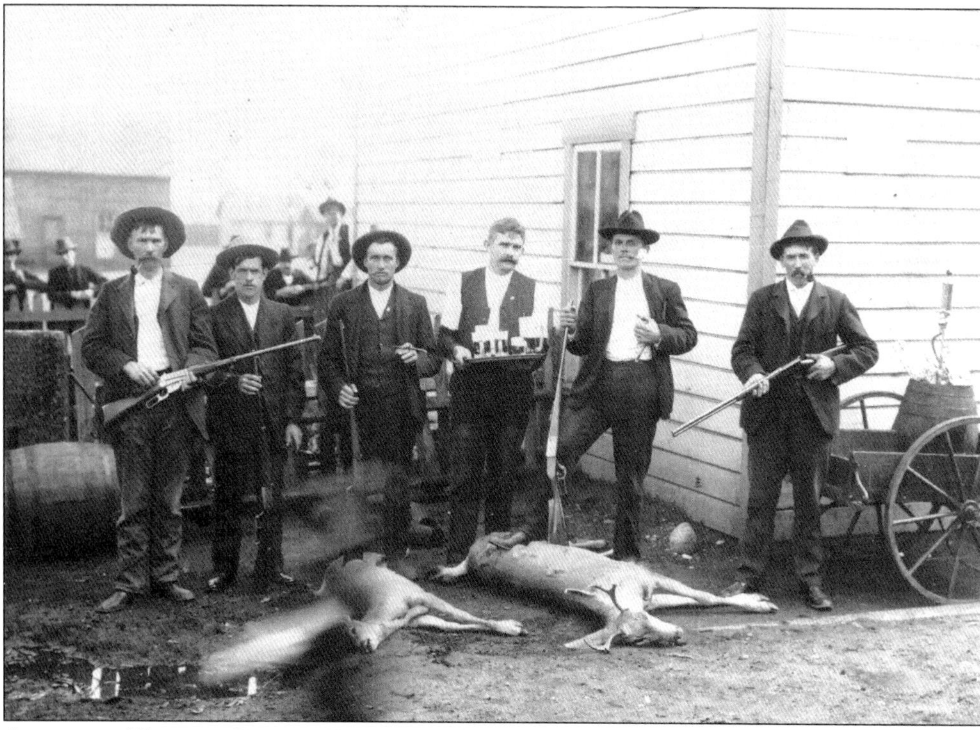

AFTER THE HUNT IN CRESTED BUTTE. Five hunters and a bartender with drinks celebrate the end of a successful hunt in 1892. These Crested Butte men relied on hunting to provide deer and elk meat for their families. Hunting season was always wildly anticipated, but many deer and elk were killed out of season.

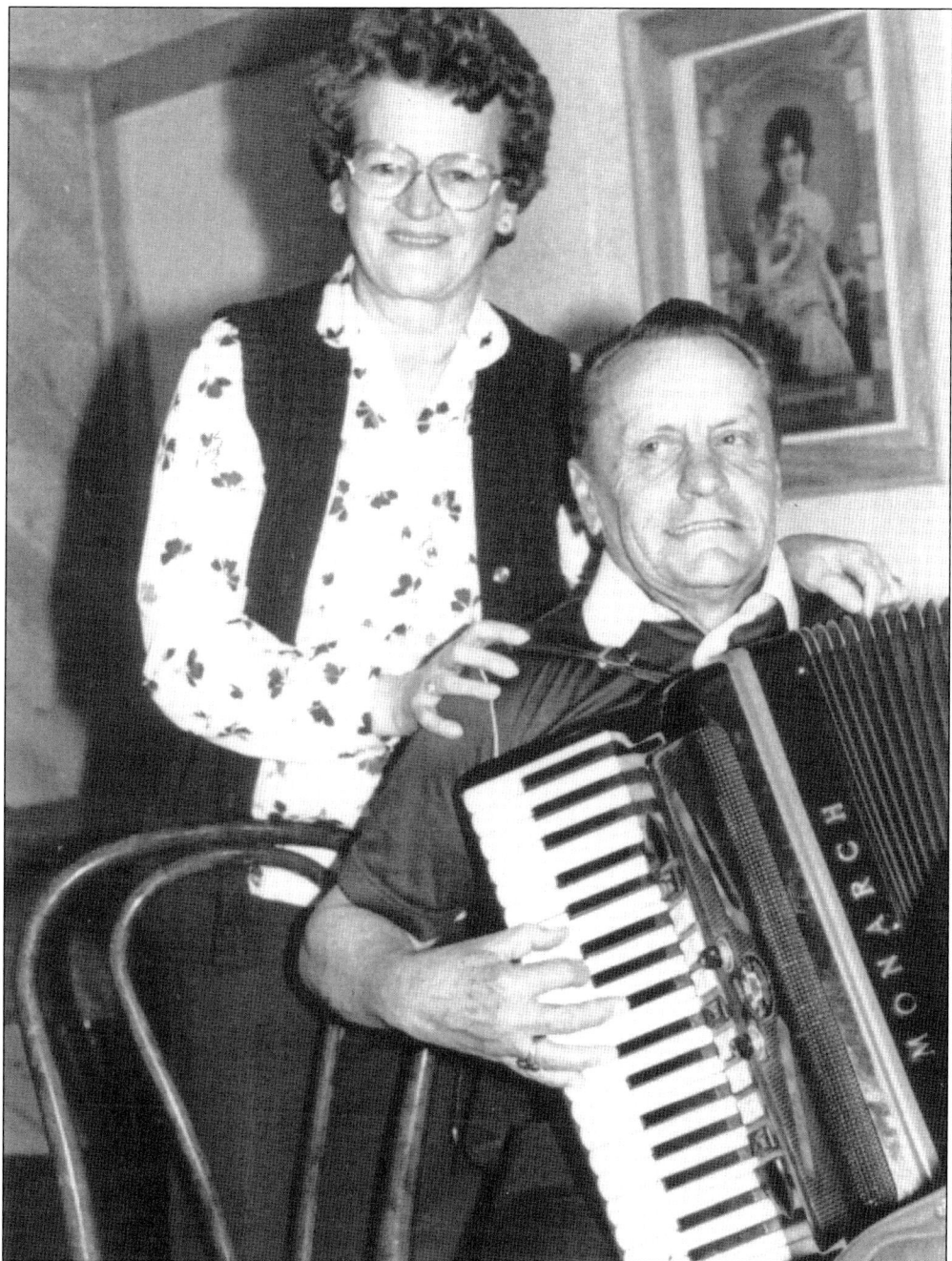

LET'S POLKA! Emil Spritzer and his wife Verl pose at the Talk of the Town Bar in Crested Butte on Memorial Day in the 1980s. Spritzer had been part of the popular Carricato band, which played in Crested Butte and Western Slope towns after World War II. When the band died out, Spritzer continued to play until 2006, always emphasizing Crested Butte's favorite dance, the polka.

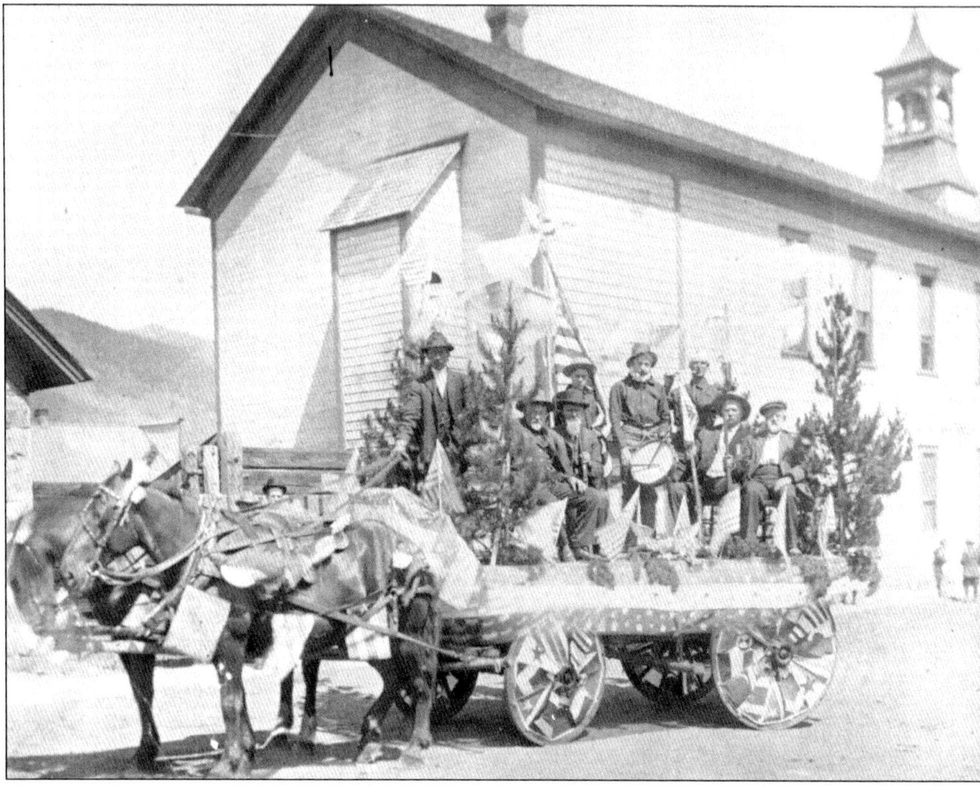

CIVIL WAR VETERANS. On the Fourth of July in 1918 in Crested Butte, ex-Union soldiers are riding on a float celebrating American independence. Today, in 2011, the Crested Butte celebration is one of the largest in Colorado and draws over 8,000 people.

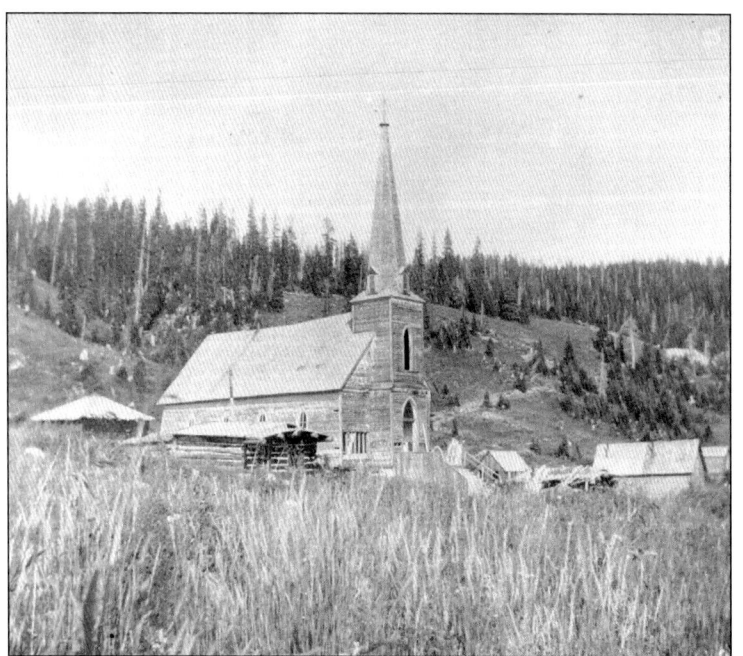

RELIGION IN IRWIN. The famous Presbyterian church in Irwin had seen better days in this 1900 photograph. Built in 1882, the church was the first in the mining camp. The church was 40 feet by 60 feet, seated 350 people, and became famous as the highest church in Colorado.

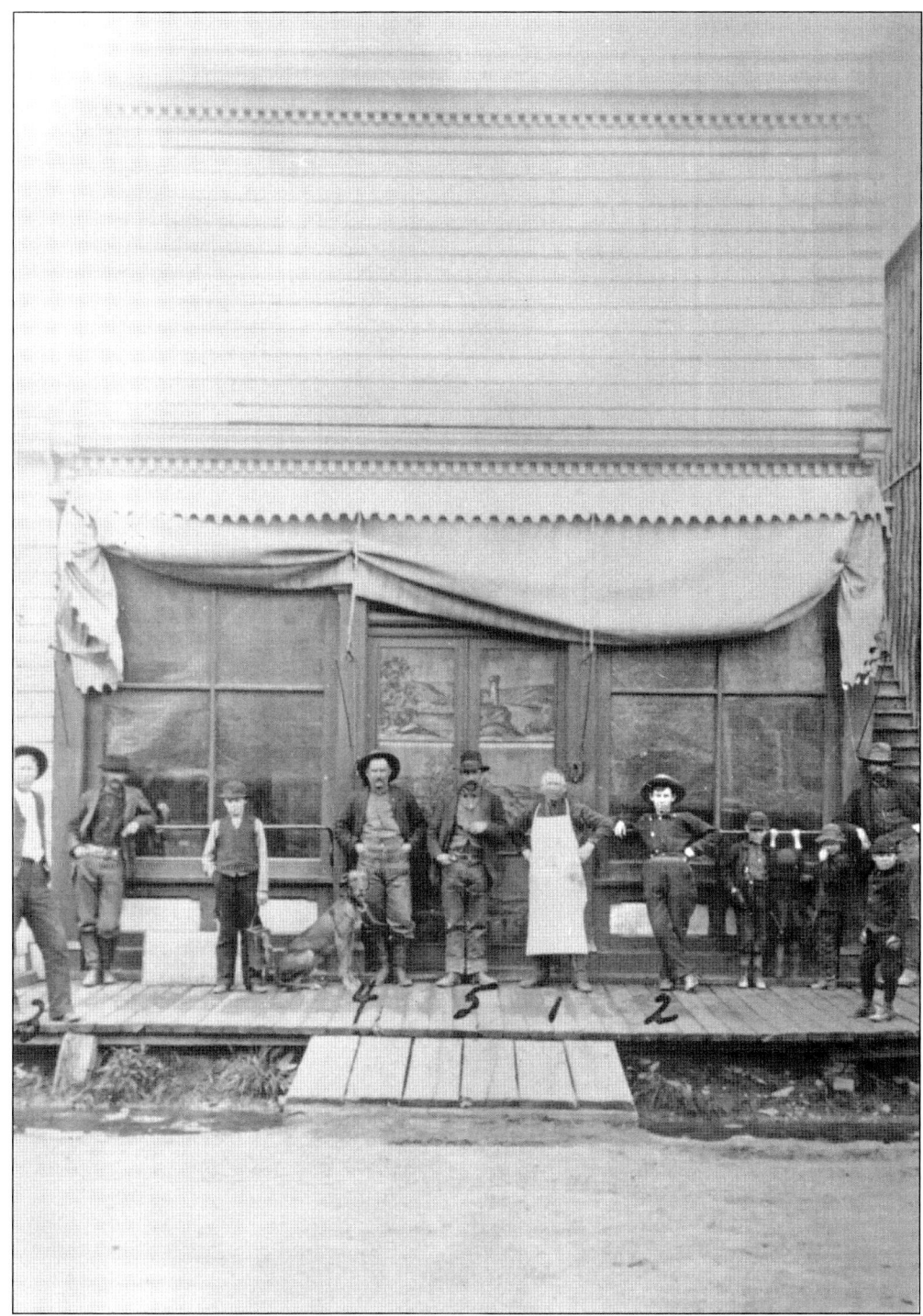

MEAT MARKET, 1884. Men, children, and one dog pose on Elk Avenue in front of Joe Block's Meat Market during the boom years of Crested Butte. Meat markets were always among the most profitable businesses in early mining camps. In this photograph are Joe Block (1), Edward Block (2), Vic Anderson (3), Bill Carroll (4), and Mike Connors (5).

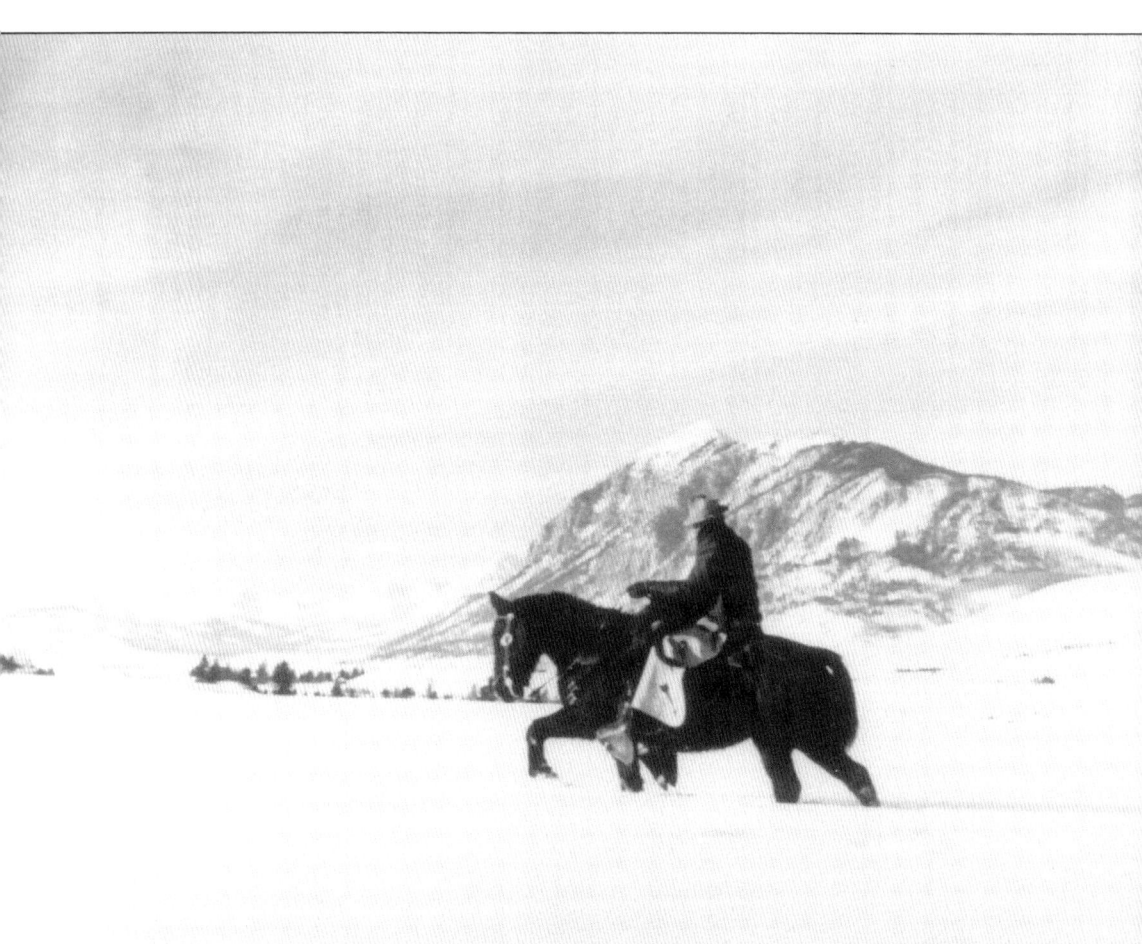

HIGH, WIDE, AND LONESOME. A lone rancher on horseback makes his way through deep snow while checking on his cows south of Crested Butte in 1940. Crested Butte Mountain provides a stunning backdrop to this scene.

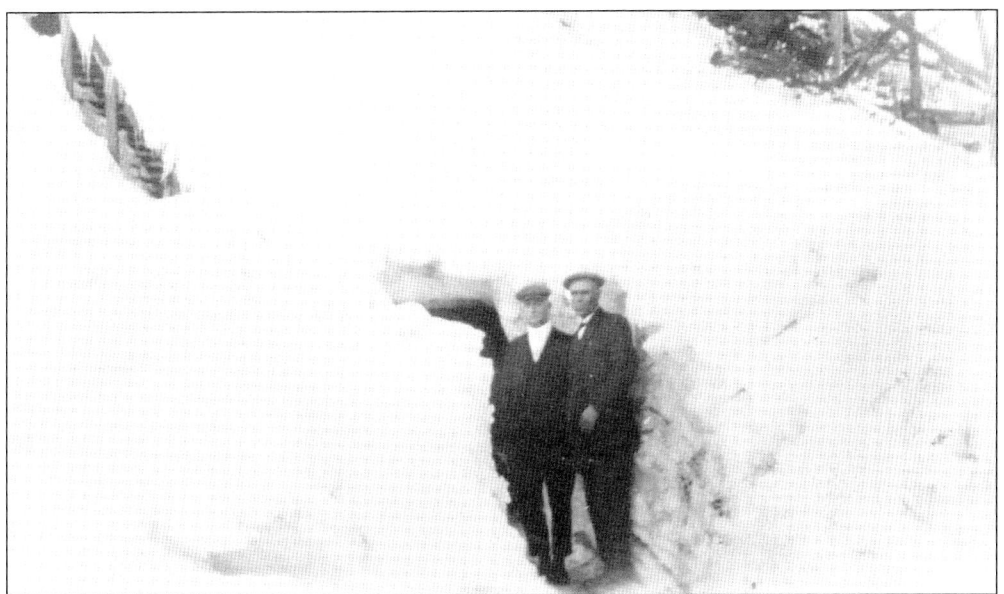

BIG SNOW IN CRESTED BUTTE. Two company officials stand in front of the portal of one of Crested Butte's many coal mines during a huge snow year in 1922. Mining coal was tough work; clearing the tremendous snow to be able to mine was equally difficult.

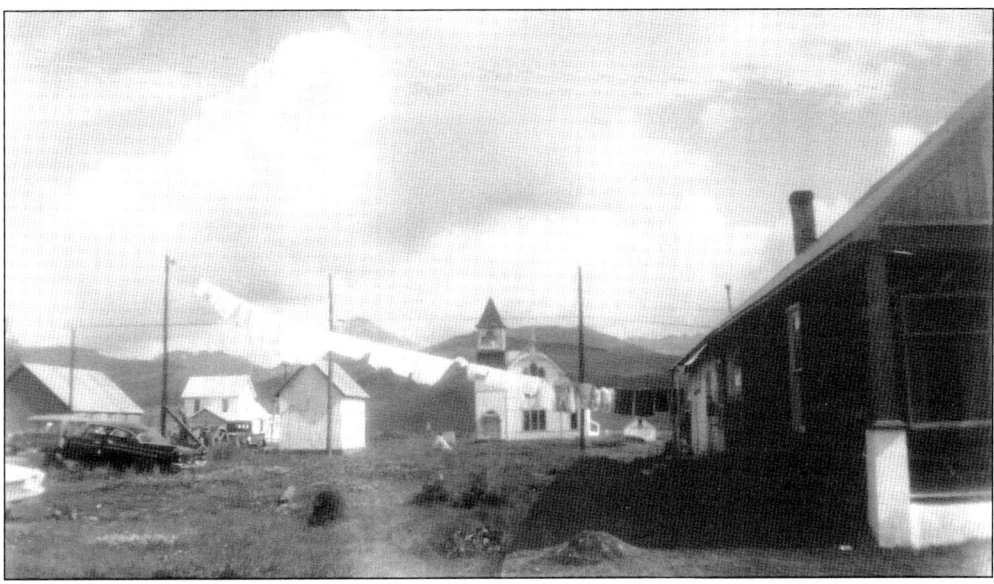

HANGING LAUNDRY. With the Union Congregational Church and Elk Mountains as backdrops, a miner's wife has hung out laundry on a clothesline. The clothes were pulled very high by a pulley because of heavy snows during winter. All women in Crested Butte did their laundry on the day the mines were closed so the smoke and pollution would not dirty the clothes.

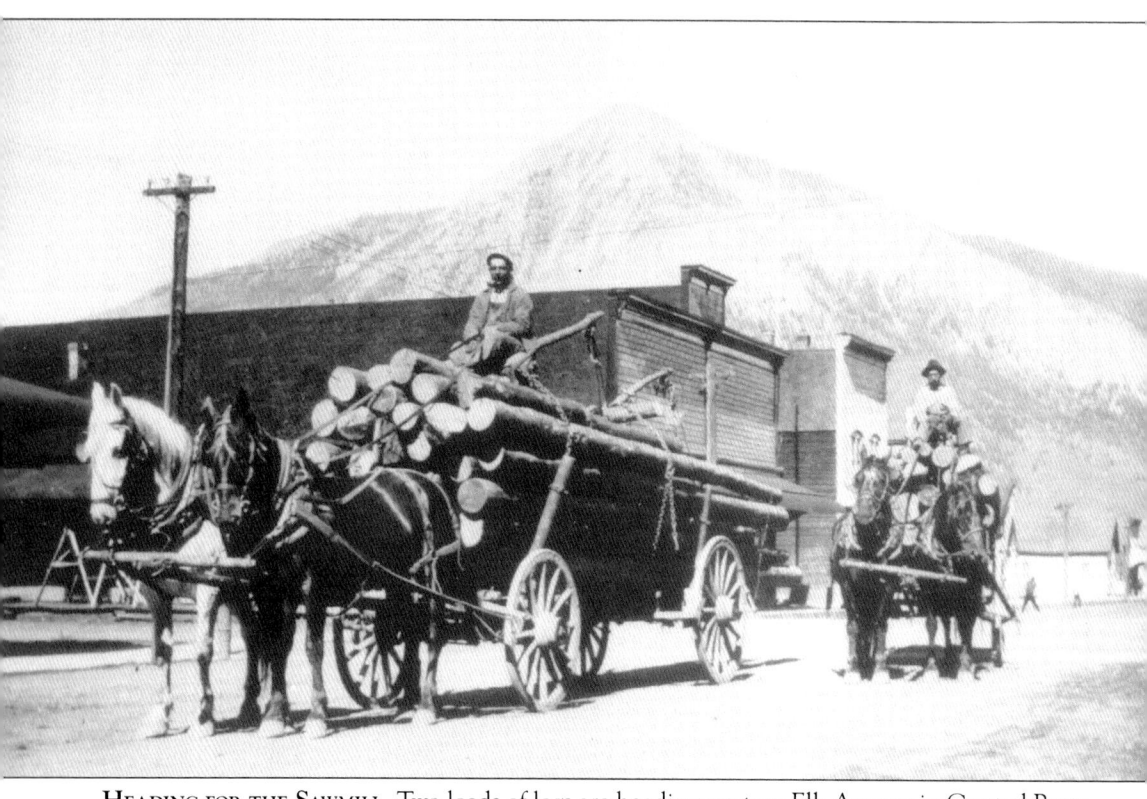

HEADING FOR THE SAWMILL. Two loads of logs are heading west on Elk Avenue in Crested Butte in 1908. The logs are going to one of the many sawmills that dotted the Gunnison Country in the early days. They were essential in turning out railroad ties, mine props, and boards for homes.

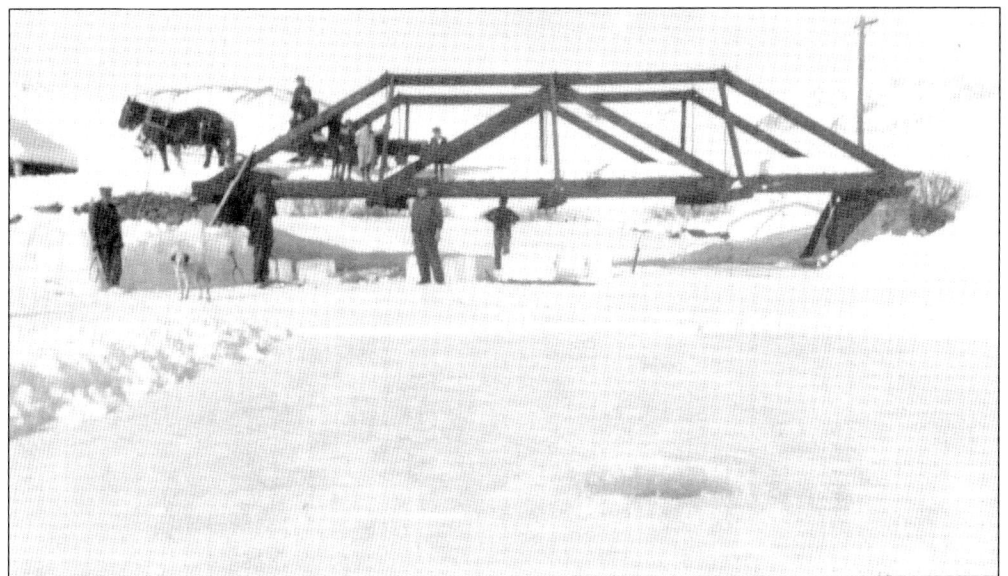

ICE CUTTING ON THE SLATE RIVER. A working party with wire saws poses before huge blocks of ice cut from the Slate River outside of Crested Butte in the 1880s. Tons of ice were cut from major streams in the Gunnison Country to preserve foods during the warm months of the year.

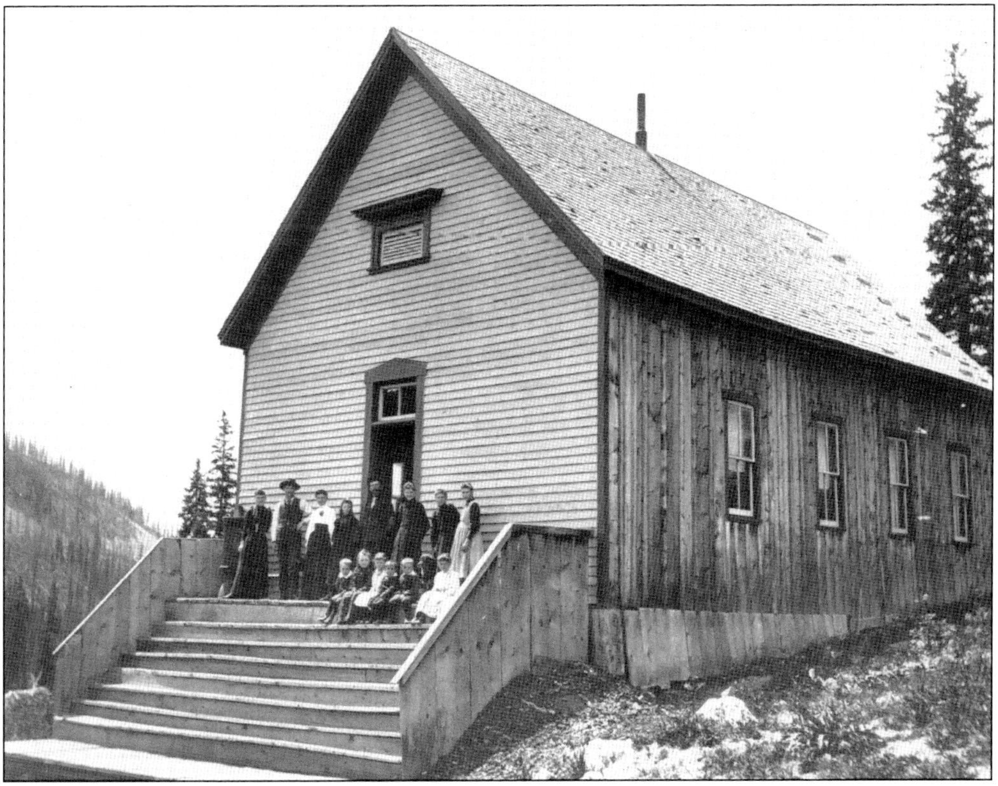

READING, WRITING, AND ARITHMETIC. It was not until 1882, three years after the start of Irwin, that the mining camp got a school. Classes were held in the summer to avoid the tremendous winter snows. One teacher handled grades 1 through 8.

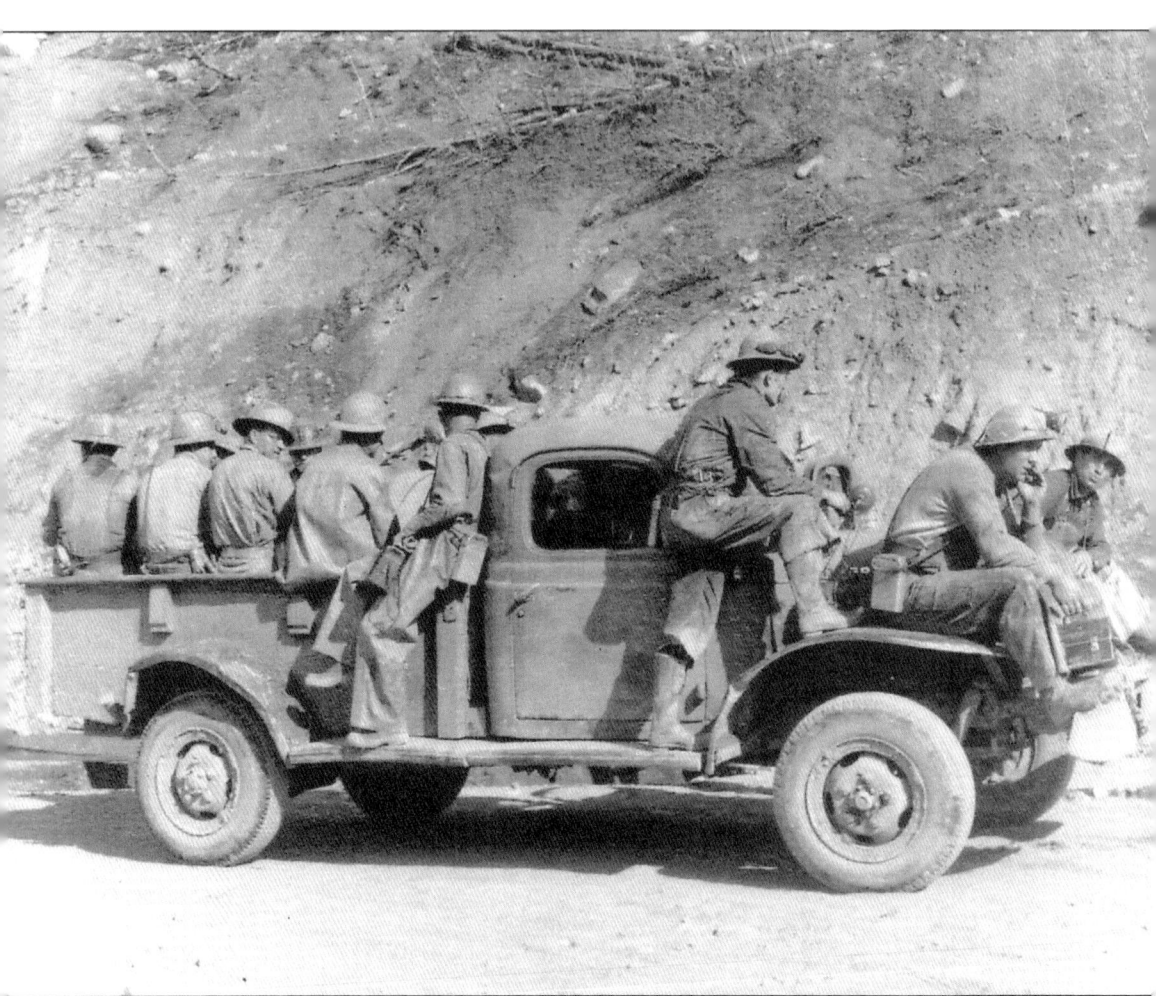

RIDING TO WORK. Keystone miners ride to work in an old, battered pickup truck on the flank of Mount Emmons, three miles from Crested Butte. One of Crested Butte's early silver mines, the Keystone was reopened in the 1950s for about 10 years and produced silver, lead, copper, and zinc.

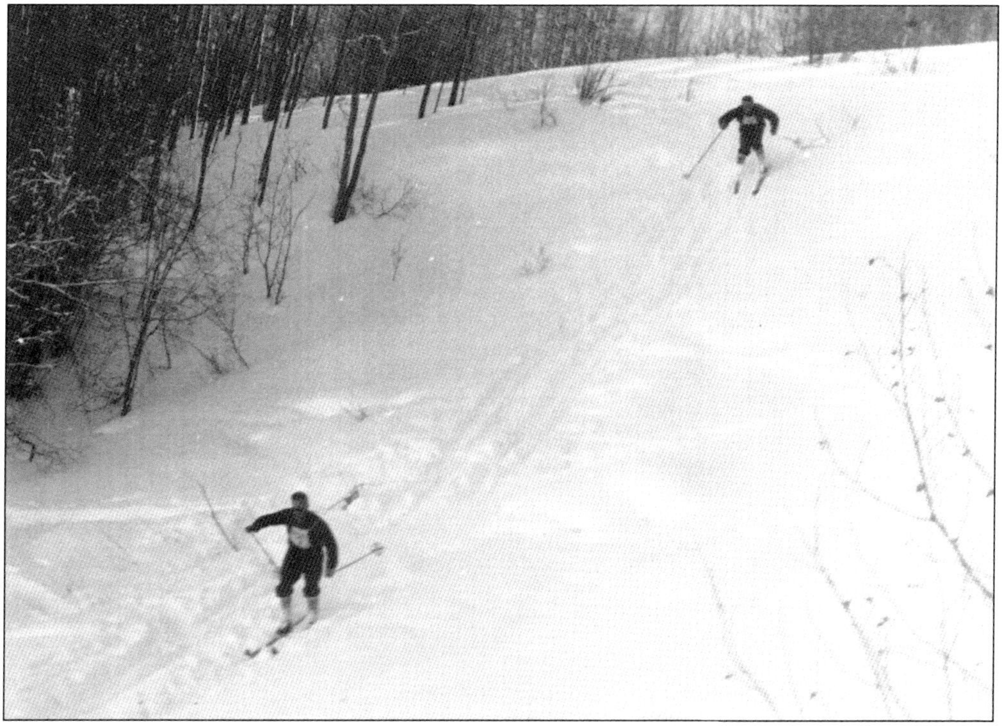

NORDIC RACE, ROZMAN HILL. Two intercollegiate cross-country skiers navigate a steep hill on the Rozman Ski Area course in 1954. Western State College, under coach Sven Wiik, turned out many Olympic skiers, and the team's major training area was Rozman Hill.

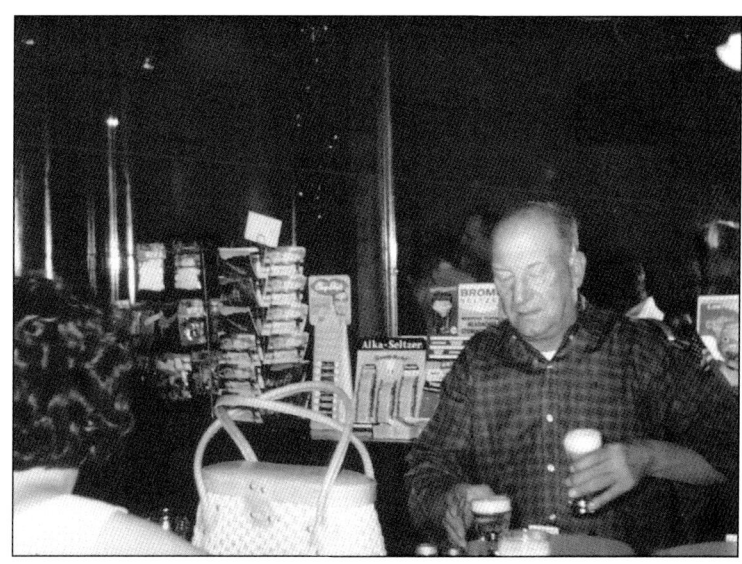

TONY'S TAVERN. Tony Kapushion serves beer at his tavern, one of the top watering holes in Crested Butte in the 1960s. The saloon building was constructed in 1929. Kapushion ran the saloon from 1951 to 1967. In 1971, the name of the business changed to the Wooden Nickel, and it remains a popular saloon in 2011.

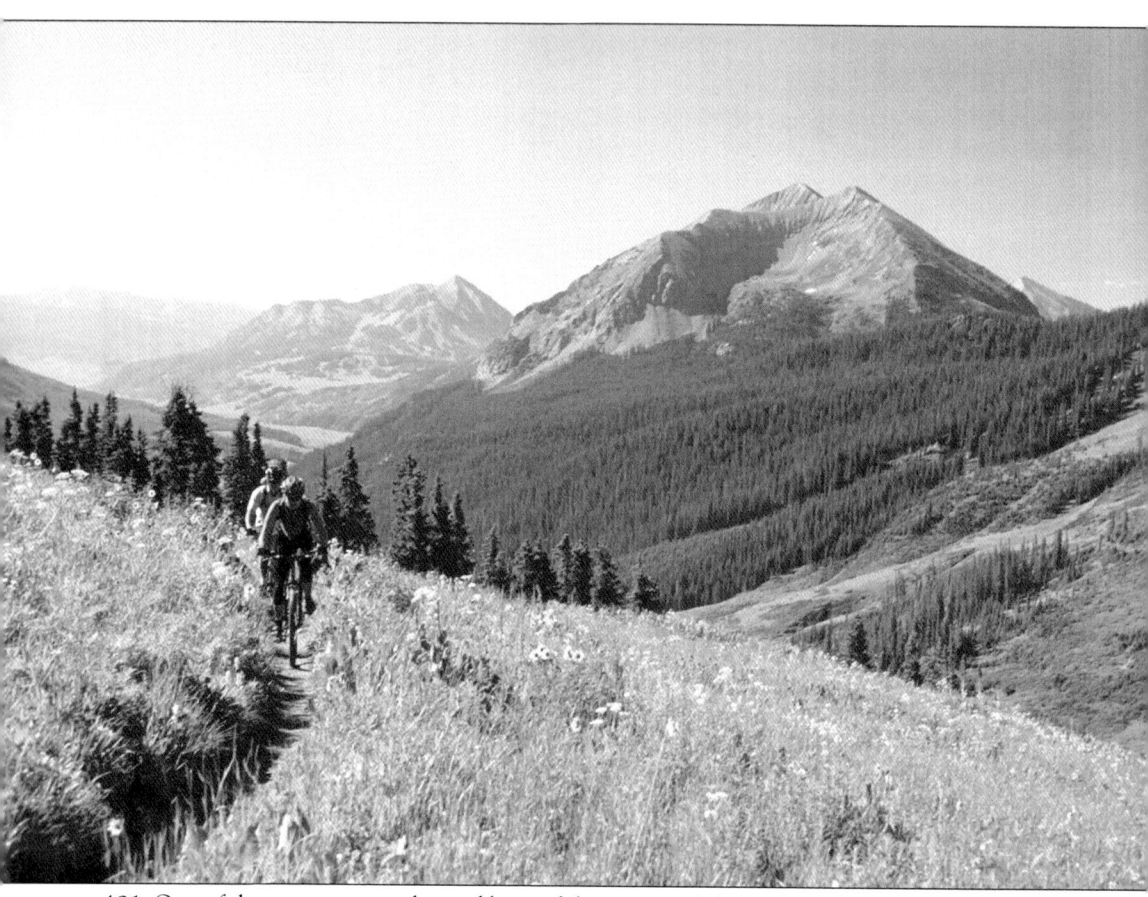

401. One of the most spectacular and beautiful mountain bike trails in the world is 401, between Schofield Pass and Gothic, north of Crested Butte. The single-track trail begins at 10,700 feet and climbs to 11,300 feet before leveling off. The foliage, wildflowers, and scenery are stunning.

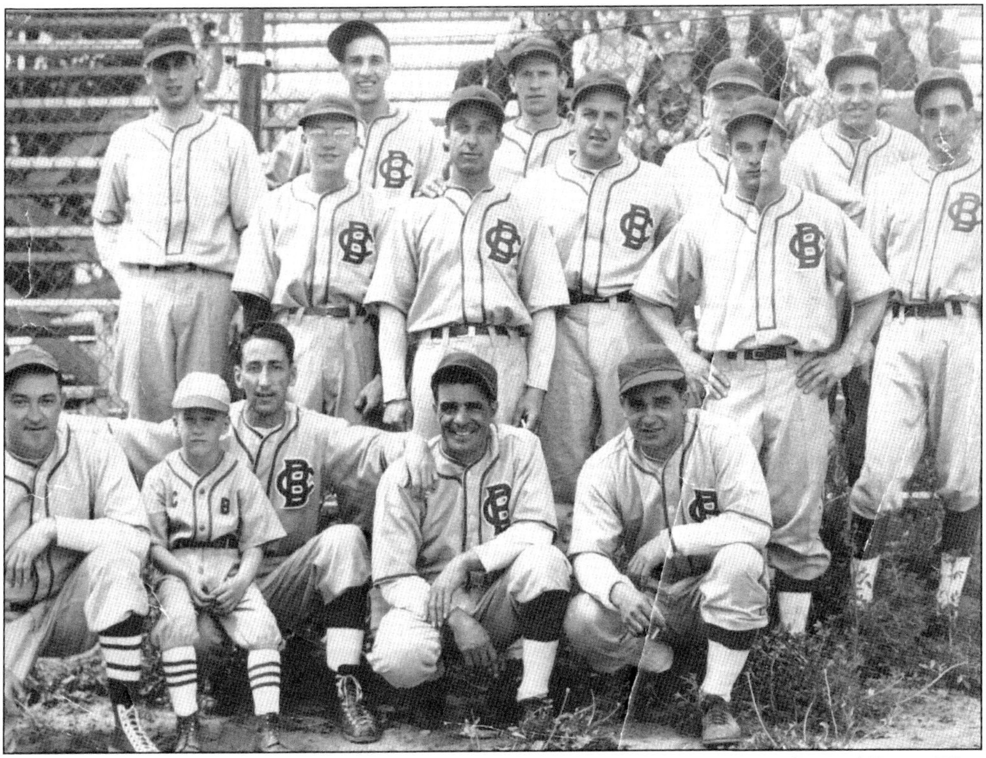

COAL AND HIGH COUNTRY BASEBALL. Baseball was always very important in Crested Butte. The Crested Butte town team is shown here shortly after World War II. The Colorado Fuel and Iron Company was the team's major sponsor. Many of the men on the team worked at the Big Mine, the coal mine owned by the company. In this photograph are, from left to right, (first row) Murph Mufich (coach), Murph Mufich Jr., Art Welch, Ernie Carricato, and Frank Carricato; (second row) Mark Byouk, Leonard Kapushion, Jake Kochevar, John Krizmanich, Pete Spritzer, Joe Savoren, Whitey Sporcich, Chick Mufich, Frank Bruno, and Otto Carricato.

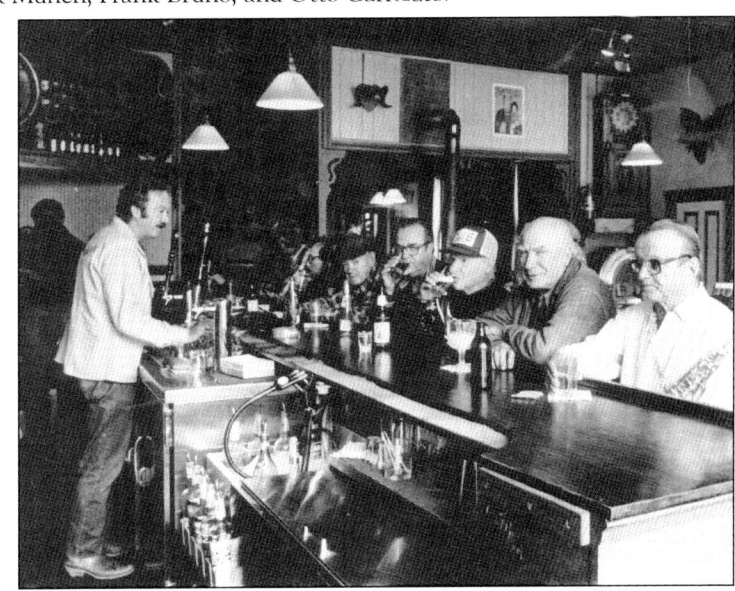

KOCHEVAR'S, 1970s. Located on the west end of Elk Avenue, Kochevar's saloon was built in 1900 by Jacob Kochevar. In this 1970s photo, Chuck Wirtz is the bartender and, from left to right, locals Pittsker Sporcich, Matt Volk, Botsie Spritzer, Joe Sedmack, and Joe Saya are drinking beer and catching up on the latest local news. The saloon is still a local hangout in 2011.

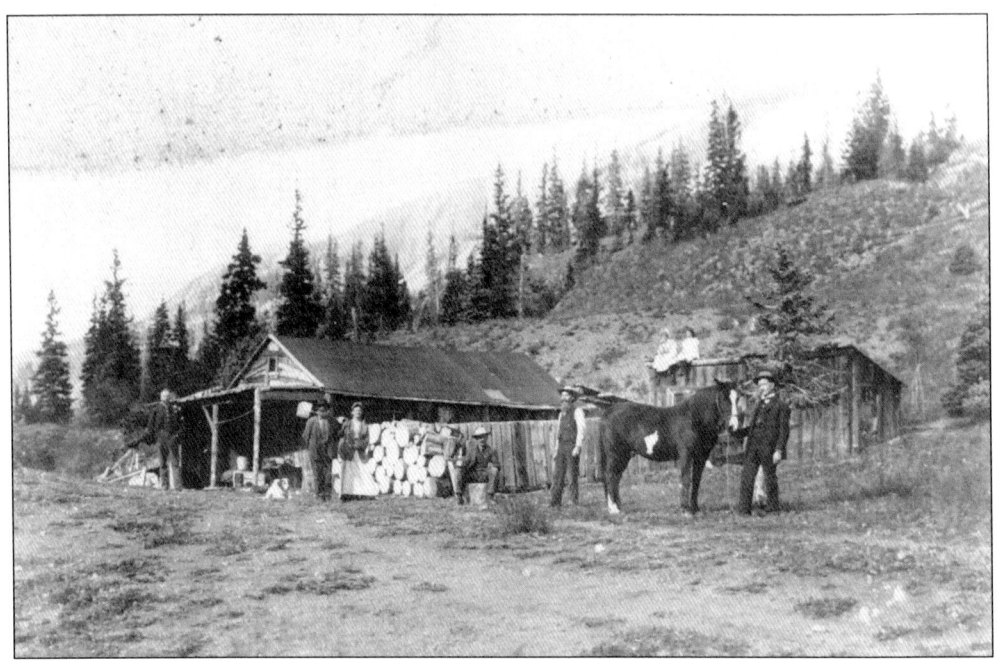

GOTHIC, 1880. Thousands of miners flocked to Gothic in the early 1880s as part of a silver boom. A few were joined by their families during the summer and fall. Most of the mining population left during the winter months, which often saw 500 inches of snow and temperatures of 30 to 40 degrees below zero.

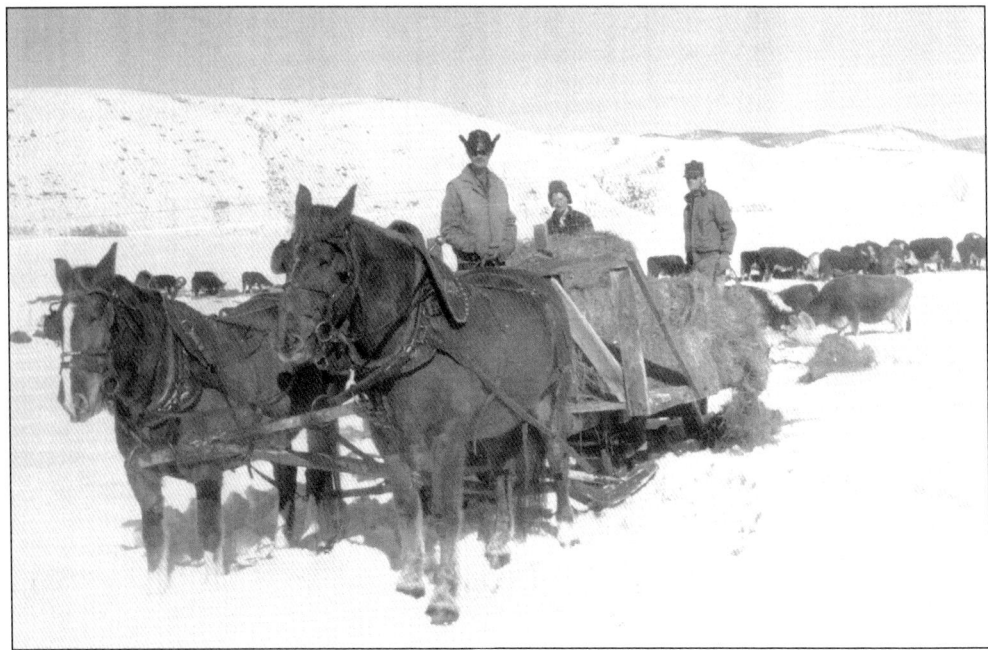

FEEDING HAY IN THE EAST RIVER VALLEY. Snow often piled up to more than 4 to 5 feet high during tough winters in the East River Valley near Crested Butte. Local ranchers fed hay to their cows by means of horses pulling a wagon with skids substituted for wheels. This scene is from the 1950s.

BIBLIOGRAPHY

Cornwall, Harry C. *The Gunnison Country, 1879-1886*. Western State College Library, Gunnison, Colorado: Unpublished manuscript, 1928.

Cortner, Sandra. *Crested Butte Stories . . . Through My Lens*. Crested Butte, Colorado: Wild Rose Press, 2006.

"Crested Butte, Colorado." *Camp and Plant* I, 20 (April 26, 1902), 337–44.

Dyer, John L. *The Snowshoe Itinerant*. Cincinnati: Cranston and Stowe, 1891.

Fails, Sandy and M.J. Vosburg. *Where The Road Ends: Stories And Images From The Heart Of Crested Butte*. Crested Butte: Riverbend Books, 2005.

Jackson, Helen Hunt. "O-Be-Joyful Creek and Poverty Gulch." *Atlantic Monthly*, December 1883, 753–62.

Lee, Bob D. *Rozman Hill Ski Area: "Where's That Angel?"* Western State College, Gunnison, Colorado: Unpublished manuscript, 1983.

Sherman, Gary. *I Forgot my Parachute: A History Of The Pioneer Ski Area*. Western State College, Gunnison, Colorado: Unpublished manuscript, 1977.

Smith, Duane. *When Coal was King: A History of Crested Butte, Colorado, 1880-1952*. Golden, Colorado: Colorado School of Mines Press, 1984.

Vandenbusche, Duane. *Around Gunnison And Crested Butte*. Charleston, SC: Arcadia Publishing, 2008.

———. *The Gunnison Country*. Gunnison, Colorado: B&B Printers, Inc., 1980.

Wallace, Betty. *The Gunnison Country*. Denver: Sage Books, 1964.

Wirth, Kelsey. *Reflections On A Western Town: An Oral History Of Crested Butte, Colorado*. Crested Butte: Oh-Be-Joyful Press, 1996.

Discover Thousands of Local History Books
Featuring Millions of Vintage Images

Arcadia Publishing, the leading local history publisher in the United States, is committed to making history accessible and meaningful through publishing books that celebrate and preserve the heritage of America's people and places.

Find more books like this at
www.arcadiapublishing.com

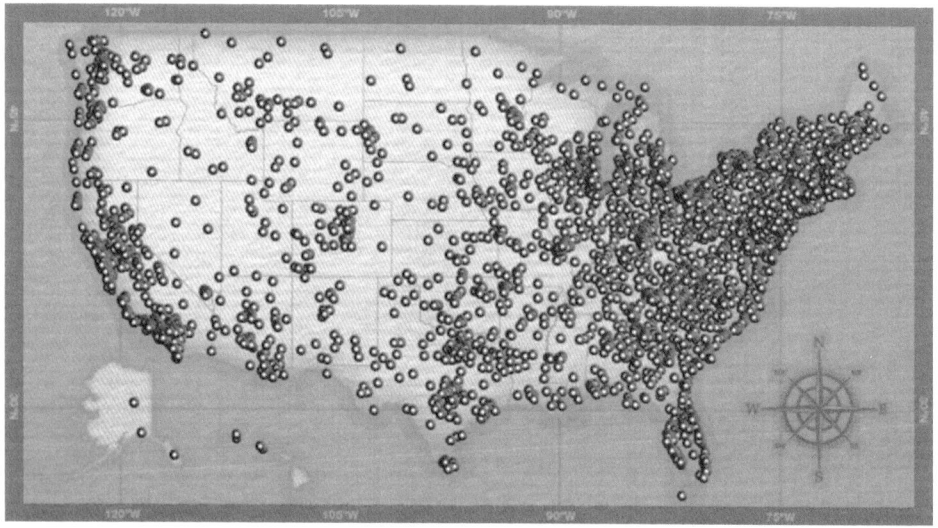

Search for your hometown history, your old stomping grounds, and even your favorite sports team.

Consistent with our mission to preserve history on a local level, this book was printed in South Carolina on American-made paper and manufactured entirely in the United States. Products carrying the accredited Forest Stewardship Council (FSC) label are printed on 100 percent FSC-certified paper.

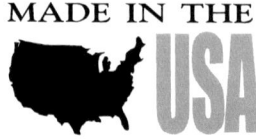